THE HERO OF DOUBT

THE HERO OF DOUBT

EDITED WITH AN INTRODUCTION BY ROBERTA MARCACCIO

TRANSLATED BY STEVE PICCOLO AND AFTERWORD BY JOAN OCKMAN

SELECTED WRITINGS BY ERNESTO NATHAN ROGERS

Maybe destiny will force you to change language, far away, and thinking will become a tiresome, complicated labour – and you will feel yourself getting lost in the others, now and then, daunted by the sound barrier of difficult words.

– Ernesto Nathan Rogers, from *Lettere di Ernesto a Ernesto e viceversa*, written between 1938 and 1939, published 2000.

Cover image: Ernesto Rogers, untitled, c. 1960

BIG DOUBTS AND LITTLE UNCERTAINTIES

ROBERTA MARCACCIO

Ernesto Nathan Rogers's most famous book, *Esperienza dell'architettura* (The Experience of Architecture), was planned for publication in 1952, though it did not appear until 1958. It was the first of three books promised to the Turin-based publisher Einaudi, the other two being a theoretical treatise and a manual, but these were never developed. *Editoriali di Architettura* (Editorials on Architecture), another collection of articles originally written for other publications, appeared in 1968 published by Einaudi. *Gli elementi del fenomeno architettonico* (The Elements of the Architectural Phenomenon) was the only title conceived and written by Rogers as a book; it was originally printed by the publishers Laterza in 1961, but Rogers's doubts over its merits led to publication being cancelled, and the copies were destroyed. This publishing history reveals something of Rogers's personality. Despite being an accomplished editor and a prolific writer (he penned hundreds of editorials and articles throughout his life), his contempt for mediocrity, in any form, meant that in his books he would often rethink everything from first principles, much as he did in his architectural projects and even in his own life.

Rogers used to say that he had 'big doubts and little uncertainties'.[1] It was a way of explaining the long pauses that punctuated his speech, which also gave him time to formulate questions and explore often contradictory answers. At times, and especially in exchanges with younger people, it was also a way of drawing a veil over his own erudition so as to put his interlocutors at ease and let them into his thought processes. However, Rogers was able to turn his uncertainties, particularly those relating to his own identity and skills, into strengths. He recognised his own weaknesses, particularly around technical drawing, and regarded it as normal to seek the help of his colleagues at the BBPR partnership, the Milan-based design studio established by Rogers with Gianluigi Banfi, Lodovico Barbiano di Belgiojoso and Enrico Peressutti. Together they would review designs, examine one another's writings, discuss teaching curricula, consider editorial lines.

It was this collaboration with his partners at BBPR that allowed Rogers to personify a new type of intellectual and professional figure, one able to move seamlessly between design, writing and teaching while embracing varying forms of knowledge and mastering different languages. In this sense Rogers's own self-effacement in the context of his personal and collaborative relations underscores a 'heroic' effort to create a culture

1 Nathan H. Shapira, 'Ricordando Rogers', in *Quaderni del Dipartimento di Progettazione dell'Architettura del Politecnico di Milano 15. Ernesto Nathan Rogers: testimonianze e studi* (Milan: Città Studi, 1993): 17–18. All translations in this text are my own unless otherwise noted.

in which architecture, and more broadly society, can flourish – a culture of collaboration between people with differing expertise, backgrounds and viewpoints where younger and older generations are able to engage in productive exchanges of ideas. This approach is now referred to as 'inclusivity' and 'interdisciplinary research', but for Rogers it was more a matter of individuals contributing their personal insights, ethical wisdom and creativity to a civic and architectural culture honest to the ambiguities and possibilities of its times. As a paradigm for current practice, the heroic and doubting traits of Rogers's persona have real merit as against the theory- and form-mongers and the tired stereotype of the architectural hero.

Inspired by a homonymous article written by Vittorio Gregotti (*Corriere della Sera*, 9 July 2009), the title of this book seeks to celebrate these very traits of Rogers's persona, while at the same time pointing out that, although largely neglected by the historiography of the modern movement, he was in fact at the heart of a profound transformation in architecture's understanding of itself in the second half of the twentieth-century – caught, as it were, between the aberrations of fascism and the utopianism of modernist manifestoes. Both fascism and some of the later developments of modernism, in his opinion, aspired to accomplish too much, too instrumentally and with too few means, and for this reason they were doubted by Rogers, a man acutely aware of the contradictory realities that had emerged from the social and economic upheavals caused by the two recent wars.

The essays in this volume, newly translated from the Italian, show how Rogers advanced this nuanced critique in his writings and trace his influence on the postwar cultural scene in Italy and beyond. Arranged largely chronologically, the texts cover a period of 33 years, from Rogers's initial adherence to fascism and his subsequent struggle as a Jewish intellectual after the proclamation of the racial purity laws to his poignant post-war reflections on the issues of reconstruction, the education of the architect and, more broadly, the architect's role in society. After my introductory essay, which explores the impact of Rogers's British-Italian heritage on his identity and career, the first translated essay in the volume is titled 'An Architect for Himself'. Written for *Domus* in 1957, this text is an account of the house Rogers had just adapted for himself which serves as a kind of brief autobiography and introduction to his personality; following this the book delves into his other writings.

The first section, 'A Shared Tongue', focuses on the early influence of fascist corporatism and historicism as reflected in Rogers's work as a student with his friends and colleagues at BBPR and in his writings for the influential journal *Quadrante*.

The second section, entitled 'The Voices of the Anonymous', brings together the texts written after the promulgation of the racial purity laws in 1939, which prohibited Rogers from writing or being acknowledged on projects under his own name. The tone of these essays is much more subdued and intimate. The confident, manifesto-like prose of the essays in 'A Shared Tongue' have given way to a style that flirts with poetry and focuses more on Rogers's inner reckoning: disillusionment with fascism, the trauma of war and the exile or loss of many family members, friends and colleagues.

The third section, 'The Editorial Voice', collects together a series of editorials written by Rogers for the journals *Domus* and *Casabella*; these testify to his open and dialogical attitude as well as his provocative editorial line, which sought to publish the works of the masters alongside the more raw and sometimes even dubious experiments of less-established practitioners. These works, Rogers argued, kept the modern movement alive precisely because they challenged its established means and methods, as well as its aesthetic, social and political rationales. Focusing on the 'heroic' period of Rogers's career and his decline towards the end of the 1950s (accelerated by the beginning of a long illness which would eventually deprive him of his voice), this section also includes some of Rogers's responses to his critics, including his famous neoliberty debate with the British critic Reyner Banham and other prominent figures both in Italy and on the international scene who took issue with his editorial and professional choices.

The final section, 'The Voices of the Generations', breaks with the chronological order of the previous sections to focus on Rogers's role as an educator and mediator between the generation of modern masters and the young practitioners and students he mentored. It was a role which he regarded as his calling throughout his life and which almost consumed him, certainly taking precedence over his practice and the editorship of *Casabella* in the final years before his death. The texts in this section help to introduce a critical essay by the distinguished scholar Joan Ockman, which bookends the volume by focusing on Rogers's tendency to think of himself in generational terms and sheds new light on the meaning of words and concepts repeatedly used by him such as *coerenza* (coherence), *continuità* (historical continuity) and *preesistenze ambientali* or *ambiente* (pre-existing conditions).

These terms, along with others such as *tradizione* (tradition), *utilità e bellezza* (utility and beauty) and *tendenza* (artistic tendency), present difficulties for translation. Rogers used them as a means of anchoring his thoughts. Not only did they, as literary *topoi*, assist him in advancing his argument in an ongoing dialogue with himself and his interlocutors, they also helped him in the forging of his own identity. None of these terms translate easily into English. Their meaning is highly nuanced and often highly elusive, even in the original Italian, which tends to be more tolerant than English of elusiveness.

One of the most difficult expressions to translate has been *preesistenze ambientali* or *ambiente*, which, as Adrian Forty has noted, has often been misleadingly rendered in English as 'context', a word which has its equivalent in Italian in *contesto*, but which Rogers (or his collaborators) deliberately chose not to use.[2] Indeed, 'context' fails to capture that which the more metaphysical *preesistenze ambientali* seeks to evoke: the importance of historical continuity, or consciousness of the historical past, as manifested by the city and as existing in the minds of the city's inhabitants. It is this idea of historical continuity that distinguishes Rogers's thinking from other arguments about architecture's responsiveness to place, such as the *genius loci* – the spirit of a place – of the English Picturesque, and the 'contextualism' debate that took place at Cornell University in the 1960s around such figures as Colin Rowe.

This is important because the same idea of historical continuity also permeates the writings of some of Rogers's most prominent collaborators, among them Vittorio Gregotti and Aldo Rossi. In the English translation of Rossi's seminal text, *The Architecture of the City* (1966), the word *ambiente* was translated throughout as 'context', obscuring, for English-speaking readers, its importance in relation to the totality of Rogers's ideas and unhelpfully suggesting a link with the 'contextualism' debates at Cornell University.

More recent translations have attempted to render *preesistenze ambientali* as 'surrounding pre-existences' (Adrian Forty), 'pre-existing conditions' (Joan Ockman) and 'pre-existent environments' (Maurizio Sabini); the latter is perhaps more faithful to the Italian,

2 See: Adrian Forty, 'Context', in *Words and Buildings: A Vocabulary of Modern Architecture* (New York: Thames & Hudson, 2000): 132-135. As Forty explains, the words preesistenze ambientali and ambiente first came to international attention in the 1954 controversy surrounding Frank Lloyd Wright's Masieri memorial in Venice (unrealised), which provoked passionate arguments, both within Italy and internationally, regarding the appropriacy of modern architecture to historic sites and about the degree to which the design did or did not take account of its surroundings.

but now carries unhelpful associations with environmental concerns, which Rogers would not have been referencing at the time of his writing. While working on this book, the temptation in English has been to paraphrase *preesistenze ambientali* and the other identity-forging terms mentioned above, each time adapting the text to tease out more precise meanings in English. In order not to lose the anchoring power and deliberate elusiveness of Rogers's terms in the texts that follow, the original Italian has been retained, sometimes accompanied by English translations.

THE MANY VOICES OF ERNESTO NATHAN ROGERS

ROBERTA MARCACCIO

Previous: CIAM 7 in Bergamo, Italy, 1949. From left Le Corbusier, Sigfried Giedion, Josep Lluís Sert, and Ernesto Rogers © GTA Archives / ETH Zurich Sigfried Giedion Papers

Vittorio Gregotti often spoke of his mentor Ernesto Nathan Rogers as the man 'who taught two generations of Italian architects how to read and write'.[1] However troubled architectural education might have been after World War II, Italian architects were hardly illiterate, but what Gregotti celebrated particularly was the fact that Rogers opened up Italy's provincial architectural culture, both by exposing it to a wider ambit of international debate and by stimulating dialogue with other cultures and disciplines – history, philosophy, poetry, geography, literature and politics. Rogers maintained a familiarity with each of these realms, evident in his mastery of the available media at the time – he exploited exhibitions, international conferences, broadcasting and, most crucially, publications, as demonstrated by his prominent role as editor of *Casabella*, which over the course of his decade-long tenure at the journal became the principal record of his influence in Italy and beyond.

Rogers shifted mainstream discourse. Challenging the break from history espoused by his contemporaries, for whom the modern movement was a kind of epic phenomenon divorced from the past and exempt from criticism, he used his involvement in the Congrès Internationaux d'Architecture Moderne (CIAM), his collaborative practice with BBPR and his parallel careers in teaching and writing to broadcast his highly controversial ideas of *continuità* (historical continuity) and *preesistenze ambientali* (pre-existing conditions). Now largely neglected by historians, his work was picked up by many of those who went on to shape postmodern discourse on both sides of the Atlantic. Rogers's ideas, in this sense, can be credited with laying the groundwork for Aldo Rossi's approach to the study of European cities; Vittorio Gregotti's speculations on the disciplinary 'territory of architecture'; Robert Venturi's creative understanding of history and the everyday environment; and Team 10's polemic against CIAM's doctrinaire approach to urbanism, even if Rogers himself was not entirely convinced by some of these developments.[2]

1 Vittorio Gregotti, 'Rogers e Casabella', in *Quaderni del Dipartimento di Progettazione dell'Architettura del Politecnico di Milano 15. Ernesto Nathan Rogers: testimonianze e studi* (Milan: Città Studi, 1993): 98–100. As a young graduate in 1953, Gregotti was an assistant on the course held by Rogers at the Faculty of Architecture in Milan and the youngest member of his editorial staff at *Casabella*, becoming editor-in-chief in 1955 until his departure in 1963. Author's translation.

2 To delve deeper into Rogers's influence on these personalities see: Manfredo Tafuri, 'Les "muses inquiétantes" ou le destin d'une génération de "Maîtres" ', *L'Architecture d'aujourd'hui* nº 181 (September–October 1975): 14–33; Francesco Dal Co, Mario Manieri Elia, 'La génération de l'incertitude', *L'Architecture d'aujourd'hui* nº 181 (September–October 1975): 34-56; Frédéric Migayrou, 'La Tendenza: Historical Backlash', in *La Tendenza: architectures italiennes 1965-1985* (Paris: Centre Pompidou, 2012); Martino Stierli, 'In the Academy's Garden: Robert Venturi, the Grand Tour and the Revision of Modernism', *AA Files* nº 56 (2007): 42–63.

In addition to the historical references manifest in his own work, what confirmed Rogers as the forefather of these new approaches was the way in which his charismatic personality embodied all the complexities and contradictions that had started to emerge in the postwar period. Part academic, part avant-garde artist, more of a militant practitioner than an ivory-tower intellectual, Rogers's tumultuous but worldly upbringing taught him to shift between contradictory roles and identities while cultivating a striking variety of interests – from architecture and art, film and photography to philosophy, sociology and politics. A natural curiosity for other disciplines would underpin his life's work.

The story of Rogers's identity is one of a struggle to synthesise a multitude of geographical, political and cultural influences. Born in 1909 in Trieste – then part of the Austro-Hungarian empire – Ernesto was Jewish and held both British and Italian citizenship. His mother was Ida Manni; his father, Romeo Rogers, was a fiercely intellectual insurance broker. His name – you might think it a kind of premonition – was a tribute to Ernesto Nathan, the distinguished Anglo-Italian Jewish intellectual and politician who, as mayor of Rome from 1907, promoted the city's first general plan to regulate rampant real-estate speculation. Later in his life, Rogers's closest collaborators would refer to him affectionately as the 'Austrian man'; born in the Trieste of Italo Svevo, Sigmund Freud, James Joyce (a family friend) and Umberto Saba, he brought to Milan – where he eventually settled – elements of Middle European philosophical and literary culture.

Rogers's childhood and early adolescence were unsettled, with the family continually having to relocate for his father's work. After leaving Trieste in 1914 and before moving to Rome, they lived in Zurich, where Ernesto attended primary school and learned to speak fluent German. Moving to Milan in 1921, he was a teenage pupil at the Liceo Parini where Gianluigi Banfi and Lodovico Barbiano di Belgiojoso, who were to become future colleagues, were among his friends. By contrast with them, however, he had doubts about becoming an architect because he believed that he had no talent for technical drawing – a complex that would haunt him for the rest of his life. Belgiojoso's father, himself an architect, managed to convince Rogers that the profession required a broader range of skills, and the three friends went on to study together at the Politecnico di Milano, where they met their future associate Enrico Peressutti.[3]

3 Lodovico Belgiojoso, 'Il lavoro di gruppo' in *Quaderni del Dipartimento di Progettazione dell'Architettura del Politecnico di Milano 15. Ernesto Nathan Rogers: testimonianze e studi* (Milan: Città Studi, 1993): 11–14.

In the culturally rich atmosphere of Milan, the young Rogers developed a lively interest in the figurative arts and became enamoured with futurism. At the same time, he was attracted to the popular national rhetoric of fascist corporatism, something that is not particularly surprising, even given his Jewish origins. In the early years of the regime, many Italian Jews served as government ministers, among them Mussolini's glamorous and influential mistress Margherita Sarfatti, the 'dictator of culture'. Sarfatti helped Mussolini to promote (and exploit) a surprisingly polyvocal intellectual climate by encouraging lively debate about the nature of 'fascist art' and the role it could play, alongside history, in shaping the identity of a nation that had been unified only since 1861.[4]

This was the climate that would first shape Rogers's reflections as a modern architect concerned with historical memory, and for whom the fascist idea of history as a malleable material that could be used to give definition to a still-fluid national identity was particularly appealing. Through his life Rogers sought to negate the anomalies of his own identity – his erratic youth, dual nationality, alleged homosexuality and his Jewish origins – explicitly rejecting any obstacle (and there were quite a few) to his self-identification with the culture he inhabited. In his twenties, for instance, Rogers decided to formally renounce his British citizenship and to naturalise once and for all as an Italian citizen, much to his father's quiet consternation.[5] He even proved reluctant to learn the language of his Anglo-Saxon forebears, as we gather from a beseeching letter from his art teacher, the painter Anselmo Bucci: 'I beg you not to get lost in the alti adagi but to go to England. In the meantime, you must learn English ... Learn it immediately. I already have the address of a teacher, a rather mature Irish lady whom I shall seduce (I will introduce you afterwards).'[6]

Ignoring Bucci's advice, Rogers would refuse to learn English until he was in his thirties, concentrating instead on the task of

4 See: Diane Ghirardo, 'Architects, Exhibitions, and the Politics of Culture in Fascist Italy', *Journal of Architectural Education* vol. 45, nº 2 (February 1992): 67–75; Giorgio Ciucci, 'Italian Architects During the Fascist Period: Classicism Between Neo-classicism and Rationalism', *Harvard Architecture Review* nº 6 (1987): 76–87.

5 Romeo Rogers wrote to Ernesto on 26 September 1932: 'As far as the issue of nationality is concerned, I would prefer and indeed be happier if you were to keep your original one. However it goes without saying that I would never say "no" if this could, in any way, jeopardise the career you have chosen for yourself.' From letters in the BBPR archive reproduced by Luca Molinari in his doctoral dissertation *Continuità: A Response to Identity Crises: Ernesto Nathan Rogers and Italian Architectural Culture after 1945* (Delft: TU Delft, 2008): 44.

6 Molinari, *Continuità* (2008): 45.

developing a 'common tongue' with his associates. Rogers's final thesis at the Politecnico was accompanied by an introduction written 'with eight hands'. In it, Banfi, Belgiojoso, Peressutti and Rogers professed their committed association, declaring:

... we believe it is not enough for an architect to build; we also feel the need to speak, to express through the synthesis of our work not just the contingencies of life but the thought and the character of the present era.

And because speaking calls for a language intelligible to most people, we have agreed, together, to seek the high road through the labyrinth of art.

We are less concerned with individual personality than we are with the personality of the work ...

If, after all the extremely subjective experiences of romanticism, we wish to avoid regressing into a dangerous Babel, then the words of individuals need to come together in a living, shared tongue.

BBPR were inspired by the anti-individualistic and collaborative spirit of fascism and by polemical practices such as Gruppo 7 (Luigi Figini, Guido Frette, Sebastiano Larco, Gino Pollini, Carlo Enrico Rava, Giuseppe Terragni and Ubaldo Castagnoli), formed in 1926 when the seven were discontented recent graduates (Castagnoli was replaced in 1927 by Adalberto Libera).[7] Gruppo 7 embraced Walter Gropius's philosophy of 'teamwork' and defined their position as 'rationalism'. As they made clear, this was not a 'pure rationalism' of the kind that was then being pursued throughout Europe, but rather one that preserved a 'classical substratum' and responded to the 'spirit (not the forms, which is quite different) of [Italian] tradition'.[8]

Faithful to the same principles, upon graduating in 1932 Banfi, Belgiojoso, Peressutti and Rogers founded BBPR – the initials of their names

7 In 1927 an essay by Gruppo 7 denounced the inability of the Milanese school to prepare students for the profession: Gruppo 7, 'Architettura (III), Impreparazione – Incomprensione – Pregiudizi' in *Rassegna Italiana* (March 1927); also published in Michele Cennamo, ed., *Materiali per l'analisi dell'architettura moderna. La prima esposizione italiana di architettura razionale* (Fiorentino: Napoli, 1973): 56–61.

8 Gruppo 7, 'Architettura' in *Rassegna Italiana* (December 1926): 849-854; see also Cesare De Seta, *La cultura architettonica in Italia tra le due guerre* (Bari: Laterza, 1983): 218-219; and Terry Kirk, *The Architecture of Modern Italy: Visions of Utopia, 1900–Present vol 2*, (New York: Princeton Architectural Press, 2005): 74–83.

deliberately weighted equally. But Rogers's otherness was not, he thought, so easily camouflaged. He remarked, 'while BBP will always have a precise sound, the R is bound to wander solitary and lost',[9] as if there remained, inscribed in the sound of their initials, an intrinsic disparity of histories, destinies and skills. Still insecure about his role as an architect, Rogers found comfort in renouncing individual creativity. Belgiojoso remembers how Rogers's complex played out in the studio: 'Sometimes, while working, he would imagine a shape that he wanted to propose and would try to express himself by gesticulating, moulding an imaginary architectural model with his hands. Aurel [Peressutti] tended to get very frustrated when this happened, and would put a pencil in Ernesto's hands, forcing him to express himself by drawing rather than talking.'[10]

The eclectic structure of the iconic Torre Velasca in Milan – BBPR's most famous and controversial building – is a perfect example of the design method shaped by these internal dynamics, a tortuous process of repeated interrogation and collaborative reworking that they called *dubbio metodologico* (systematic doubt). At each stage the four different voices of the associates would inform and reform aspects of the project – as demonstrated by the multiple in-progress variations of the design, moving from a sleek and functional tower in steel and glass towards the heavier concrete mass that would culturally summarise Milan's layered historical context.[11] The tower's vertical columns evoked the ribbing of the neighbouring Duomo, the pitched roof with protruding vertical stacks resembled domestic chimneys, while the muddy colours of its surfaces referred to the tonalities of old Milan. Built on a contained lot, and thus detached from the surrounding buildings, it compensates for its reduced footprint with its impressive height, with the floor plates widening towards the top, reaching out to the edges of the site. This solution increased the market value of the residential units at the top; the narrower part beneath was reserved for offices.

9 Ernesto Rogers, Trieste, 2 October 1938. From letters in the BBPR archive reproduced by Luca Molinari in *Continuità* (2008): 103. An anxious Rogers writes to his colleagues at the BBPR about his fears regarding the promulgation of the racial purity laws and the resulting ban for Jewish people from making work or making their names known.

10 Belgiojoso, 'Il lavoro di gruppo', *Quaderni del Dipartimento di Progettazione dell'Architettura del Politecnico di Milano 15. Ernesto Nathan Rogers: testimonianze e studi* (Milan: Città Studi, 1993): 17–18.

11 For further reading on the Torre Velasca see: Gerhard M. Kallmann, 'Modern Tower in Old Milan', *Architectural Forum* nº 2 (1958): 109–111; Giuseppe Samonà, 'Il Grattacielo piú discusso d'Europa, La Torre Velasca', *L'architettura. Cronache e storia* nº 40 (February 1959): 658–675, 713–714; Studio BBPR, 'Tre problemi di ambientamento: La Torre Velasca, un edificio per uffici e appartamenti a Torino, Casa Lurani a Milano', *Casabella–Continuità* nº 232 (October 1959): 4–27; Manfredo Tafuri, *Storia dell'architettura italiana 1944–1985* (Milano: Einaudi, 2002; first published 1982): 68–69; Luciano Semerani, 'Torre Velasca, Milano' in Marco Biraghi and Alberto Ferlenga, eds., *Architettura del Novecento*, vol. III (Torino: Einaudi, 2013), 708–714.

Studio BBPR, Lodovico Belgiojoso, Enrico Peressutti, Ernesto Rogers, Torre Velasca, Milan, 1952–1958, detail © Architectural Press Archive / RIBA Collections

Torre Velasca foregrounded by the campanile of the Church of San Gottardo, Milan, 1950s
© Monica Pidgeon / RIBA Collections

The fact that the Torre Velasca, the first Milanese skyscraper built in reinforced concrete, did not conform to planning regulations was evidently not a problem. BBPR were deeply embedded within the wealthy Milanese bourgeoisie, and powerful enough to sway the decision of the authorities.

Though insecure as a designer, Rogers nonetheless emerged as a leader within BBPR, relying on his strengths – his prominent editorial and public roles and his talent with words – to define the practice's direction and profile. For example, in a series of presentations and articles on the Velasca published in *Casabella*, he placed emphasis on the dubbio metodologico, the design process through which the tower had gradually acquired its characteristic physiognomy.[12] Built in reinforced concrete using the most contemporary industrial materials, the tower also had to fit into a historically sensitive urban area by absorbing and reinterpreting the cultural and formal repertoire of its surroundings – its *preesistenze ambientali*. In this way Rogers deliberately used the project to call into question the idea that the outward appearance of a building could be regarded as a faithful indicator of its modernity. And in taking the visual out of the equation, he reminded his contemporaries that modernism was not so much a style as a way of designing in accordance with modern methods of construction and by adopting a dynamic approach to problems.

The idea of looking beyond the external experience of a building was something that Rogers had started to appreciate during his time at the Politecnico di Milano, studying under the guidance of figures like Ambrogio Annoni and Piero Portaluppi. Annoni's history course, rather than aiming at a purely stylistic reading of past architectures, proposed an investigation of the aesthetic and constructive reasons for buildings. His unorthodox case-by-case approach to preservation was underpinned by a mode of inquiry whereby one had to use one's own best judgement, combined with rational method and artistic sensitivity, to tackle the problems at hand without referring to preconceived ideas or ideological strategies about what and how to preserve. An essay that Rogers wrote

12 See *Casabella* nº 232 (October 1959). This issue was prompted by CIAM '59, the congress in Otterlo, the Netherlands, that had precipitated the organisation's demise and at which Rogers's presentation of the Torre Velasca was severely criticised for failing to express a contemporary aesthetic and functionality. This episode prompted Rogers to respond with an editorial entitled 'CIAM at the Museum', followed by several illustrated pages describing the Torre Velasca, whose design stages are well documented, along with other achievements of the BBPR studio: Casa Lurani in Milan and the building in Corso Francia in Turin. All of this is prefaced by an article written by BBPR with the significant title 'Clarification', which explains how works so different in appearance are in fact the product of the same design method.

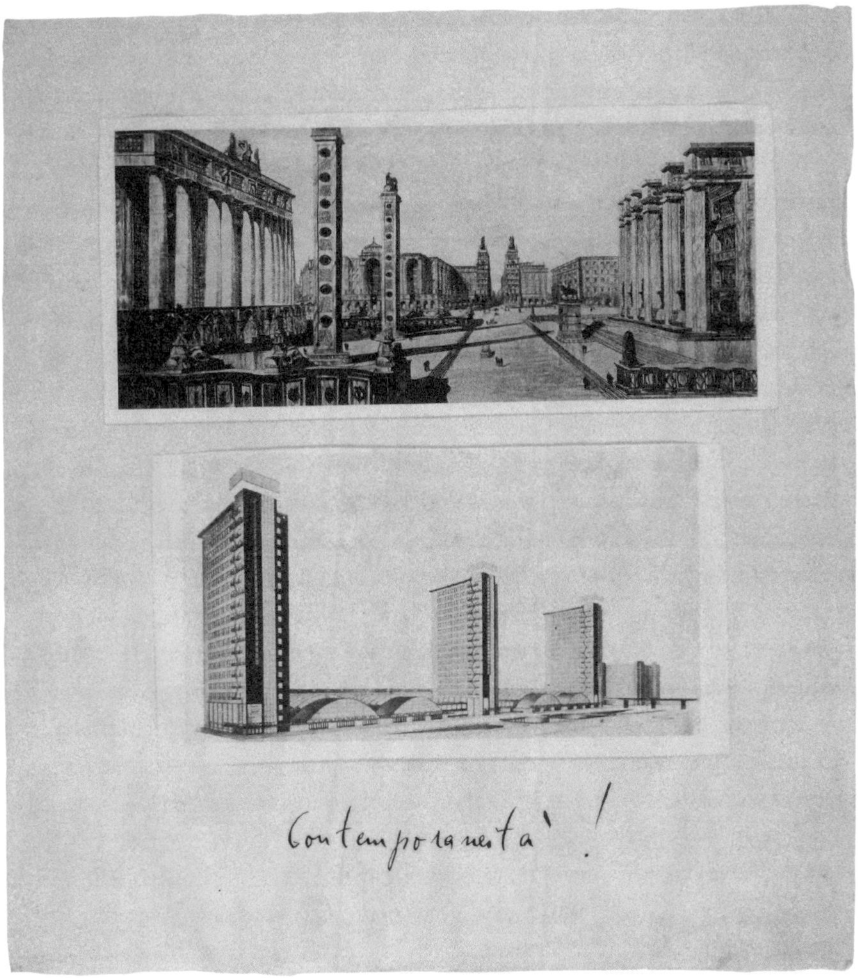

A page from Ernesto Rogers's notebook as a student © Giovanni Bonfanti

for Annoni's course is illustrated with a series of Wölfflin-inspired photographic juxtapositions. The images were cut out from books that he owned and assembled in rudimentary collages – even as a student, it seems, Rogers refused to analyse architecture through the sketch. Through these images he began to display a distinctive editorial approach as well as a certain freedom in juxtaposing past and present.[13]

In those same years, between 1930 and 1932, and in parallel with his studies, Rogers published about 30 articles in *Le arti plastiche* – a magazine of art criticism edited by Vincenzo Costantini. Rogers mainly reported on art exhibitions in Milan, but he also wrote on architectural themes, and particularly on the work of Le Corbusier, Bruno Taut, Henry van de Velde and Auguste Perret. In the reflections on contemporary architecture published in Le arti plastiche, there were overlaps with the essay that Rogers had written while on Annoni's course, both clearly expressing ideas, fuelled by the febrile atmosphere of the 1930s, that would flourish in his later writings. The ambiguity of the fascist regime's cultural agenda allowed room for multiple competing images of the state, sparking inflammatory debates that played out in contemporary magazines like *Casabella*, then edited by Edoardo Persico and Giuseppe Pagano, or Giò Ponti's *Domus*, both published in Milan; or Marcello Piacentini's *L'Architettura*, the official mouthpiece of the state architects' syndicate in Rome; or *Quadrante*, edited by Pietro Maria Bardi and Massimo Bontempelli, with bases in both Milan and Rome. With varying degrees of tolerance, all of these journals encouraged the expression of different points of view, spanning from the classicism of Piero Portaluppi through the refined Milanese *novecentisti* (twentieth centuryists), to the futurists and the avant-garde rationalism of Adalberto Libera and Giuseppe Terragni. These contrasting voices would coalesce to define a uniquely Italian strand of modernity – mercurial and continuously in crisis.

Through his writing, Rogers thrived in this intellectual milieu and, together with his associates, he became affiliated with its principal actors, starting with the circle around Pietro Maria Bardi, a distinguished writer, art critic and gallery owner whose connections would give Rogers entry to the wider international networks of CIAM. Bardi was an early adopter of the argument that modern architecture could serve the fascist regime's pursuit of rapid industrialisation and modernisation, as attested by his articles for the Milanese paper *L'Ambrosiano* in 1930.

13 See Michelangelo Sabatino, 'Ernesto N. Rogers studente. La scuola, i libri, gli scritti', *Casabella* nº 688 (2001): 76–83.

The co-founder, with Bardi, of *Quadrante* was the novelist and playwright Massimo Bontempelli. In the three years of its existence, from 1933 to 1936, *Quadrante* would galvanise contemporary Italian culture, politicising architecture and transforming its practice in interwar Italy. Militant and fiercely intellectual, the journal managed to draw Italian politicians, practitioners, academics and patrons into a cohesive movement that advanced the cause of modern architecture, adapting its principles to Italian culture while simultaneously promoting Italian modernism to the rest of Europe (and to South America, where Bardi was to flee with his wife Lina Bo Bardi after World War II). The *Quadrante* circle used a variety of means to stimulate cultural debate, staging exhibitions at Bardi's Galleria d'Arte di Roma and the Galleria del Milione in Milan, attending international congresses (every Italian delegate to CIAM contributed to the journal), inviting figures such as Le Corbusier to give lectures, building temporary installations at national expositions and participating in official and professional boards. Giuseppe Bottai – who was at various times the Minister of Corporations, Minister for Education and Governor of Rome – was a supporter of the journal – while the industrialist Adriano Olivetti (one of rationalism's key patrons) frequently argued in *Quadrante's* pages in favour of the corporate development of fascist politics; BBPR and Gruppo 7, among others, published urban plans based on those principles.[14]

Years later, reflecting on the rather dubious start to his career within *Quadrante's* circle, Rogers would write: 'We based ourselves on a syllogism which went roughly like this: 'fascism is a revolution, modern architecture is revolutionary, therefore it must be the architecture of fascism.'[15] In 1938 there was a sudden wake-up call for Rogers with the enactment of the racial purity laws. He was obliged to disassociate himself from all work at the studio and was banned from publishing under his own name. His diary – 'Lettere di Ernesto a Ernesto e viceversa' (Letters to and from Ernesto and vice versa), see page 73 – stands as a poignant record of his inner turmoil during this period. A few years later, in 1941, Giuseppe Pagano, then editor of *Domus* and *Casabella*, courageously offered Rogers a public platform while keeping his identity secret. A column in *Domus*, 'Confessioni di un Anonimo del XX secolo' (Confessions of a Twentieth-Century Anonymous Person) allowed

14 For a detailed study of *Quadrante* and its circle of architects, critics, artists, and patrons see: David Rifkind, *Battle for Modernism: 'Quadrante' and the Politicization of Architectural Discourse in Fascist Italy* (Venice: Marsilio, 2013).

15 Ernesto N. Rogers, 'Catarsi', *Costruzioni Casabella* nos. 195–198 (December 1946).

Rogers to take sardonic (if not explicitly political) swipes at the distortion of fascism's progressive ideals. These veiled critiques would be short-lived, however. After only nine instalments, his name was leaked to the authorities, and the series had to stop.

Belgiojoso relates that after the proclamation of the racial purity laws Rogers wandered the streets of Milan, evidently shattered and predicting an apocalyptic end not just for himself but for all Jews and for the nation as a whole – a striking reaction, given his measured nature and his obstinate determination to stay in the country. He eventually left in 1943, urged by his friends to flee to Switzerland.[16] But this was in no sense an idle retreat. During his exile he strengthened his ties with the international set, including Sigfried Giedion (the theoretical and political mastermind of the CIAM), Alfred Roth and Max Bill, who offered Rogers a first refuge at his house-atelier in Zurich with other intellectuals including Alfred Thomas, Hans Arp and Max Ernst. In 1944 Rogers began to teach theory of architecture and urbanism in the Italian section of the University of Lausanne, where courses were taught to and by the growing community of fugitive intellectuals. Among the Italian expatriates were prominent political figures like Luigi Einaudi and Amintore Fanfani, as well as Adriano Olivetti, all of whom were to play major roles in Italy's postwar reconstruction. In 1945 he was also teaching at the Haute École d'Architecture in Geneva, while writing articles on education and reconstruction for the *Bulletin du Centre d'Etudes pour le bâtiment*, which he co-directed. These first teaching and editorial positions, along with the 'Dear Ernesto' letters and his column for *Domus*, are significant in that they mark the emergence of a more singular voice, evolving from the 'shared tongue' that Rogers had established with his partners at BBPR, and clearly oriented towards the international scene. While Rogers was sheltering in Switzerland, all members of BBPR became involved with the anti-fascist movement, and both Banfi and Belgiojoso were deported to the Nazi concentration camp at Gusen. Banfi, tragically, did not survive.

After Italy's liberation in April 1945, Rogers returned to Milan to reconvene with Peressutti and Belgiojoso, ready to breathe new life into BBPR and into Italian architecture. The associates were among the founding members of the Movimento di Studi per l'Architettura (MSA), devoted to the propagation of CIAM principles in Italy, and the Casa della Cultura, which sought to further the causes of freedom and justice through a dialogue between disciplines – involving artists, journalists, doctors, philosophers,

16 Lodovico Barbiano di Belgiojoso, 'Alcuni Ricordi', in Serena Maffioletti, ed., *Architettura, misura e grandezza dell'uomo. Scritti 1930–1969* (Padova: Il Poligrafo, 2010): 20.

engineers, scientists and politicians. Meetings of the Casa della Cultura drew some of the most important figures in European culture, among them Alberto Moravia, Sibilla Aleramo, Jean-Paul Sartre, György Lukács, Henri Lefebvre, Bertolt Brecht and Jürgen Habermas.

This convergence of interests was already a distinctive trait of Milanese culture during the fascist years, in the circles gathered around *Quadrante*, *Domus* and *Casabella*. In the years following World War II, as Umberto Eco noted, architects, urban planners, designers and editors came together as 'the critics and interpreters of an industrial bourgeoisie with a radical-socialist inclination, trying on the one hand to master the problems of science, technology and industrial production, and on the other to modernise Italian visual culture'.[17]

In this context, Rogers was able to move seamlessly between activities at the MSA and the Casa della Cultura, between writing, teaching and practice, constantly fusing politics, philosophy and culture. Taking on the directorship of *Domus* in 1946 was something of a strategic move that allowed him to position himself in the postwar political debate.[18] The declared aim of *Domus* had always been to revitalise architecture, interiors, industrial production and the decorative arts in keeping with both the culture and the climate of Italy, and without overlooking topics of interest to women – stereotypically the arts of homemaking, gardening and cooking. Since its founding in 1928, *Domus* had waged a war of words on strict functionalism, with Ponti and his neoclassicist colleagues arguing that houses were not 'machines for living', as Le Corbusier called them, but rather sanctuaries of stylish beauty and refined comfort that provided 'the setting for Italian life'. During his brief tenure, Rogers reasserted this domestic theme by adding a subtitle – 'La casa dell'uomo' ('The house of man') – to the journal's name, and he gave *Domus* a fresh look, embraced new cultural trends and sought out the collaboration of intellectuals and writers such as Elio Vittorini and Alberto Moravia. He also used *Domus* to expose Italian culture to international debates, while at the same time arguing against the reduction of modernism to a mere 'international style' – one that was erasing history and context and increasingly applied in speculative building projects.[19]

17 See: Umberto Eco, 'Preface', in Vittorio Gregotti, *Il territorio dell'Architettura* (Milano: Feltrinelli, 1966, third edition): v–vii. Author's translation.

18 In summer 1945 Gianni Mazzocchi, the publisher of both *Domus* and *Casabella*, asked Rogers to take on the editorship of *Domus*. During the war Gio Ponti (founder of the magazine) had joined another publishing house, Garzanti, where he started the magazine *Stile*, and Giuseppe Pagano (editor of *Domus* in 1933) had died.

19 See Luigi Spinelli, 'La *Domus* di Rogers 1946-1947' in Chiara Baglione, ed., *Ernesto Nathan Rogers 1909-1969* (Milano: Francoangeli, 2012): 71–78.

The polemical tradition of architectural criticism in Italy – first established with *Quadrante* and Pagano's and Persico's contributions to *Casabella* and *Domus* – continued unabated after the war. In the Rome-based journal *Il Mondo*, founded by Mario Pannunzio in 1949, texts by the likes of Leonardo Benevolo and Ludovico Quaroni would appear alongside contributions by the archaeologist Antonio Cederna, who ignited a bitter, passionate political battle against the real-estate speculators who were wrecking historic city centres. If Cederna's polemics raised awareness of issues of quality – or the lack of it – in postwar reconstruction, his attitude towards modern architecture was intransigent. He argued that the modern city had to develop alongside, and not above or inside, the historic one. This clearly set him at odds not just with Rogers, whom he called a *regista invadente* (an intrusive director),[20] but with the Roman critic Bruno Zevi, who was using the pages of *Metron* and *Architettura* to argue against the preservationists who would turn the historic city into a museum, as well as to focus the debate around the issue of reconstruction, particularly in terms of urban planning.[21]

In his first editorial for *Domus* in 1946, and in line with the Milanese tradition of criticism, Rogers's newly found individual voice emerged clearly as he questioned the role that a magazine could play in the desolate context of postwar Italy.[22] 'Words too are construction material. And even a magazine can aspire to that status', he resolved, and went on to consider the problem

20 In 'Il regista invadente', *Il Mondo* (9 October 1956), Antonio Cederna criticises BBPR's recently completed restoration of the museums in Milan's Castello Sforzesco. Moving away from both the neutral backdrop of the gallery-like 'white room' and the contextual 'period room', BBPR (like other Italian architects of their time such as Franco Albini and Carlo Scarpa) had experimented with the idea of scenography, mixing history and the present, blurring the boundary between artworks and props, removing works of art from heavily decorated walls or cabinets so that they could shine in their own right and be fully experienced by the visitor. For Cederna and other critics, the display at the Castello Sforzesco was overly contrived and too subjective in its fictional reinterpretation of history.

21 For a more comprehensive overview of the landscape of architectural publications in postwar Italy, see: Marco Mulazzani, 'Le riviste di architettura. Costruire con le parole', in Francesco Dal Co, ed., *Storia dell'architettura italiana. II secondo Novecento* (Milano: Electa, 1997): 430–443; Vittorio Gregotti, *New Directions in Italian Architecture* (New York: Braziller, 1968): 38–41; Pippo Ciorra, *Senza architettura: Le ragioni di una crisi* (Roma-Bari: Laterza & Figli Spa, 2011): 77–89; and Giorgio Ciucci, 'Le riviste di architettura fra il 1945 e il 1965', *Rassegna di architettura e urbanistica* nº 146 (May–August 2015): 31–45.

22 Julia Banfi, Gianluigi's wife and Rogers's close collaborator at both *Domus* and *Casabella*, recalls how, 'flicking through the pages of *Domus* after 45 years, I am amazed at the fact that in four months, in a completely destroyed Milan where almost everything was missing, we were able to publish 64 pages of that magazine. Obviously, in spite of the devastation, there was in us and in all Italians, in fact in the best Europeans, such a desire for rebirth, such a belief in the right moment to realise new ideas in architecture and social life, and, to use a word that has unfortunately fallen into disuse, such an extraordinary commitment. The house of man was to be reinvented (many of us had lost ours and were living more or less huddled under one roof) without class distinctions, or so we thought.' Source: Julia Banfi, 'Esperienze con Rogers: Quadrante, Domus, Casabella', in *Quaderni del Dipartimento di Progettazione dell'Architettura del Politecnico di Milano 15. Ernesto Nathan Rogers: testimonianze e studi* (Milan: Città Studi, 1993): 19–21. Author's translation.

of reconstruction from a number of perspectives – economic, social, technical, cultural and ideological. Assigning the verb 'building' both a literal and metaphorical sense, he put the need to provide shelter for a homeless population on the same plane as the more metaphysical problem of mending Italy's social fabric by forming 'a taste, a technique and an ethics'.[23] The interiors he published in Domus during these years reflected practical solutions, such as the use of standardised, mass-produced furniture or prefabricated construction elements, but they also projected the vision of an ideal home, combining tradition with modernity. Photographs in *Domus* would often depict eighteenth-century furnishings next to items made in tubular steel, and would always include books, everyday objects and other tokens of human habitation. In this humanistic editorial line, and particularly in his strategic use of writing, Rogers strove to revive a tradition of combining architecture and literature at the highest level, using one to support the other – a tradition embodied by Leon Battista Alberti, the historical model that Rogers continuously referred to.[24] Years later, Rogers would clarify: 'I am no philosopher or literary-man, I am an architect who reads literature (and the poets) and writes, but who essentially designs and proves himself on the construction site.'[25] And yet behind his usual self-deprecatory tone, Rogers maintained a firm belief that intellectual enquiry and historical consciousness constitute the foundations of artistic and professional practice, the load-bearing material for any architect's work.[26]

True to this idea, when, in 1953, he became editor of *Casabella*, he promised to dedicate the magazine 'to the polemic surrounding vital topics', once again affirming that 'one builds no less with passionate discussion and the honest exchange of opinions as with tangible

23 Ernesto N. Rogers, 'Programma: Domus, la casa dell'uomo', *Domus* nº 205 (January 1946): 2–3. See page 125.

24 Less than two years later, this program, as aptly noted by Joan Ockman in her *Architecture Culture: A Documentary Anthology* (New York: Rizzoli, 1993), proved too challenging for the magazine and Rogers's appointment was terminated while the editorship of *Domus* returned to Ponti. In an editorial written in January 1947 titled 'Nota ai lettori' (Note to Readers), Rogers is already giving signals of emerging tensions with the publisher saying: 'This magazine, which some find too "bourgeois" and others too "progressive", costs us a lot of effort, an effort that far outweighs the results. Last year we published twelve issues: the editor showed us diagrams of each one's fate, like a midwife worrying about a child's physical fate; we in the editorial office showed him letters from all over the world, which flattered and encouraged us to continue along the path we have begun.'

25 Ernesto N. Rogers, 'Introduzione alla prima edizione', in Luca Molinari, ed., *Esperienza dell'architettura* (Milan: Skira, 1997: 8; first edition, Torino: Einaudi, 1958).

26 After less than two years, his appointment at *Domus* was terminated and the editorship returned to Ponti. Rogers took a break from editing and practising, travelling between 1948 and 1949 across the UK, USA and especially in South America.

materials.'[27] His first act as editor was to rename the magazine *Casabella Continuità*. Through the simple appending of the word continuity – an act clearly not without provocative intent – Rogers completely transformed the journal and helped to trigger a momentous shift in architectural research, which turned away from abstract expressionism and the question of new towns to focus on the problem of the war-torn fabric of historic city centres. *Preesistenze ambientali*, the metaphysical term Rogers used to identify this issue, would from that moment on haunt Italian architectural discourse, resonating well beyond the Alps. The banner 'continuity' was an exhortation to understand the modern movement as a 'continuous revolution' rather than a codified style; as a process which, as noted by Gregotti, is 'critical rather than organic with respect to society, and whose continuity lies in its ability to constantly critique itself to bring its own contradictions into consciousness and eventually overcome them.'[28] As Rogers stated in his first *Casabella* editorial, continuity 'means historical awareness, awareness of an essential tradition or *tendenza*, which, for Pagano and Persico, as for us, lies in the eternal variety of the spirit hostile to any sort of formalism, past or present. Dynamic continuation and not passive copying: not mannerism, not dogmatism, but rather research that is free of preconceptions and consistent in its methods.' Continuity, for Rogers, was therefore not about the past, but about the future. And tradition was something not to be passively inherited but rather to be constructed every day.

This layered idea of 'continuity' is manifest across several strands of Rogers's work as editor: in the way he built on the efforts of Pagano, who had transformed the original *La Casa Bella* into a critical journal;[29] in the consistency of his approach towards the various creative disciplines, from painting to film, sculpture and philosophy; in his references to pre-war Italian rationalism, rescuing it from the taint of fascism, and to early European modernism, restoring its connections to historical precedents. Continuity is also evident in the way Rogers saw his editorial work as complementary to, and even a mimesis of, the architectural project. As Gregotti observed:

27 Ernesto N. Rogers, *Casabella Continuità* nº 199 (December 1953–January 1954): 2–3.

28 Vittorio Gregotti, *Quaderni del Dipartimento di Progettazione dell'Architettura del Politecnico di Milano 15. Ernesto Nathan Rogers: testimonianze e studi* (Milan: Città Studi, 1993): 99. Author's translation.

29 Designers and critics who had already written during Pagano's editorship, such as Giulio Carlo Argan, Pier Luigi Nervi and Mario Labò, also contributed to write for Rogers's magazine.

... a magazine, as Rogers taught us to understand it, is constructed within a given set of constraints, through complex collaborations and daily, patient work that closely resembles the design process. At the same time, its result can only be fully appreciated in the long run, as a whole, as a series. The task of a magazine is to take what is happening around us as a kind of material, to create a critical distance [to help us make sense of reality], just as an architectural project should aim to do. A magazine must constantly take sides, just as a project must do so with its own tools. A magazine qualifies its line by what it chooses and what it excludes, by what it writes and what it writes against.[30]

Rogers's continuity was also a pragmatic response to the political situation in Italy. To address the severe housing crisis, the government had created the Gestione INA-Casa, a programme that diverted money from welfare provision into social housing, in the process largely defining the face of Italian architecture in the 1950s. The legal basis for the programme was the Piano Fanfani of 1949 – a seven-year plan for reconstruction drawn up by Amintore Fanfani, who had spent time with Rogers in exile in Switzerland. In addition to specific design recommendations, the plan implicitly criticised the monotony of modernist rationalisation and standardisation, calling instead for an urbanism that evoked spontaneity and 'genuineness'. It also had the explicit objective of boosting the economy. By deliberately keeping construction at a preindustrial, strictly manual level, it allowed for the 'absorption' of unskilled workers who had remained unemployed after the war.

As Giulio Carlo Argan remarked (in the exhibition catalogue of the 1952 RIBA exhibition on 'Italian Architecture'), 'problems of form have always played an extremely important part in Italian culture... Just as political conditions have mandated that questions of ethics are often presented in the guise of aesthetic issues, so in Italy the modern movement's stylistic problems have always taken precedence over ideological concerns.' In this sense Roman *neorealismo* and Milanese 'continuity' emerged as answers to the Piano Fanfani. *Neorealismo* emerged directly from its political context. The term extended beyond the domain of cinema and literature, coming to describe an architectural movement based on an informal and picturesque organisation of the plan and on the use of traditional materials for detailing, as exemplified by the Tiburtino complex in Rome (1954). In a context of austerity, neorealismo

30 Gregotti, *Quaderni del Dipartimento di Progettazione dell'Architettura ...* (1993): 99. Author's translation.

choreographed a populist, regressive utopia. Its ex-novo, pseudo-rural vernacular was intended to appear as the product of layers of historic sedimentation – a sop to residents who had relocated to the city from Italy's depopulating countryside.[31] Milanese 'continuity', on the other hand, was an attempt to find a middle ground between modernist constructive principles and a formal expression that could 'dialogue' with the masses by means of historical references and quotations.[32]

Rogers used his talents as an editor to encourage his young collaborators at Casabella (Giancarlo De Carlo, Aldo Rossi, Vittorio Gregotti, Gae Aulenti and Giorgio Grassi, among others) to study historical figures whose work challenged the canonical reading of architectural modernity (such as Adolf Loos, Auguste Perret, Henry van de Velde, Peter Behrens, Alessandro Antonelli and the architecture of the French Enlightenment). However, some of these attempts to incorporate history and regional traditions into modernism met with great resistance, particularly when some of his collaborators started to pursue their own subjective and introspective investigations using discrete fragments freely selected from the whole repertoire of architectural history – a shift that in some ways echoed the one that took place in film around the same time, as the work of formerly neorealist directors like Federico Fellini and Michelangelo Antonioni took on a more existentialist and oneiric tone.[33] Needless to say, some prominent figures in architecture took exception to this development, accusing Rogers of betraying modernism and contributing to an 'infantile regression' to historical references and eclectic forms of composition.

In the wake of this criticism, Rogers's role as an educator would also come under attack.[34] Italian institutions had always been wary of his pedagogical methods, on account of his tendency to integrate political and historical references. Another black mark was his reluctance to deliver certainties: in lectures he would frequently tell his students 'I'd like to reveal to you new horizons ... and let you move towards them under your own steam. These are limits that not even the Grand Masters of modernism can surpass.' Before gaining some level of

31 Bruno Reichlin, 'Figures of Neorealism in Italian Architecture (Part 1)', *Grey Room* nº 5 (Boston: The MIT Press, Autumn 2001): 78–101.

32 As observed by Manfredo Tafuri, *Storia dell'architettura italiana 1944–1985*: 20–21, 75.

33 See Paolo Portoghesi, 'Dal Neorealismo al neoliberty', *Comunità* nº 654 (1958): 69–79.

34 Rogers's roles as editor and educator were closely related; he dedicated several editorials to pedagogy (particularly towards the end of his tenure), and many of his students were invited to collaborate with *Casabella*: first Vittorio Gregotti and Gae Aulenti, followed by the 'young' Silvano Tintori, Aldo Rossi, Guido Canella, Giorgio Grassi and Aurelio Cortesi.

acceptance at home, he would first have to teach at many prestigious institutions abroad – in Lausanne, Geneva, London and at Harvard, where Walter Gropius proposed to make him his successor as Dean of the Graduate School of Design. It was only in 1952 that Rogers joined the faculty of the Politecnico di Milano, inheriting the course on 'stylistic characteristics of architecture' that had once been the preserve of his own teacher, Ambrogio Annoni. He would have to wait until 1964 to become a full professor.

Rogers had developed a teaching approach alongside Gropius through their association at the CIAM conferences, beginning with the one at Bergamo in 1949. He and Jane Drew, working together on the CIAM Educational Commission, had devised a pedagogy based on dialectics, teamwork, international exchange and dialogue between disciplines. The commission invited CIAM members to open their ateliers to students who could thereby broaden their practical and technical experience. Notably, they also argued for the need to study the history of architecture, not in isolation but in direct relation to the immediate problems of design practice. It was here, however, that their opinions diverged. Gropius argued that '[h]istory studies should be started in the third year rather than in the first, to avoid *intimidation* and *imitation*.'[35] Rogers found this demand ironic, in that it was advanced by 'people like Gropius (and other masters) who, despite knowing history very well, were not intimidated by it and did not feel compelled to imitate, but rather found it contributed substantially to their progressive ideas. So why deprive the young of an element necessary to their training?'[36]

To introduce younger generations to the discourses of CIAM congresses, the commission headed by Gropius and Rogers also assembled a global faculty and established a CIAM summer school. The

35 Walter Gropius, *Scope of Total Architecture* (New York and Evanston: Harper & Row, 1955): 53–56. Gropius feared that when 'the innocent beginner is introduced to the great achievements of the past, he may be too easily discouraged from trying to create for himself. As soon as he has found his bearings, however, through self-expression in workshop and studio, history studies are a welcome means of refining his thinking without luring him into an imitative attitude.'

36 In *Gli elementi del fenomeno architettonico*, Rogers writes: 'Since I consider myself a disciple of Gropius and not a slavish mannerist, I have tried to develop, either by dialectical contrast or by direct refutation, some statements which are typical of the generation of which he is the highest representative in the field of the education. Of these statements, the one that is furthest removed from my own thinking is the following: "Modern architecture does not consist of a few branches of an old tree, but is a new plant rising directly from the roots." It will be seen that the affirmation of the continuity of history ... is what gives this essay its character and is the essential reason why I wrote it. It should not seem paradoxical if I say that one must know history in order to forget it and become oneself. Indeed it is evident that forgetting is not oblivion, a disappearance, but a conscious, critical activity.' Author's translation.

BBPR Studio in via dei Chiostri, 1939 © GTA Archives / ETH Zurich Sigfried Giedion Papers

first session took place at the Architectural Association (AA) in 1949, with Rogers as an invited juror. That same year he was appointed as a visiting tutor at the AA, a school whose vitality and seemingly unstructured set up simultaneously fascinated and upset him. What Rogers absorbed from his encounter with the 'orchestra of students and the chorus of the AA' was a certain pre-existing climate of dissent. For him these were 'the most rebellious, the most obstinate and pretentious students': he referred to them affectionately as the 'we don't agree' gang.

So successful was Rogers's stay at the AA that the then principal, Robert Furneaux Jordan, made an informal exchange agreement with him, whereby the other BBPR partners would come in turn to the AA as visiting teachers, while a succession of AA students would spend a term based at BBPR's Milan studio – a sort of ad-hoc proto-Erasmus exchange. And indeed, by the early 1950s, Rogers's connections had made BBPR's studio – much like his own house in Via Bigli – the Italian base for various foreign architects linked to the international CIAM circuit. It was not uncommon to enter the door of Via dei Chiostri 2 and find personalities such Alvar Aalto, Walter Gropius, Le Corbusier, Richard Neutra, Tomás Maldonado, Edgar Kaufmann Jr, Sigfried Giedion, Bernard Rudofsky or Alfred Roth; the studio was also regularly visited by artists like Alexander Calder, Lucio Fontana and Saul Steinberg, or by entrepreneurs such as Adriano Olivetti, writers like Eugenio Montale, philosophers such as Enzo Paci, and the circle around of the journal *Aut Aut*, the Italian laboratory of phenomenology (to which Rogers himself was a frequent contributor).

All the subsequent CIAM summer schools, between 1952 and 1957, were held at the Istituto Universitario di Architettura di Venezia (IUAV) in Venice under the direction of Rogers, Franco Albini, Ignazio Gardella and Giuseppe Samonà. The initiative had an important impact in Italy, its emphasis on research, regional planning and student–faculty collaboration contrasting sharply with the traditional, style-based methods of Italian academia. CIAM's host school, the IUAV, would change its curriculum and to some extent become the new Milanese school, attracting Rogers and other BBPR partners, as well as members of the CIAM and the MSA.

Rogers's presence was one of the elements that prepared the ground in both Milan and Venice for the student turmoil of the late 1960s, partly because his approach to education combined the study of architecture with an extended exploration of the city, art, literature, philosophy, cinema, sociology, urban geography and, above all, politics,

Enrico Peressutti, Lodovico Barbiano di Belgiojoso, Ernesto Rogers and Saul Steinberg (from left to right) at the Labyrinth Milan, 1954. BBPR and Steinberg had collaborated on the Labyrinth installation in Parco Sempione for the X Triennale © Architectural Press Archive / RIBA Collections

but also because he embodied a certain polemical stance. 'One needs to have architecture in one's guts', he would tell his students.[37] In an era of rampant rationalism, that must have sounded like quite a provocation. Nor did he shy away from confrontation, even at the cost of straining his professional relationships. We can see this in his staunch defence of the Torre Velasca at the eleventh – and, not coincidentally, the last – meeting of CIAM at Otterlo in 1959, and in the fierce dispute over 'neoliberty' waged by Rogers and Reyner Banham in the pages of *Casabella* and *The Architectural Review*.

Though the term neoliberty was first coined by Paolo Portoghesi in 1958, the argument around it had begun some time before with the publication in *Casabella* nº 215 (April–May 1957) of an article by Aldo Rossi on liberty and some historically charged works of the Turinese architects Roberto Gabetti and Aimaro Isola. Rogers's editorials viewed the work of his young collaborators through a critical lens, but that was not enough for Banham, who in 1959 accused the whole contemporary Italian scene of a 'retreat from modern architecture'. Banham reserved his most acerbic remarks for the 'excessive, indulgent' Milanese, who reminded him, he said, of the destitute couple in Vittorio de Sica's film *Miracolo a Milano*; before food or shelter, they wanted a crystal chandelier. Rather than bringing about aesthetic and social renewal, the Milanese had changed little 'beyond the detailing and some amelioration of space standards'.[38] In response to this attack Rogers sarcastically labelled Banham the 'keeper of the frigidaires', mocking his fondness for new domestic appliances and his blind faith in technology. Though Banham was able to read Italian, Rogers suggested he had failed to interpret it correctly, his language skills not being adequate to the task, and invited him instead 'to make a direct reading of Ruskin, who was a great Englishman, without bothering with lame interpretations of Marinetti' and other contemporary manifestations of Italian culture.[39]

In the same neoliberty exchange Banham labelled Rogers the 'hero-figure of European architecture in the late 1940s and early 1950s'. For Banham this was the ultimate rebuke, dismissing Rogers as out of step with his time and with the cultural revolution brought about by

37 See Francesco Gnecchi Ruscone, 'Un'amicizia nella scuola e nella vita', *Quaderni del Dipartimento di Progettazione dell'Architettura del Politecnico di Milano 15. Ernesto Nathan Rogers: testimonianze e studi* (Milan: Città Studi, 1993): 15–16.

38 Reyner Banham, 'Neoliberty. The Retreat from Modern Architecture', *The Architectural Review* nº 747 (1959): 231-235.

39 Ernesto N. Rogers, 'L'evoluzione dell'architettura. Risposta al custode dei frigidaires', *Casabella Continuità* nº 232 (October 1959): 2.

mechanisation, which had 'permanently altered the nature of domestic life and architecture'. Banham's choice of words illustrates how Rogers's arguments had been misconstrued by the English-speaking world. In a radical break from the established modernist discourse, Rogers understood 'progress' as a state of constant crisis and interrogation (much like the Italian intellectual climate of the 1930s), with different voices negotiating a variety of positions to enrich modernist discourse and move it forward. At the time, the British still clung to the much more Whiggish view of a clear, unchecked line of progress through time.

The debate continued at the Otterlo CIAM in 1959, where Rogers gave a presentation on BBPR's Torre Velasca, justifying the building's eclectic structure as the outcome of functional and technical considerations on the one hand, and of a historical analysis of the *preesistenze ambientali* on the other. The backlash was violent, though hardly unexpected. Rogers was attacked by Team 10 members Jaap Bakema and Peter Smithson, who declared that the Velasca was a formalistic exercise and a dangerous model for imitation. To these accusations Rogers famously replied: 'There is one main difficulty that I see and that is that you think in English.' The irony, of course, was that Rogers was not averse to thinking in English himself – by his own admission, his favoured concepts of tradition and *preesistenze ambientali* were indebted to the work of the poet T. S. Eliot, for whom 'The historical sense involves a perception, not only of the pastness of the past, but also of its presence.' But his Anglo-Saxon interrogators remained unconvinced, and the confrontation at Otterlo exposed the irreconcilable differences between the English and the Italian contingents.[40] Rogers's vision of modernism as 'a truly international language sprung from mutual understanding' – the words are from his inaugural editorial for *Casabella* in 1954 – now appeared fundamentally out of reach.

Rogers's dialogue with an English-speaking audience continued to prove difficult. One year after Otterlo he submitted to Harvard's Belknap Press a collection of essays whose translation he had personally funded. The response from William Warren Smith, a senior editor, was less than encouraging: 'There are many items which will have to be shortened or eliminated ... e.g., there are references to the positions of architects under fascism, which are "old hat" and would be unlikely to interest English-speaking people ... or references to the postwar political scene too parochial to be left in... One chapter is a sentimental lament

40 The exchange is recorded in Jürgen Joedicke, ed., *CIAM '59 in Otterlo: Documents of Modern Architecture* (London: Alec Tiranti, 1961): 92–97.

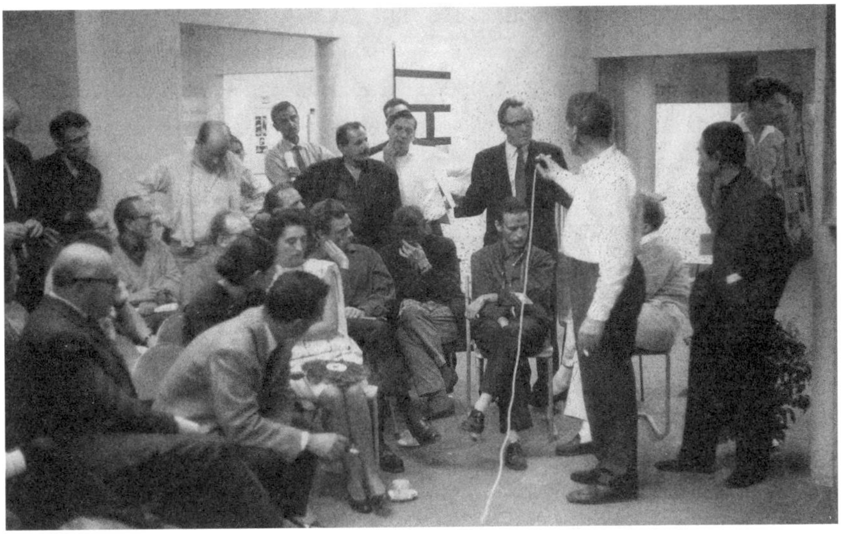

A meeting at CIAM II in Otterlo, Netherlands, 1949. Rogers is seated on the left in the foreground, in the group are also (from left to right) Peter Smithson, Jacob Bakema, Alison Smithson, Georges Candilis, Shadrach Woods, Aldo van Eyck, Giancarlo de Carlo, Kenzo Tange © Bakema, J.B. Archief / Het Nieuwe Instituut

over a friend and colleague who died in the war and will certainly have to be omitted.'[41] Perhaps unsurprisingly, the anthology was never published. Rogers's international reputation continued to decline, hastened in 1965 by a changing of the editorial guard at *Casabella* and the ascendancy of a new generation of architects, including Aldo Rossi, Carlo Aymonino, Giorgio Grassi, Luciano Semerani, Francesco Polesello and Francesco Tentori. Rogers's loss of this editorial role coincided with the onset of a prolonged illness that would severely impair his professional life, and tragically, for several years, completely deprived him of his voice before his premature death in 1969.[42]

Fifteen years earlier, a characteristically self-deprecatory Rogers had lamented to his friend Luciano Semerani, 'I'm 50 years old and I've achieved nothing: I don't own a house, I don't have a family, or a position within a university, I haven't realised any major works or published a book yet.' Things would soon change. Within a couple of years he had completed a building that would dominate European architectural discourse. While remaining central to that discourse in Italy through his editorship of *Casabella Continuità*, he would also enjoy a succession of academic appointments at some of the world's most prominent schools and publish his first book with Einaudi.[43] He would even, soon afterwards, buy a beautiful house in Milan's Brera neighbourhood, which was a favourite part of the city for Stendhal, an author particularly cherished by Rogers.

One must therefore always judge the extent of Rogers's achievements – and particularly his literary efforts – against the parallel extent of his own self-doubt. A master of understatement throughout his career, he shied away from the pomposity of titles such as 'historian' or 'theoretician', refusing to fix his words in a treatise or compose a systematic narrative of the history of the modern movement. He chose

41 See Luca Molinari, *Continuità: A Response to Identity Crises: Ernesto Nathan Rogers and Italian Architectural Culture after 1945* (Delft: TU Delft, 2008): 243.

42 Rogers died at Gardone, Lombardy, on 7 November 1969 and was buried in his native Trieste.

43 In 1956 Rogers was awarded an Honorary Fellowship by the American Institute of Architects and, to mark the occasion, he toured the USA to lecture at several universities. Rogers's seminal book, *Esperienza dell'architettura*, developed since 1950, was published in 1958 and, the following year, he held the Chair of Italian Culture at the University of California Berkeley. During the late 1950s and early 1960s he was also offered teaching posts, although unable to accept the invitations at MIT, Harvard, Yale, and the Hochschule für Gestaltung at Ulm (Germany). Having lectured extensively in Italy, Europe, in the USA and in China, he spoke at the International Design Conference in Aspen, USA, in 1957 and gave a lecture on Le Corbusier at Columbia University in 1961; in 1963, he was inducted as Honorary Fellow of the Royal Institute of British Architects.

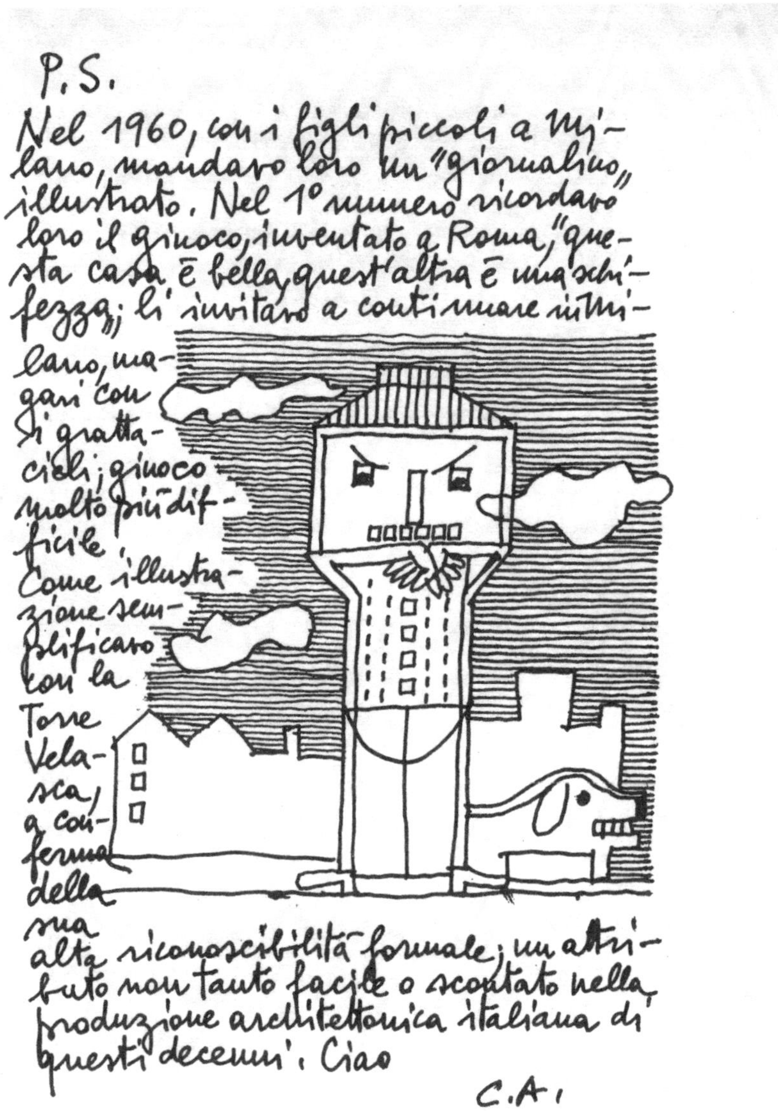

Carlo Aymonino, Torre Velasca, from *Zodiac* 3, 1960

instead the editorial, the lecture, the article in a journal or the epistolary exchange to give voice to his reflections. These traces, samples and soundbites, dispersed in notes, periodicals and the memories of his interlocutors, have been selected and assembled in books on only a handful of occasions: *Esperienza dell'architettura* (1958), *Gli elementi del fenomeno architettonico* (originally printed in 1961 but not published until 20 years later) and *Editoriali di architettura* (1968); a number have appeared posthumously in new translations in Joan Ockman's *Architecture Culture 1943–1968* (1993) and in Serena Maffioletti's *Architettura, misura e grandezza dell'uomo* (2010). For this reason, Rogers has been largely neglected by historians, who have taken his self-deprecatory attitude literally, thus allowing him to draw a veil over his own heroic efforts to 'humanise' the work of the great modernist masters and open them up for contemporary criticism and debate.

Nearly 60 years after the death of Ernesto Nathan Rogers, now that the dust has settled on the polemics that undermined his reputation towards the end of his many careers, this book aims to celebrate this complex and controversial figure in a first-ever English anthology of his writing. It goes without saying that the act of translation brings with it certain objective difficulties, which are tied not only to the nature of the languages in question, but also to Rogers's complex relationship with English culture, which throughout his life was something both irreconcilably alien and suffocatingly familiar.[44] Of course, at the same time there is an obvious irony in the idea of 'reading' Rogers's voice in English, an unnatural form for him, whereas his Italian always 'flowed fresh, precise, clear, immediate' and with 'such a firm unity between thought and expression that the two could not be told apart', as he wrote in the 1940s. Now we are forcing Rogers to change language and face what he termed 'the sound barrier of difficult words', but with the sole purpose of allowing his voice, and his doubts, to reverberate and to reach new audiences.

44 Perhaps one of the main difficulties has to do with the 'beauty' of Rogers's writing, which often seems like a seductive amalgam that introduces a certain vagueness of meaning. In fact, even after a careful reading, one is left with the feeling of not having completely solved Rogers's riddle – a characteristic that doesn't translate easily into the more pragmatic English language.

In the mid-1950s, after 20 years of drifting from hotel to hotel, Rogers finally settled in a nineteenth-century building in Via Bigli, in the historic centre of Milan. This text, written for *Domus*, is his account of the house he had just adapted for himself and is in many ways a kind of autobiography as well as a testament to his idea of *preesistenze ambientali*, whereby traditional elements, the substratum, are reactivated by additions selected according to personal values, thus creating a new, original work.

On the ground floor there is a succession of three small rooms, parallel to the internal garden, with French windows opening onto it; on the upper floor are the studio and the bedroom. The rooms are lined with Madagascar panama canvases hung from rails that conceal the wall with shelves, a mobile bar and a wardrobe. The floors are covered with rugs and mats from Montenegro. The many paintings are by Giuseppe Capogrossi, Alexander Calder, Roberto Sambonet, Max Bill, Bruno Munari, Fernand Léger and Le Corbusier. The furniture consists of a few simple pieces, some designed by Rogers himself, others inherited. The objects, of no particular value, were bought by him on his many travels around the world or in antique shops; they represent his life and 'resemble [his] humanity.'[1]

1 On a different occasion, in his first editorial for *Domus* n° 205 (January 1946): see page 131, Rogers wrote: 'I want to have a house that resembles me (in a flattering way): a house that resembles my humanity.'

AN ARCHITECT FOR HIMSELF

DOMUS NO. 326, JANUARY 1957

My house: the house of a bachelor is, like his life, a trifle incomplete, but there are certain advantages to be derived precisely from the nature of this condition; in other words, a certain nonchalance and at the same time the organisation of a coherent discourse undisturbed by the tastes of others.

For 20 years I lived in one hotel or another, and everyone told me I should have a home of my own, if only because I was an architect. The one I finally have is not mine, but it is for me; I can no longer understand how I managed to live for so long as a wanderer, outside this shell that is now as necessary for me as a suit and shoes.I have the good luck to live in an area of Milan known to Stendhal, an author I particularly cherish; when I go back to read his work, I feel as though I am moving through my own rooms. If he describes the Milanese gardens (some remnants of which can be seen through my windows), it seems as if he has come to visit me and is marvellously recreating what I see every day.

It might seem strange that it is harder for an architect to design a home for himself than a house for other people, but this task is actually a way of giving concrete form to [the maxim] *cognosce te ipsum* (know thyself) that - as we know - is the most important and unsolvable challenge an individual can set for himself.

There are no such things as ideal houses, only those that have been made according to the needs of given moments in history: the rest are utopias. For this reason I have tried to turn to the fullest possible advantage the givens of the situation: to interpret them in my own way, not perceiving them passively but rather taking possession of them and transforming them in line with my own practical and spiritual needs. When a building is constructed, the essential issue is inserting it into the *preesistente ambientali,* the existing setting, whether natural or historical; likewise, the arrangement of an interior should not be considered separately from the character of the host construction or from the natural landscape (if there is one) that enriches the setting.

The modernity - the actuality - of this work lies in the personal values embodied in this insertion. And one needs to know a sufficient amount about oneself to be certain of interpreting life in its every aspect. Had I been able to redesign the rooms of my house from scratch,

Ernesto Rogers's private flat in a 19th-century building in the historic centre of Milan, 1957
© Fondo Casali / IUAV Archivio Progetti

I would have tried to create something similar to what I found in this old building in the heart of Milan.

It goes without saying that the first negative limit (of this reality that, as a whole, is very positive) was that I had to impose a certain discipline upon myself, financial and otherwise, in order to avoid my desires running away with me. Actually, I do not own a single object of particular material value: from my parents' home, destroyed in part by the sad circumstances of poverty and in part by Nazi barbarity, I have inherited very few things, which are rather like the keynote of my emotional intonation. The rest is made up of objects purchased in the course of my many travels or in the recesses of antique shops I visit either out of curiosity or in a professional capacity.

I do not like technique except as a means to express poetic sentiments, but I can't stand badly made things. Though simple - and maybe precisely because they are simple - the few furnishings I have designed demand skill on the part of their makers: therefore I have entrusted them to Piero Frigerio of Cantù, who works with the love and skill of an ancient Italian artisan; and I am also grateful to him for having given me the chance to realise so accurately the things I have imagined.

The paintings are all gifts from the artists, who have shown their affection for me over the years. One day a colleague, examining a shelf with Peruvian, Greek and Brazilian pottery, remarked in jest that: 'it seems like the home of an explorer'. I have discovered nothing, not even myself, but I took this definition as a compliment: at least it seems to jibe with the secret aspirations of my dreams. In my dreams I am, naturally, a much better architect.

A SHARED TONGUE

Rogers's final thesis at the Politecnico di Milano was accompanied by this introduction, written 'by eight hands'. In it, Banfi, Belgiojoso, Peressutti and Rogers declared their association and commitment to one another, inspired by the anti-individualist and collaborative spirit of fascism as well as by Walter Gropius's philosophy of 'teamwork'. Shortly after writing this manifesto, they founded BBPR – the name formed from the initial letters of their names.

As the last survivor of BBPR, Belgiojoso has often offered perspectives on and memories of the group's internal dynamics. In one of his many accounts, he recalled that their four graduation projects, which, according to the institution's rules, had to be produced individually, were developed together and presented with common graphics, even in the details. 'From then on' – he added – 'our collaboration intensified. [...] We had different characters and family backgrounds, but we also had some common denominators in our personalities that allowed us to translate our work together into a common form of existence.'[1]

This way of working, as Manfredo Tafuri clarifies while reflecting on BBPR and similar types of association which were flourishing in Milan and Rome at the time, was in sharp contrast to the 'functional division of labour' that prevailed in more conservative circles. 'For these young groups, teamwork was chosen as a means of fostering human and professional relationships which, through the continuous debate of ideas, allowed them to attain a rigorous moral dimension and develop a cultural and professional objectivity that stood in stark contrast to the careless and amateurish behaviour of old and new generations of conservative academics' – of the kind ruling the universities and the profession during the fascist years and beyond.[2]

1 Lodovico Belgiojoso, 'Il lavoro di gruppo', in *Quaderni del Dipartimento di Progettazione dell'Architettura del Politecnico di Milano 15. Ernesto Nathan Rogers: testimonianze e studi* (Milano: Città Studi, 1993): 11–14. Author's translation.

2 Manfredo Tafuri, *Ludovico Quaroni e lo sviluppo dell'architettura moderna in Italia* (Milan: *Edizioni di Comunità*, 1964): 29–30.

Previous: From left Ernesto Rogers, Enrico Peressutti, Lodovico Belgiojoso, Gianluigi Banfi with their mentor Piero Portaluppi, 1930s © Fondo Peressutti / IUAV Archivio Progetti

PRESENTATION OF DEGREE PROJECTS

WITH GIANLUIGI BANFI, LODOVICO BARBIANO DI BELGIOJOSO, ENRICO PERESSUTTI

PUBLISHED IN *ESPERIENZA DELL'ARCHITETTURA* (TURIN: EINAUDI, 1958)

POLITECNICO DI MILANO, JULY 1932

Architecture is the sublimation of the necessities of life; it is the art that defines time in space.

Being modern simply means existing; being rational means little more than possessing the *sine qua non* for existence.

Being architects - i.e., artists - is something else entirely.

We will not therefore boast of such qualifications, just as elsewhere we would not boast of being honest men.

What is a man if he is not honest? And likewise, what is an architect if he is not logical?

We have a higher aspiration: we believe it is not enough for an architect to build; we also feel the need to speak, to express through the synthesis of our work not just the contingencies of life but the thought and the character of the present era.

And because speaking calls for a language intelligible to most people, we have agreed, together, to seek the high road through the labyrinth of art.

We are less concerned with individual personality than we are with the personality of the work. It matters little to us if a building is said to be by 'this architect' or 'that architect' if the monument does not communicate its own soul. A house has first and foremost to be a house; whether it is 'mine' or 'yours' is less important.

An artist, if he is truly an artist, always leaves some trace of himself in his work, and we believe this sign will be etched more deeply when the artist is less intent on making his mark.

This is the principle that informs our projects, and it requires each of us to sacrifice our own personal ambitions. Extreme individualism is not just, in many cases, thinly veiled egotism, but a generator of signature or whimsical oddity; in defying logic and aesthetics, it damages society.

If, after all the extremely subjective experiences of romanticism, we wish to avoid regressing into a dangerous Babel, then the words of individuals need to come together in a living, shared tongue. The artwork will be original, not when the artist has capriciously placed his own superficially ornamental seal upon it, but when the clear equilibrium of the organism expresses the inner essence and newness of the interpretative concept.

We have felt the need to start by saying these things, so that the uniformity of our guise will not seem like inner poverty, but rather will serve as a reminder - if only as something to aspire to - of the Franciscan maxim that teaches us to be simple on the outside in order to shine from within.

This article is an edited version of a speech Rogers gave at the eponymous international conference, organised by *L'Architecture d'aujourd'hui* and held in Milan in 1933, with speakers including Peter Behrens, Victor Horta, Clemens Holzmeister and Auguste Perret. The text was published in the same year in *Quadrante*, the magazine edited by Pietro Maria Bardi and Massimo Bontempelli, which often featured articles and projects by BBPR and which, during its short-lived existence (1933–36), completely transformed the practice of architecture in fascist Italy, organising the most prominent practitioners and patrons of Italian rationalism into a coherent movement that championed modern architecture as an explicitly fascist mode of construction – as the many references to Mussolini's speeches in this text by Rogers testify.

This is also one of Rogers's first texts on education, a subject he would return to throughout his life. He prefaced his most important book, *Esperienza dell'architettura* (1958), with a reflection on the architect's craft and ended his writing career with a short article on 'some principles for the architect' (*Lineastruttura* nº 1, 1966). Other contributions on education are: 'Problemi di una scuola d'architettura' (*Bulletin du Centre d'Etudes pour le bâtiment*, 1944); 'Lo stato dell'arte' (*Domus* nº 210, 1946); 'Per gli studenti d'architettura' (*Domus* nº 213, 1946); 'Chi siete voi?' (*Venezia Architettura* nº 3, 1953, see page 279); numerous editorials in *Casabella Continuità*, mostly written towards the end of his tenure and containing reflections on the training of architects and the university (a selection of which is collected in the last section of *Editoriali di Architettura*, 1965); and finally, *Gli elementi del fenomeno architettonico* (Rome–Bari: Laterza, 1961, see extracts on page 307).

THE FORMATION OF AN ARCHITECT

QUADRANTE NO. 6, OCTOBER 1933

We enter school with one hope, leave it with another, and die still with nascent aspirations. This is our fate, and this should also be our credo - always to be pushing the finishing line forward, never satisfied that we have done enough.

We go to school with our childish illusions of 'what I want to be when I grow up', and the school has the task of sending us back into the world as useful men.

We are artists, but we do not want this lofty title to imply an egocentric and anarchic individualism. Like any other citizen, we have to be active cells in society, performing a specific function within it - a profession. We are art professionals specialising in architecture.

For five years, the school oversees the mining of our souls and our brains: it has to guide us as we tunnel along a path to reach our precious ore, bring it to light, refine it, so that each of us can give our best to society.

Artists are born, but architects, painters and sculptors are made. The art of philosophers is intuitive, but it is an abstract art; the arts are intuitions developed through the acquisition of knowledge - study is required.

The truth is inside each one of us: we carry it like a bud within us; the school has the task of watching over its marvellous development and helping it to happen. School and students must engage in the deftest Socratic dialogue to uncover the truths hidden in the youthful soul.

The static academy gives way to the concept of a dynamic, shaping school. Since art cannot be 'taught', the school must instead supply all the means necessary to acquire the techniques of the art - to furnish the possibility of practising it.

In this way, the tension that often exists between the generations will vanish, because the students will view their teachers not as high priests of some infallible dogma, but rather as the baptisers of their own creations, while the teachers will find in their students not a reiteration of their own stylistic prejudices, but rather the perpetuation of their hopes.

In an era of political realism in which it is boldly asserted that 'treaties are not eternal',[1] we artists and critics, too, must fearlessly acknowledge the continuous flow of life, running along the riverbed of history and relentlessly sweeping aside the barriers of convention.

We no longer believe in the inviolable families of the metopes and triglyphs, the bucrania and cornucopias, just as we no longer believe in the dusty symbolic languages of the defunct masonic brotherhoods.

We need to look life in the face, to approach it, to run with it; we need to represent it in our work, adhering to its spirit.

There is but one dictum, and that is to be modern – not like the ivy that attaches itself to something and clings on until death, but like the primroses that bloom as the snow melts, approaching spring with unshakable faith.

Every tradition is valid to the extent that it offers energy for the present, but every tradition should be resolutely jettisoned when it fuses with prejudice: the dogmas of Vitruvius and Vignola, at this point, are prejudices.

The spirit counts, forms count for less; the school can guide spirits, but it cannot imprint brains: it has to reveal the problems of life, not solve them for us. Art is love, architecture is love, one cannot impose a way of loving, one cannot teach how to love, or love in someone else's stead.

1 This is a reference to a well-known remark by Mussolini, first made when he was a deputy in the Italian parliament, repeated later in speeches or interviews when he was Prime Minister and finally included in his famous Declaration of War speech on 10 June, 1940, when, having withheld formal allegiance to either side in the war between Germany and the Allies, the dictator of Italy had a change of heart and declared war on France and Great Britain. Addressing the Senate on 5 June 1928 he justified his foreign policy as follows: 'No treaty has ever been eternal, because the world moves, peoples are formed, grow, decline and sometimes die: the eternity of a treaty would mean that at a given moment, by some monstrous miracle, humanity had undergone a process of mummification, in other words, had died.'

The assistance we demand of a school is similar to what a child asks of its parents: 'Mama, give me your hand. I want to jump'. The mother does not jump for the child, she gives him her hand and says, 'Land on your toes, not on your heels, and bend your knees.' She teaches the technique. By technique I mean not just those things that grant us knowledge of the material world but also, and especially, that which teaches us to know ourselves and the world of the spirit – the world of the greats who came before us, be they saints from St Francis to St George, or artists from Fra Angelico to Caravaggio.

'Love, Reverence, Obedience, Perseverance' – these virtues, which Cennino Cennini describes as fundamental for art, must unite those who teach and those who learn in a shared humility, in a willingness to sacrifice individual ambition for the supreme purpose of life, which is to serve.

In life, after five years, we gain the title of Doctor of Architecture, the word *dotto* indicating someone learned, a specialist.[2]

A medical doctor takes a person's pulse and says, 'Get some air, rest and do not smoke', and to please the doctor the good patient may deny himself such pleasures. We say, 'Fresh air, light, simplicity', but a good client may turn away and grumble: 'These kids are nuts!'

No, we are not nuts, we are sick and tired of seeing our faith described as fanaticism, of seeing our concerns, our problems, our research derided and scorned. Those living postulates of Darwinian theories are only happy when they're surrounded by pinchbeck gilding and fake coats of arms.

The time has come to put an end to all that, to the dusty melancholy of the past.

We should not be afraid of clients or pander to their pretensions with fake embrasures and other tricks. If the walls are thin, it is the task of the architect to take advantage of that thinness; if the house is cheaply made, the artist has to find a poetic take on such

2 In Italy anyone who has a university degree in any subject can be addressed with the title *Dottore* (Doctor).

parsimony. And don't use references to tradition to mask your own creative impotence: the fable of the fox and the grapes will do just fine to skewer anyone who poses as a superman.

Modern architecture – a rational architecture that effectively reconnects the art of building with its reason for being – is no job for idlers. Let's not split hairs about the word 'rational'. Of course, this improper term, which we use reluctantly, should not be interpreted in an absolute, dogmatic sense. We could just as easily say 'functional'.

Functional is the opposite of sentimental, just as classical is the opposite of romantic, or the twentieth century the opposite of the nineteenth.

Of necessity, modern architecture translates the economic into the ethical, and the ethical into the aesthetic – a dual process of conversion that bears witness to its relevance in an era in which all resources are directed towards the solution of the social problem. Mussolini outlines the architecture of his own political beliefs with words we might paraphrase to express our own convictions as artists.

He puts it like this: 'We are for the collective meaning of life and we want to reinforce it [even] at the cost of the individual life: in doing so, we do not go so far as to transform men into cyphers, but we consider them above all in terms of their function in the State.' Functional citizens, functional architecture.

And just as we reject those who want to place false pilaster strips behind the pillars of society, so we do not allow hypocritical arches that pretend to be bearing a load while concealing the strength of reinforced concrete beams.

There has to be one direction in life.

Great steps have been made, including here in Italy, on the correct course for this century.

In Italian architecture schools - and I speak with particular knowledge of the one in Milan, which I had the pleasure of attending for five years - the academic mildew is dispersing and fresh air is circulating in the lecture halls.

In life, the public is observing with growing attention and less distrust that forward-looking artists, and indeed many mature architects, are trying to advance beyond their own past by aligning themselves with the young.

The Italian national anthem is *Giovinezza* (Youth). We certainly would not deny youth to anyone, even at the age of 80, if they prove their ability, but above all we do not, under any circumstances, want our own young people to be denied at the age of 20.

THE VOICE OF THE ANONYMOUS

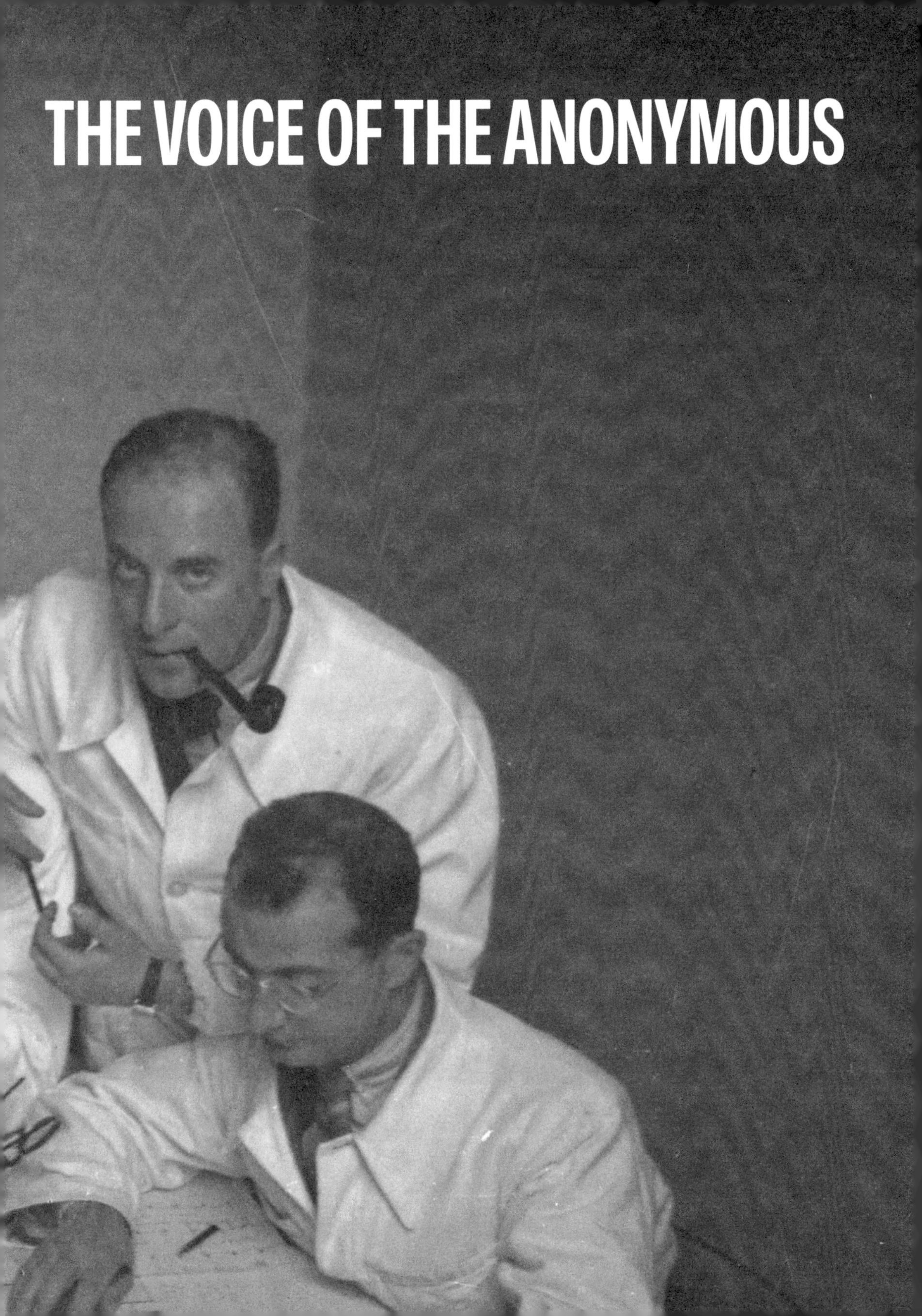

The series comprises 42 short letters dating from 1938 and 1939, typewritten and with handwritten corrections. The letters were initially found by Michelangelo Sabatino in the Bonfanti archive and subsequently compiled by Luca Molinari as *Lettere di Ernesto a Ernesto e viceversa* (Milan: Archinto, 2000). A selection also appears in *Architettura, misura e grandezza dell'uomo* (Padova: Il Poligrafo, 2010), along with a poignant note by Rogers found by Serena Maffioletti in the BBPR archive among copies of the letters from which she had selected:

If the sadness that pervades these writings may seem excessive and unbearable to some, may I be forgiven, for they are meant to be a testimony of my soul at a time when, having lost everything I had in the world, I have become very rich inside, with so many tears, so much suffering, so many memories, so many hopes, that it seemed right and humane to share them with others who might find strength to endure their own sufferings.[1]

The letters in the selection that appears below were written by Rogers following the promulgation of the racial laws on 19 November 1938 that banned Jewish people from making work or making their names known, effectively prohibiting them from existing in the public space. The young Rogers, 'an architect of almost 30 years old', and one of the leading figures of modern Italian architecture, was suddenly erased from the firm's letterhead, from the magazines to which he contributed, and his name expunged from the documentation of projects he was involved in, all of which he was forced to abandon.

Through these letters, Rogers begins to distance himself from fascism. While the letters contain no direct references to the regime or to historical events, this process takes place through a painful internal dialogue with a 'multiple Ernesto', described by Luca Molinari as 'a sum of different personalities that follow one another, crowding the scene, disturbing and provoking the narrating ego, forcing it to constantly open the windows and doors of the soul, to expose forgotten secrets and sorrows.'[2] The letters that follow offer a glimpse of Rogers's agonised reckoning.

1 Author's translation.

2 Luca Molinari, 'Alcune note al margine' in *Lettere di Ernesto a Ernesto e viceversa* (Milano: Archinto, 2000): 8. Author's translation.

Previous: BBPR at work in the 1930s in the studio of via Borgonuovo. From left Enrico Peressutti, Lodovico Belgiojoso, Ernesto Rogers and Gianluigi Banfi © Fondo Banfi / IUAV Archivio Progetti

DEAR ERNESTO

WRITTEN BETWEEN 1938 AND 1939

1

Dear Ernesto,

On this November day, solitude brings me closer to you; I return to find you here once more, just like when I first discovered you inside me – my image in the mirror.

Time has passed, bringing dawns, sunsets, loves, suffering and the laborious birth of my art.

In those days I was a pale young man, skinny, with a thatch of hair over an ample, sloping brow; I observed the life of others without understanding, never realising that it was by suffering that I lived, that suffering was in fact life itself (the heat of the flame).

How many conversations we have had since then, you and I, until my breath veiled the mirror and you left me on my own, a body without a shadow.

As the years went by you became stronger, and little by little I seemed to learn how to turn a smile into laughter so that my mouth, up to then always a bit lopsided, softened into a more equable expression.

But not yet having reached 30, this is not the time to write my own biography; forgive me, Ernesto, if I have led thoughts back to the past at a moment so laden with anguish of its own.

Have we ever been so sad, in all the time we have been acquainted?

A multiple series of moats rings the castle of my life: I cannot escape.

I have only you, Ernesto; give me strength, persuade me that I have no need of the world, because as long as I breathe I embrace the Universe and as long as I dream the Universe is in me.

See you tomorrow! I'm drowsy; who'll fall asleep first, you or I?

Ernesto

5

Ernesto,

You are as hateful to me as a cloven devil, as bad company: if I need you I cannot find you, and if I ask you for advice you're like an echo and repeat my words; if I look into your eyes I see what ails me in your pupils; you are like the moon in the well, an object of luxury without substance.

~~'My God, help me'~~ [sic] Neither does any God exist in me to help us.[3]

E

3 None of the letters comment on this directly, but a distant God hovers over everything, ultimately unhelpful. In spite of (or perhaps because of) his secular upbringing, religion was a persistent source of difficulty throughout Rogers's life. (The lines through text appear in the original manuscript).

6

Dear Ernesto,

My apologies for the other day.

It really is impossible to feel a toothache for someone else; you can feel sorry for him, console him, but in the end it's the guy with the rotten tooth whose cheek swells up.

This is an elementary observation, yet it comes to mind only when you have your own troubles, which I saw before me as I told good and dear, close, brotherly friends 'of my abysmal woes' [sic], of my ills, my problems: yes, they were moved, disappointed, indignant, very indignant; they said they suffered in their spirits the same insult I had to bear, but which of them, even had they so wished, could have swapped places with me?

So I come back to you, Ernesto, poor Ernesto: you who feel cold when I am cold, and thirst when I am thirsty, and when you smoke a pipe it is my pipe you are smoking: our pipe.

E

14

Caro Ernestino,

Today I write to you, the boy from my childhood.

I find you stored away with jealous care in my parents, my brother, in me and in the hearts of so many loving people.

Dear Ernestino, so full of curiosity, you were always asking 'why?' about everything; now I'd be able to give you loads of answers, I could tell you how clocks work and I could explain how children are born without having to confuse you with lies, and I could speak to you about pain as an everyday thing, telling you about myself, without having to go looking for it in the story of Little Red Riding Hood.

You know these things Ernestino, you are inside me, but the Ernesto who is still with his grandparents, now confined to their tomb, doesn't realise that *you* have become Ernesto, so he continues to ask 'why?' and to chase his hoop along the borders in the garden. (The chrysanthemum beds.)[4]

Have a sweetie.

Ernesto

4 In Italy (as in other European countries) the chrysanthemum is a flower associated with mourning.

26

Dear Ernesto,

I had lost the notebook containing these letters: I was so upset, almost as if I had gone mute, roaming the maze of memory to reach back to your words and mine.

I stared at you to read the secrets in your eyes, but I got dizzy and fell into the pond with your image in it; the water rippled and I could no longer see you. And then I got out and collapsed, desolate, beyond the pond's blind orbit, like someone trying to find inside himself the beloved voice of one departed, longing to hear a shout, chasing, but hearing nothing but the wind and the sound of his own voice.

Now these pages are here: I feel less alone, and your face again forms itself on their surface.

Ernesto

30

Oh Ernesto,

Why did you believe it?

Today is not a continuation of yesterday, and tomorrow, impossible to guess at, will emerge suddenly from the dark.

You believed the clouds were heralds of storms, that the rainbow announced fair weather, that fine words were preludes to good deeds.

You gave your heart to those who promised to hold it beside their own – together they would beat more strongly – and you never realised that they were stealing your life.

Yet I am proud that so many times you have overcome, in acts of faith, the reasoning I set before you to put you on your guard, and I forgive you for having led me to this extreme limit of disappointment. While they, the liars, are condemned to no longer recognise themselves (their souls are shrunken in their corpulent bodies), you remain Ernesto – the proof being precisely this disappointment, which looms as large as the hopes do.

At this point, to express myself I am forced to use infinitive verbs – to be – to suffer – to love – to die – because, reliving today the happy hours of yesterday, they feel empty and I don't think they ever existed outside this present.

But the present is already projected into tomorrow. And tomorrow? Ah, that does not exist, Ernesto, if not as a possibility inside us; but not all men will have it: their falsehood drags them back towards the past, with its stink of putrefied oaths.

Ernesto

40

Dear Ernesto,

Your speech flowed fresh, precise, clear, immediate: there was such a firm unity between thought and expression that the two could not be told apart.

This always happens when you speak Italian.

Sweet, beloved language; what else could you use to say '*mam*ma'?, to say '*tutti, io*' [everyone, me]?, to say 'Ernesto'?

In the ears it is a sound like a song that surrounds my whole life and leads it lightly among the life of others.

Maybe destiny will force you to change language, far away, and thinking will become a tiresome, complicated labour – and you will feel yourself getting lost in the others, now and then, daunted by the sound barrier of difficult words.

You will come to me, you will speak to me, even voicelessly, from inside, near the heart that beats, and you will tell me your secrets in Italian, and a whole nation will rise up and you will seem to have a blue sky above you and a garden around you, of thorny roses; yes, a rose garden.

Yours, E

The four articles that appear here are taken from a series written for *Domus* by Rogers between 1941 and 1942. In *Esperienza dell'architettura*, which includes only the first and ninth instalments, the 'Confessions' are preceded by these words:

One day in 1941 I ran into Giuseppe Pagano in the Galleria in Milan: at the time he was the editor of both Casabella and Domus. He asked me, somewhat absently: 'Why don't you write anymore?' I expressed my surprise that he did not remember that this was prohibited. I proposed writing about my painful experience as an anonymous person. Pagano, generous and courageous as always, immediately accepted. When we reached the ninth chapter I had to stop, because my name had got around.[1]

Although short-lived, this column for *Domus* and Rogers's 'Dear Ernesto' letters are significant in that they mark the emergence of a more singular voice, evolving from the 'common tongue' he had developed with his partners at BBPR that was clearly oriented towards the international scene. Reproduced here are the first, seventh, eighth and ninth instalments, which offer a taste of Rogers's sardonic (if not explicitly political) swipes at the distortion of the progressive ideals of fascism in an attempt to expose its dehumanising nature and appeal to the consciences of his contemporaries.

1 Author's translation.

DOMUS, 1941–1942

Presenting the Anonymous Person
***Domus* No. 158, February. Reprinted in *Esperienza dell'architettura* (Turin: Einaudi, 1958) 1941**

I know: it is sad to be anonymous: it sends a sort of chill down your spine, a chill that is all yours, that comes not from outside, but from deep within you.

You feel lonely and you seem to be mute and unable to speak your name to others, or perhaps they are deaf and cannot hear it; yet you feel that you are Giovanni, or Maria, or Ernesto, or Pietro, or Natalina. And then you also know your surname and lots of other things about yourselves: that you have suffered because your mum was ill or your wife was unfaithful, or because of kids, and above all you know what ardour you have inspired around everyday labour. No one will ever give a name to this pain, it will pass in men's midst without a face.

But I want to comfort you because I also know that in such solitude so much humanity throngs that if you were to have a name, it would not dare to take on your features and would remain closed off in itself.

You resonate with everything that happens to those who live around you, pale at the suffering of others, flush at their joys.

All the wealth (and, of course, the miseries) that are sown by an epoch and do not take root in the fenced field are yours, are mine, of the indefinite man, the nameless man.

And this harvest is so substantial that we end up, we anonymous people, having a personality that is enviable for the multiplicity of its experiences. (Like certain aunts who, while listening to a multitude of confiding nieces and nephews, have lived all their lives wrapped up in their own, and when these aunts pass away they leave a great emptiness: for me, Aunt Virginia was like that, but you too, I am sure, have also known such an aunt).

Names keep vigil in History, they are in books, amidst dates, on street signs, even far from their works; Anonymous, though, cannot leave works behind and only when you approach the remains of his labour do you grant life to him, as in dreams.

Consider the importance of these facts, respect them: they are aspects of eternity.

When you go to the antique shop and move a painting resting on the floor, leaning against a wall with its ragged and patched corners, you awaken Anonymous.

When you brave the cold to penetrate with your gaze a pamphlet found on a vendor's stand, you liberate an anonymous person from among many others.

The song of the fishermen over the seas is the voice of Anonymous. It is he who has lost the ultimate substance of his own physical being, lacking the boundaries that, with a name, distinguished him from other beings.

The fruit of labour remains solitary. Solitary.

We know nothing of his Beatrice, his travels, his ailments, but when the guide to the cloister says: 'These columns, ladies and gentlemen, differ from each other: observe!', you become aware of his tribulations when you notice that one column writhes like a serpent towards its capital where despair is shouted from the mouths of monsters and then you compare it to its neighbour, which is covered in golden tiles, and has fronds draping joyously from its top.

Each anonymous person has put his stamp on his own life and he alone knows what it is and how much it has cost in sufferings. Hail to he who worked with Giotto under the Franciscan vaults of Assisi and bowed over the work beside him; and praises to the scholars who after such arduous efforts to define his personality, drawing conclusions from the colours, called him 'the master of feathers' because of the particular way in which he provided angels with wings.

I want to be the painter of feathers. You will find me when you want to fly, but, if you act presumptuously, I will clip your wings, with no fear of creating new Lucifers.

On the bus we are elbow-to-elbow, and our mingled breaths cloud the windows: you are with me a man of the twentieth century, the illustration of a page of History: customs and traditions.

My chair, which I designed and had made with great care, and your chair, which you purchased at the antique shop and which seems hideous to me, are nevertheless relatives, for we have breathed and exhaled the same air together: they will be piled up together in the storerooms of future antiquarians. (Oh, but what a horrible thought: the antiquarians of the future!)

And yet, please remember that, as a river flows over stones, we create a 'style' every day: this is how we live, whether we are someone in an office, someone riding on a bus or the lady from the mezzanine. And it makes me angry that I never see you read a book, or think, or transform sufferings. Your toothache is annoying me, but it could lead to your chair becoming a handsome one – it depends on you. Why don't we help each other to live? Who knows what enormous constructions could result from so much pain: at the very least, if you were subjects of the pharaoh, the pyramids could be achieved or perhaps something even better if you were able to put your own stamp on it and assert yourself – a grand cathedral with its sculpted pinnacles and statues: each of you with a halo, and with the name of a saint rather than your own.

I, Anonymous, you see, has a great fear of descendants and I do not want, as a result of your misdoing, my chair to remain eternally hanging from the ceiling of a storeroom, without hearing one of your grandnephews, a son of a son, of a son, of one of your many sons, my dear Doctor, finally exclaim: 'Nice lines, excellent steel; re-upholster the seat and send it to my house: it is a fine twentieth-century specimen, an example of … style.'

If all together we cannot manage this, we will have accomplished nothing, believe me, and it will be your fault, down to your fads and, above all, your egotism.

It is a big responsibility to have a name, but also quite a responsibility not to have one.

I will tell you, but not today, the many reasons for our inadequacy, and I want to be cruel, I will tell you, as I look into myself; that is why I have started by confessing to you; after all, I am Anonymous, I am one of you.

The Responsibilities of the Anonymous
***Domus* no. 167, November 1941**

The fortunes of Names and the Anonymous are like the fortunes of words.

Example: seeing a young woman pass with great legs and what not, you may often have used this linguistically imperfect but utterly understandable expression: *Perbacco che siluetta!* (For the love of Bacchus, what a silhouette!)

Now that is a twisting plunge into the past, that makes us go up and down, turning this way and that as if on a roller coaster. I won't conceal the fact that I suffer from dizzy spells.

Follow me on this journey. We'll take two routes: one to find Bacchus, the other to find the origin of the word *siluetta*.

You know that Bacchus was a pagan god who oversaw the grape harvest, orgies and many other activities. In those days people having a good time would, in a Bacchic frenzy, shout out excitedly '*Bacchus evohè*'

Bacchus, believed to be immortal by the ancients, is dead, but his spirit is still restless because in order not to offend our God and speak His name in vain, especially where impure thoughts are concerned, we exclaim '*perbacco!*' and Bacchus rises again, but this time, wrongly, in the shape of a curse.

The word *siluetta* is the Italian version of the French *silhouette*, for which one Étienne de Silhouette is responsible.

This gentleman, born in Limoges in 1709, was a councillor at the Parliament of Metz, a commissioner of the East India Company and the French finance minister. He wrote 'General Idea of Duty and Morals of the Chinese', 'Voyage in France', and other books. He fell out of favour, due to his stinginess, I understand, and was lampooned in caricatures with simply drawn outlines, hence the use in French of the word *silhouette*, which later came to mean any profile, especially that of the female body.

Did you know that? I didn't, I must confess.

These words contain an entire drama, a precipitate of history: you see a god reduced to an exclamation that is not even blasphemous, and a forgotten functionary of the 1700s finds his way into our unwitting current discourse. A Name that becomes almost Anonymous, and an Anonymity elevated to a Name, almost quintessentially. Had the two of them known about this fate when they were still alive they might have been much more careful about what they did and, if aware of this extension every action of ours can have in History, who knows whether they might not have been more cautious in how they conducted their lives, or at least more determined to leave behind not only a lasting reputation, but also one that would be clear and honourable?

It is a known fact that Bacchus was a rather laid-back god, so in the end his inglorious fate should come as no surprise.

But in the end, what have I been able to glean about that other, by now utterly forgotten Monsieur Silhouette, whose name I have wrenched out of its hibernation in Anonymity amidst the pages of a dictionary? I've found nothing about his books on the morals of the Chinese in the 1700s, nor about his other achievements, but only his stubborn avarice, the last remaining simulacrum of his existence. As Anonymous, this state of affairs worries me. Our thoughts (even our secret ones) transform into gestures, gestures into works, works into myth. In the sphere of myths, then, there is a fertile multiplication, a melding of imagination with History, where other concatenations of thoughts, gestures and works arise, blended with each other, to take on new reason and consistency of life in the heavens or the abysses.

Ideas that were once luminous become obscure, but then in the darkness phantoms spring up and jostle until they find the wherewithal to become real and appear alongside us.

Across the centuries Anonymous whispers the word so that it travels from person to person, each repeating it in his own way (do you remember the game in which many children form a circle and attempt such an exercise?): '*vitulus, italos, italo, italiano, italiano...*' So many centuries and so many Anonymities for the acanthus leaf arrive at the top of the Corinthian capital.

Sentiment complicates the linear development of logic and winds, flowing around it, so that the mind loses its way; thus in architectural thought the decorative bough is grafted onto the stem, and Anonymous, who becomes distracted, even for an instant, from the dogma of reason, is like someone who has unwittingly switched the points so that many trains, with their cargos of human beings, are diverted towards mysterious destinations.

Anonymous, I repeat, has great responsibilities: he invents new languages, erects and destroys temples, makes peace and war. Even wars are my fault, your fault.

Why must we always pick a bone with others, as if all of them, even the Names, were not part of us, created by us?

One can find the example of Monsieur Silhouette amusing, and no harm done, but just as he is responsible for, at the very least, an expression in our language, so we, anywhere and always, are responsible for the gestures and works of others.

Peace comes when each of us knows how to find it, otherwise it is bloody war: an inner war - a contagion infecting individuals in which each person is contaminated before infecting himself and then infecting others - is waged on the battlefield, with cannons firing from either side.

The Personalities of the Anoymous
Domus no. 170. February 1942

Today I was filing my thumbnail: I was reminded of my grandfather, who died many years ago.

If I did not take care to round that thumbnail properly with the file, it would resemble his, growing wide and straight between two borders of pink flesh.

This might have been the only thing I didn't like about my grandfather, because I did like the kind, warm gaze of his chestnut-brown eyes through his spectacles with the peaceful composure of certain housewives standing at the window after their chores are done; his pointy beard was handsome, transforming the placid impression given by his eyes and, together with his solemn nose, giving him a hieratic physiognomy protected by the vault of the cranium over his slender figure, like certain domes on modest, out-of-the-way churches, where God is nevertheless present.

I miss all that, yet in that thumbnail I resemble him. Oh, but if I look at myself my eyes are those of my mother; hers are so beautiful, veiled and tempered by the pupils, much more opaque than those of my father's family; I have the forehead of my Uncle Carlo; the healthy, clean and tightly serried teeth of Aunt Lidia; I also have something of Uncle Marcello and Uncle George; from my cousins Gino and Bianca I've taken my slow gait, and the sudden bursts of energy come perhaps – who knows – from my poor dead brother.
All of them, and many others I don't know, can be found in my tastes and attitudes; I don't know, for example, from whom I have the pleasure I take in proportions, but my love of bright colours comes – I am certain – from my grandmother, Maria, just as my appreciation of seascapes is from Aunt Alice; the book mania from Dad; the aversion to cats from Aunt Gilda, that good soul, who passed it on to my mother along with a half-real, half-fake silver table trophy.
As you can see, I am a mosaic, and each person has contributed a small tile to give me body and colour.

When one thinks about how little of oneself has been generated from just that self, it is tempting to lose faith in the potentiality of actions, since it seems that they must be the servants of these inner and outer features.

Maybe it is that Don Juan ancestor who makes me gaze longingly at pretty girls, rather than a free impulse springing from my own heart.

Who wafts sentiments of pity skyward? Is it really me, or is it instead my dear Aunt Emma, who wants to deliver me to the threshold of paradise?

If you think about it - I repeat - you feel like an anthill busy with the to-ings and fro-ings of creatures carrying food and feeding each other and living and dying; a dreadful itching rises from the soles of the feet to the top of neck: it's horrible. Then you no longer understand whether you are seeing yourself with the eyes of others, or the others with your own eyes. It is a doubt that can make even the most well-balanced spiritual edifice tremble.

The drama of the self is pluralised and overflows in the drama of being.

He who attempts to shape the clay of his own inner person with his own hands feels his nose being pinched and his neck being stretched by mysterious hands that change the features where thoughts take form.

So we guard all the more jealously that last nucleus that apart from aunts, cousins and ancestors makes us aware in ourselves of that small package that is our Name: a true, unique, sole and almost sacred legacy we have to offer up to God.

Our faults and merits, all the possibilities of our life, are concentrated in this solitary part.

Here a narrow opening in the boulder of Being leads to the passageway of our free action.

So be careful, because it is easy to block or ruin it, but Giacomo

Leopardi made use of it so that 'The Infinite' gushed forth (while Monaldo, his father, poor fellow, just grumbled); from here flows sanctity, from here surges wickedness, from here emerge the yes and no, the *alea iacta est* [the die is cast] that makes History ... from this little opening through which each of us can make himself heard for what he is, what he wants or believes himself to be.[2]
I remind you of the wise words of Eupalinos: 'In execution, there is no such thing as detail', so if someone wants to give a face to his anonymous substance, he should patiently set to work.[3]

Will you pardon me? It is not therefore out of pure vanity that I round my thumbnail; this too is important, and it's a good idea to file it down. Otherwise, what would I have, of myself, if even my thumbnail belongs to someone else?

2 The famous Italian Romantic poet Giacomo Leopardi (1798–1837) was sickly and confined to his family home in Recanati for most of his life. In one of his most famous poems titled 'L'infinito' (Infinity) he describes the view of the hills and sea that he enjoyed from its gardens and expresses his longing for space and escape.

3 This is a reference to Paul Valéry's 1922 text *Eupalinos: or, The Architect*, which imagines a new Platonic dialogue between Socrates and Phaedrus elaborating on how creating forms is a prerequisite for self-knowledge; detail is everything where creation (or construction) is concerned.

The House of the Anonymous[4]
Domus no. 176, August 1942. Reprinted in *Esperienza dell'architettura* (Turin: Einaudi, 1958)

'The ant and the moth have cells for each of their young, but out little ones lie in festering heaps, in homes that consume them like graves.'

Harken to the warning of Ruskin, who after 70 years emerges from his tomb to reawaken in our consciences the troubling problem of the house of man.

Years, centuries, millennia pass, the gods are born and pass away, the gaudy mansions and manors of the powerful are erected, and fountains, theatres and markets, but man has still to learn how to construct an abode for himself: a home for each, for you, for me, for Anonymous. *Homo sapiens* should blush with shame before the humblest creatures of the earth. A grave, inexplicable shortcoming. Progress and civilisation? Don't make me laugh: it is all a pompous performance!

Why so many monuments bigger than us, if we then have to borrow a shelter against the elements and the darkness of destiny? To pay rent on the planet: how humiliating!

Anonymous wants a home of his own, he wants it, I tell you, he wants it.

He will not content himself with hiding behind the ornate falsehoods of facades: you dare to call these homes?

I know how you live, poor man or rich man, I have entered your house, I dine at your table, I breathe the odour of browning onions filtered by dusty drapes, I hear the squeals of the woman next door, and I have rummaged through your drawers.

4 Anticipating a recurring theme in Rogers's writing, that of the home, the description of the house that Anonymous imagines for himself is almost like a proposal formulated by Rogers and enabling him in some way to participate in the competition to design an ideal house organised by Pagano and featured in *Domus* nº 176. In this issue, Rogers' text is accompanied by proposals by Peressutti, Banfi and Belgiojoso, among others.

Were the masterful beaver to wind up in your house ... what embarrassment! Even the snail would blush!

The shame is not exactly yours, not exactly mine, but it is of humankind and, therefore, it becomes our own.

From these pages where I have confessed so many disappointments, might Anonymous not make a wish, a pledge? After the war I would like to whisper something in the ear of my fellows more or less like this: 'Move the rubble, and build your house, now is the time; you have dawdled sufficiently over the pyramids, the arenas and the domes. Show the world who you are and what you are worth.' I want to be real, to live; I want houses where that is possible.

I see my house. Look: you see it when you glimpse, on the distant hills, multi-coloured patches amidst the twining vegetation. This is my ideal house: far from yours, far enough for me to sing out of tune without you hearing me, yet close enough for me to greet you with a wave, and you respond.

It grows from the ground like a plant, yet it reigns over nature, the assertive footprint of man.

A piece of land below, and above a piece of sky: among the infinite flowers, some release their scent just for me, and at night a section of stars - among their infinite number - lights up for me.

My house's countenance fluctuates with the changing seasons;
it changes its leafy branches, renewing itself every spring;
in the summer it benefits from the coolness of the woods; colourful in autumn, it allows itself to be cloaked by snow in winter, beneath which my family is germinating, waiting for the sun.

The walls are boundaries, rather than obstacles, to the outside world: they all open outwards, close, stand ajar, eyes with eyelids and eyebrows or, perhaps, pores that breathe in the universe and expel harmful humours.

My house is a body, like my body, a repository of suffering and joy, lying next to your boundary.

Bodies that are not interpenetrable.

Let us respect the weeping and laughter that give life to Anonymous within his walls. He asks for no other property.

If you pry with indiscreet eyes through my window, you will look into my eyes and snatch the secret.

The flower I offer every day to the portrait of my loved ones blooms each day inside my heart; do you know that?

The slippers and robe I scatter in the room reflect my inner disorder: stress, anguish, worries, ideas.

I am cheerful and my house smiles; the wind blows against the walls and my whole being resists it.

The house is mother to me like the womb that protected me before I came into the world, a loving refuge, a warm abode, nourished by a single impulse springing from love and the same blood.

Thus every man should have his house by the same right of nature that gave him a mother and for the obligation to repeat the miracle for his children.

Against the pitiless voracity of time, grant me this place with my roots, which encloses a space that is mine.

I do not ask that my house be eternal but that, like an embrace, it be closed.

A fixed point in the mutable universe to which I can refer in my travels without, at night, having to focus my gaze to get my bearings from the pole star. Otherwise, son of humans, I will continue to envy the snail for six thousand years, and more.

The antifascist activities of BBPR led, on 21 March 1944, to the incarceration of Banfi and Belgiojoso. Imprisoned first at the penitentiary of San Vittore and then in the camps of Fossoli and Bolzano, they were deported to Gusen, a satellite of Mauthausen, where Gianluigi Banfi was to die on 10 April 1945, just weeks before the camp's liberation on 4 May that year. In this text Rogers remembers his friend and colleague and celebrates Banfi's exemplary contribution to modern architecture.

REMEMBERING GIANLUIGI BANFI

REPRINTED IN *ESPERIENZA DELL'ARCHITETTURA* (TURIN: EINAUDI, 1958)

QUADERNO DEGLI STUDENTI DELLA FACOLTÀ DI ARCHITETTURA DI MILANO, NOVEMBER 1945

My dear Giangio, how can I talk about you in this journal of young comrades without addressing you directly, as if I were writing you a letter, one of many over the course of our lives?

We have never believed in death, have we? Nor are you dead today, even if I speak of you as someone so far away that tears come to my eyes as I search for you. I cannot talk about you without also talking about 'us' - Lodo [Belgiojoso], Aurel [Peressutti], myself. From the moment that work bound us together, we had just one name: 'Bibipierre'. We were so proud of that! And we were delighted when other people got us mixed up: we felt as though we could multiply each other's existence.

So it should not be seen as vanity if, instead of simply commemorating you, the words I address to you refer to our friendship, filling the vase to overflowing - the vase I'd like to be filled with flowers and placed in front of your portrait.

When we met we were two curly-haired young boys in sailor suits (at the same school, Giuseppe Parini). Our mothers were the sort that came to pick up their offspring almost every day - '*Buon giorno, signora*' and '*Buon giorno, signora*' - but then we went our separate ways: we didn't hit it off immediately. It was only a few years later that we became close, our ever more sparky banter forming a bond between us among our companions. We were, indeed, very cheerful, always laughing, joking and playing tricks (just the thought of it moves me, as such things seem so impossible now).

Dear Giangio, memory transports me. We both failed the first year of architecture school. There our friendship intensified as the result of a shared passion for artistic endeavour. Then, joined by Aurel and Lodo, we began to hope and despair as a quartet - in architectural projects, in life projects.

When the four of us won our first competition, what joy we experienced (but we also lost in so many)!

For many years we would gather together around a particular drawing, our faces lit up by the sun (and often by the stars). Our first studio: the ping-pong table at your parents' house in Via Moscova.

Ernesto Rogers's drawing of himself and his partners at BBPR © Fondo Peressutti / IUAV Archivio Progetti

Then Via Borgonuovo with the scent of oleanders in the garden. And then, finally, the cloisters of San Simpliciano, where we defended ourselves against the slings and arrows directed at us, united behind the white walls, in our white shirts.

You, me, Aurel - we had all lost our mothers. But Aurel and I found solace in your son's eyes and in Lodo's children.

Confronted with the racism that wanted to force us to be different, we allowed ourselves a bitter smile.

Nothing could divide us, everything strengthened our union: the successes and the sacrifices, the praise and the criticism, friends and enemies. For fifteen years (of articles, discussions, exhibitions, projects, constructions) we fought together for our ideal of architecture, to which was added, ever more clearly, that other ideal that now radiates from you and guides us.

Dear brother, in our midst you were the embodiment of optimism, tireless and incontestable energy, moral and material generosity.

Our youth would have finished with you had you not left us to continue what you believed in.

The vandals who scattered your ashes from the Gusen camp at Mauthausen certainly had no idea that they would become fertile ground.

[J]ulia's weeping is not in vain: she will teach your son to know you in the flowers and fruits of new gardens.[1]

1 The Julia referred to in the text is Banfi's widow, Julia Bertolotti Banfi, who later worked with Rogers at *Domus* and *Casabella*. She discusses their collaboration in 'Esperienze con Rogers, *Quadrante, Domus, Casabella*', in *Quaderni del Dipartimento di Progettazione dell'Architettura del Politecnico di Milano 15. Ernesto Nathan Rogers: testimonianze e studi* (Milano: Città Studi, 1993): 19–21.

Like Rogers's father and Gianluigi Banfi, Giuseppe Pagano died in a concentration camp, paying the ultimate price for his early association with fascism.

The text that follows is the most important of the many pieces Rogers wrote about his friend and mentor; it was originally published in a monographic issue of *Casabella*, edited by Franco Albini and Giancarlo Palanti and dedicated entirely to the magazine's former director. In addition to extracts from Pagano's writings, notes, letters and poems, and a selection of his works and unfinished projects from the last years of his life, the issue included contributions by a number of his friends and collaborators, who pieced together Pagano's biography and provided commentaries on his activity as a writer and polemicist. Rogers contributed a touching profile of Pagano's moral travails, from his early convinced adherence to fascism to his dramatic disillusionment, similar to those of a whole generation of young Italian architects, including Rogers himself and his colleagues at BBPR.

CATHARSIS

REPRINTED IN *ESPERIENZA DELL'ARCHITETTURA* (TURIN: EINAUDI, 1958)

COSTRUZIONI CASABELLA NO. 195-198, DECEMBER 1946

Why make a blanket apology? We show respect to the dead (and the living) by giving them the truth.

This is the truth and it must be told, even if it is uncomfortable to hear: Italy's modern architects were, to a greater or lesser degree, part of fascism; even those who did not openly pledge allegiance collaborated through some of their work – exhibitions, buildings, magazines.

The past cannot be altered. What is needed is the courage to talk about it.

The truth is that two of the best among us were the most active in this wrongdoing: [Giuseppe] Terragni and Pagano, the former an instinctive artist, the latter a gifted intellectual with razor-sharp critical faculties. Terragni's Casa del Fascio in Como was revered outside Italy as one of the most representative works of architecture of our time; Pagano, editor for many years of this very magazine, *Casabella*, which (along with *Quadrante*, for a much shorter period) was one of the clearest voices of conscience of architects, engaging with the political dimension of art.

I do not mean to sharpen weapons to be placed in the hands of my enemies. I will be specific, keeping to solid ground: that way the position of Pagano and of many other modern Italian architects can be clarified in a neutral tone.

Each followed his own path determined by his own nature and culture; only a few stayed away from this torturous route. The tragic end of Terragni, his brain addled by the horrors of the Russian campaign, prevents us from looking further into his particular case, but the others, sooner or later, will have the chance to define the terms of their own inner intellectual and moral integrity.

The contribution many could make to our national redemption is of great significance. We will name only the martyrs: [Luca] Beltrami, dead amidst his partisans; Banfi, dead at Mauthausen; not to mention Belgiojoso, who miraculously returned from that hell, and others who in various degrees dared to rebel (dear [Giorgio] Labò, executed by the Germans in Rome, was always an anti-fascist).

But here I want to talk about Pagano.

They may have been acquainted for years, but Italy's modern architects were not able truly to become friends until they were able to reveal to each other how they had rejected fascism. This is what happened between Pagano and me.

I hope I will be allowed to remember this friend with the unbiased sincerity that he so appreciated, and to sketch a profile that may be incomplete (because there are many things I do not know) but I hope is not too far removed from reality.

I want to talk about Pagano the man, who laboured until the light hidden in the crevices of his heart could begin to shine; this light may now fall on those who are left behind.

Pagano is a special case among us: partly because he was of a different generation, ten to fifteen years older, which had an effect on his cultural training, but mainly because of a distinctly passionate temperament which propelled him from one side to the other, towards the bad as well as the good, beyond our shared experiences.

Do you remember him? He was tall and well-built, yet his clean-shaven face with its constant pallor might have brought to mind a Benedictine penitent, had not the dark hair and piercing eyes, behind his big glasses, confirmed the inner character of a feisty Dominican.

His were not the slender hands of an architect or a writer, used to lightly wielding a pencil, but were instead those of a sculptor, gnarled and practical, accustomed to shaping clay.

And the way he dressed reflected his character: a bit eccentric but not lacking in refinement; with his beret pulled down over his forehead and his fine wool jacket, he might have been taken for a foreign student, one of those you see in the Latin Quarter. And yet, for all that, there was nothing bohemian about him.

An artist type, yes.

At 50 he had more vitality and passion than a boy of 20. Ambitious? Certainly, if the word can be used without any slight to an intelligent man who believed himself capable of achieving his goal.

An idealist, not a utopian: this idealism of his, this vitality, made him feel more comfortable with younger people than with his contemporaries; while ambition spurred him on to be their champion.

Perhaps he was not a master, in the deeper sense, because his political manoeuvres and his taste for debate, for swordplay, aroused suspicion, putting people on their guard. While this did not prevent others from following him (or seeking his company) it did hinder the quieter exchange that should be possible between master and pupil.

He energised people, and when given the opportunity to direct a group show (the Esposizione aeronautica italiana, for example), he became a generous orchestrator, bringing out the best in all concerned.[1]

If I have lingered over this description of Pagano the man it is because it is a necessary basis for understanding everything that followed. I will also mention his cultural background: the son of an archaeologist, he grasped the nature of things and loved them with a physical passion.

Giuseppe, an 'irredentist', volunteered to fight in the other war and (perhaps revelling in his own courage) earned himself four blue ribbons.

So this is where Pagano came from: his political life branched out from here, and from an equally innate but certainly healthier social conscience, with the two concerns gradually changing places in importance. The initial general misunderstanding of fascism among Pagano's generation can be explained in these terms; in his

1 The Italian Aeronautical Exhibition, held at the Palazzo dell'Arte in Milan from June to October 1934, documented the entire history of Italian aviation from Leonardo da Vinci's drawings of helicopters to the record-breaking Italian seaplanes of 1933. It was one of the most important celebrations of the 20 years of fascism in which prominent Milanese architects, such as BBPR, Marcello Nizzoli and Edoardo Persico, Gio Ponti and Franco Albini, were called upon to collaborate under the supervision of Giuseppe Pagano.

particular case, however, there was something more: the declared need for a dictatorship was consistent with some aspects of his character, and you will discern motives of a psychological order in the brief sketch I have given here.

Had his political (rather than artistic) consciousness been more astute, Pagano could have been a Marxist.

But his activism, while it prompted him to make polemical attacks on the system from within, did not, for most of his life, allow him to take a more morally committed stand - one less compromised by the historical moment which would have forced him into exile or onto the road towards conspiracy at even greater personal risk. The activism that gripped Pagano was also shared to some extent with younger modern Italian architects of that period; as I have said, even if they did not participate in the regime as he did, they did not remain immune to it. The reason for this must lie - and I am not saying this in an attempt to make excuses for any of us - in the heartfelt need to match the ideal world of our own construction with three-dimensional reality: the tangible expression of immanence, which keeps it alive.

It took us a while to realise that out of love for love itself we risked begetting a child born of prostitution.

Pagano's faith in architecture pushed him down a dangerous path - making him first a collaborator, then a dissident and finally an opponent. A fire burned within, a fire he identified with the highest spiritual values, and to keep it going he fed it with the finest fuel he believed life could offer, never noticing that the flames mingled the sacred, the profane and even the damned.

It was a grave error, but it was the sin of pride of a prodigal, or rather, generous son - one who in the end did not hesitate to sacrifice his own life.

His writings - they will make you emotional as you read them again - trace all the stages of the path towards his own Calvary, with the necessary falls along the way. Those falls, if they made the Son of God more human, make every man with spiritual aspirations submit more consciously to his destiny.

The fascism of the modern architects (putting aside Pagano's personal actions) coincided with the polemic for rational architecture, beginning in 1932, and developed in tandem with it. It was a handful of artists wagering their own spiritual heritage in a game of cards played with a gang of avaricious tricksters. We can be accused of many sins, the first is that we were ingenuous, gullible, but then there is something more serious: our egocentricity led us to create absurd syllogisms around art and politics, roughly in these terms: fascism is a revolution, our art is revolutionary, therefore fascism should adopt our art.

Because fascism was never a revolution, but a reaction, as we all sooner or later (and usually not much later) came to understand. It is not difficult to imagine how much suffering this illusion caused (I'm alluding to Pagano here, but the same applies to many of us). In essence, Pagano's polemics tilted against the windmills of this illusion (though by this I certainly do not want to suggest that he was a Don Quixote).

He forged ahead, driven by his faith as an artist, and could not understand how ideas that were so honest and so clear could run into so many obstacles. He let fly with anathemas when he himself was the heretic. He believed that others had betrayed Mussolini's will to construct, even though he was the one who had dismantled the foundations of that flabby and presumptuous edifice planted by Mussolini and his minions on the shoulders of Italians.

The true architect of Mussolini was [Marcello] Piacentini.

Neither Pagano nor his friends, who wanted simple, rational cities, could become architects for the regime, whereas that academic profiteer, rhetorician and sycophantic courtier did so effortlessly. From his very first writings in *Casabella*, Pagano attacked his adversaries: the likes of [Ugo] Ojetti, [Ardengo] Soffici, [Guido] Sommi Picenardi and, after some delay, Piacentini. These names take on the value of symbols, though initially Pagano treated them more like old fogies than rogues: Mussolini, whose anthem was 'Youth', would be bound to notice the fresh spirit of the new generation of Italian architects, or so Pagano hoped. And indeed, as the controversy over architecture reached fever pitch with the competition for the design of Florence train station,[2] Mussolini, in his Chamber of Fasces (a chamber allowing no debate), praised the most daring entry, and with it the designs for Sabaudia, an experiment in modern urban planning.

In *Casabella* Pagano wrote an article entitled 'Mussolini saves Italian architecture'. Our hopes were at their highest then, because – like fools – we thought we could save the people by giving them comfortable, healthy and beautiful homes.

In some instances optimism is a serious sin, even worse than naivety.

We remained ensnared by this skilfully cast net, while the sharks circled just outside it. This was 1934.

So we wasted our energy on competitions, with Pagano always defending the progressives against the reactionaries. And while we were talking about the Golden Section, truth in construction and social (maybe even 'cooperative') architecture, those reactionaries got down to business.

If you look through the issues of *Casabella* from those days you will divine the generous hand of Pagano: if a colleague produced even a small work that was in line with his ideals, he would immediately enter the fray on their behalf, shielding them from attack while wielding a scythe against the choking weeds of the state, hoping to make them yield to the evidence of a more luminous truth.

It is not my role here to analyse case by case Pagano's aesthetic arguments, which were often expressed in very precise critical language. Nevertheless, I would like to recall just a few of those most

2 The construction of Florence's railway station in 1933–35, and the controversy surrounding it, was one of the key moments in the architectural debate and wider struggle for supremacy between the rival movements in fascist Italy, marking the culmination of the success of the rationalist front. Angiolo Mazzoni, the most prolific architect and engineer of railway stations under fascism, was originally entrusted with the project. However, following fierce and widespread criticism of Mazzoni's project a public competition was held in 1932 and won by the Gruppo Toscano, the regional branch of the MIAR (Italian Movement for Rationalist Architecture). Exemplifying rationalist principles, the Gruppo Toscano's building had a low horizontal mass, bare and compact, and a façade devoid of any decorative elements. Mussolini himself endorsed the project with a famous speech in defence of modern architecture, in which he declared that fascist architecture had to be modern, clearly distinguishable from the styles of the past, and that the style and form of buildings had to reflect their function. Despite this pronouncement, he would soon change his tune and increasingly favoured monumentalism in architecture.

relevant to the theme of this piece in order to demonstrate the clarity of his moral position on architecture and to show how, little by little, as he consciously moved further away from the political sphere, these principles came to instil (despite various reversals) a clearer sense of his own political duty. He was offended by the wastefulness of the regime, and by the insolence of Sommi Picenardi, who passed judgement on art in the pages of *Regime Fascista* with no qualification other than his senior membership [of the fascist party]. He was concerned about the private ownership of property, which posed so many obstacles to the solving of urban planning issues, and proposed sensible reforms.

Then, when impotent provincials, citing tradition, wanted to cut Italians off from fertile exchange with European thought, Pagano became intractable.

He gave no quarter to the monumental architecture of the adulators, instead taking every opportunity to urge the state, private investors and architects to adopt honesty in construction as a sign of their higher ethical standards. Such moralising might appear surprising, coming from someone who let pass many other more serious aberrations and abuses on the part of our wretched leaders, but this temporary blindness was the only way Pagano could keep alive his fading hopes in those times – and rewind, ever more tightly, the spring of his passion, which was ultimately destined to snap.

His past orthodoxy gave him some leeway with the censors, but little by little his dissident tone became more resolute, disillusion making his language more bitter still. At first, he was able to convince himself that Mussolini was really on his side and had been forced to surround himself with a mob of tricksters for reasons outside his control. But the evidence of the dictator's proclivities, of his constitutional weakness for certain kinds of character, became increasingly clear. Imperialism, autarky, the alliance with the Germans, racism – all were unmistakable signs of a world that could not be reconciled with that of a true intellectual.

Do you remember those articles? No architect, and in my opinion no-one else in the field of culture, was writing such courageous words at that time. The scribbler [Giuseppe] Pensabene, that *riempitore di destri* (filler of latrines), was his unworthy opponent, an apologist for the regime, backed by all the Axis politicians, handcuffs at the ready.

The dissident, sustained by one last glimmer of hope, became more cunning, deploying a dialectical approach: what he thought of as fascist art bore no relation to the stuff that generally bore that name, yet he continued to identify it as such.

A speech given at [the School of] Mystical Fascism is typical. Keeping something in reserve? Others would call this taking a 'tactical position'.[3]

Temperamentally obliged to remain within the system, to comply with the games of the laymen, this '*clerc*' stubbornly continued to pick his way through the minefield of the regime, where his own explosive devices mingled with those set by his opponents to trap him.

Julien Benda would accuse him of 'treason'. And it was precisely in this '*trahison des clercs*' that Pagano's story would unravel, along with the dramas of many other bewildered intellectuals.

In Italy he was certainly one of the last to fight back through these systems of dialectical opposition, as even his architect friends - one-by-one - abandoned him.

To our great sorrow, when war broke out he volunteered. It was the final act of a man incapable of restraint, who, needing to possess his woman - architecture - paid no attention to whether she was wearing a white or a red camellia in her hair. He could not stay away. So why not throw himself more worthily into opposition? Clearly this was another error, but one of judgement rather than a moral error - at least within the ethical framework that Pagano's sense of integrity required.

3 Until 1942, when he resigned, Pagano was director of the art department of the School of Fascist Mysticism in Milan whose primary goal was to train the leaders of the fascist party in a spiritual understanding of fascism.

Once again, then, he was unable to extract himself sufficiently from a false doctrine to see that the problem lay not just in its application but in its fundamental principles (as if political science and practice were not symmetrical terms with the same origin).

The pages of his diary in which he recounts his reasons for volunteering offer a moving confession: out of the tangle of his old beliefs, stirring like fronds of seaweed in the murky depths of his soul, Pagano attempts to separate out his nascent feelings with the care of a gardener who knows that in order to cultivate a new, more fragrant flower, he must first prepare the ground with coarse manure.

If I have enlisted as a volunteer, I have done so advisedly, calculatedly (yes, also calculatedly, if the desire for integrity is calculation), to demonstrate that I am ready even to risk death in war to preserve my independence as a man and an artist in the face of the political siege that is pressing in on us, suffocating, confusing and humiliating us, badgering us into herd-like conformity. If we wish to restore the prestige that intellectuals have lost, we must act and accept all the risks of the game. Only in this way can we hope for a true revolution, a true moral cleansing, a true rebirth of the values of our Mediterranean Italian identity as the logical consequence of this fanatical stealing, hypocritically and clumsily disguised as a humanitarian, legal and racial undertaking.

These were the conscious motives that drove Pagano, but once again we can see more deep-rooted reasons, determined by his nature. We read the next lines: 'I cannot remain impassive in the face of this spectacle. The dilemma, for now, must be resolved this way. In an "active" fashion. God forbid I should settle into the standard routine of grumbling.' Once again, activism.

So, bearing these and other illusions of redemption, he departs, already convinced that he is risking everything for a bad cause, in the hope of surviving to further a better one, as a man and as an artist.

This was an untenable position, and Pagano must have known it. In the meantime, from his occasional contact with clandestine cells on his visits to Milan, he came to understand that there was another option for those who wanted to take action, that the revolution lay on the other side, that he could not achieve his aims and fulfil himself without hoping and preparing for the defeat of the fascists. People like Sommi Picenardi, Ojetti, Pensabene, Soffici and many others I will not name here, took no action, symbols not by chance of an equal corruption of art and morals.

So Pagano's anti-fascism began here, and it was more a rediscovery than an evolution (and even less a conversion): it was, ultimately, a synthesis. His long and carefully reasoned study, '*Presupposti per un programma di politica edilizia*' (Requirements for a policy of construction), first published in extract form in March 1943 and then reprinted in *Casabella* in June that same year, is his 'manifesto'. Worthy of praise for addressing technical considerations, it establishes an unequivocal moral and political position that corresponds (truly, this time) to the high ideals of the artist as well as the needs of citizens. It is an impassioned plea 'for a decisive test by which the field of construction and architecture might also be rescued from this indecisive, sterile, vain and compromised bureaucracy that is stifling the free and eternal laws of progress...'

During the period of dictatorship he could not have been any more explicit; that 'also' was to cost him dear - the magazine was impounded. Above all, the 'also' stood for a renewed consideration of the terms of the dialectic with which his conscience had grappled for so long.

Then came 25 July [the fall of Mussolini]. The August issue of *Casabella* appeared with a splendid editorial, 'Our Position', in which Pagano, with great sincerity and in a lofty tone - almost like that of an encyclical - evoked the past, took stock of the present situation and urged future reconstruction.

No exegesis of this piece is necessary here, as its essence is contained in these few sentences: 'Our disagreement focused especially on the field of architecture and the figurative arts, but the tide of our offensive against academicism, against conventional rhetoric, against the servile immorality of exclusive architecture, has gradually swelled and overflowed into much more extensive spheres: first, into the field of ethics, and finally into politics.' This is lucid thinking, worthy of a man turning to look back and gather breath midway through a long climb.

But the fascists remained in power, under [Pietro] Badoglio, and Pagano, knowing how far he had to travel to reach his destination, could not escape his concern: 'what we have seen in these days is the first act of a drama that is still in progress; the way in which it ultimately unfolds will decide our future.'

Who can fail to hear in these words a premonition of his fate? And as if that were not enough, listen to his conclusion: it touches the very hearts of all those of us who have survived.

With this political clarification of our consciences as artists and as men I urge my colleagues and friends to be ready for the life of tomorrow, for that practical and personal action that will take place in undoubtedly exceptional circumstances and will require from each of us a very high level of moral commitment, an absolute obedience to the voice of our conscience, an unswerving adherence to the mission that each of us has chosen, devoting our whole life and art to that fine way of 'paying in person' – of self-sacrifice – that our men of the Risorgimento, from [Carlo] Cattaneo to [Carlo] Pisacane, have appropriately taught us.

I hope it will not seem like vanity if I include a portion of the letter Pagano wrote to me during that same period, as the only reason for doing so is to contribute to the story:

At this point I am being swept along by youthful euphoria, just like in the good old days when I was 20 or even younger. We must keep a watchful eye, a hunger for the truth, a desire for selfless action and sacrifice. We must not simply stand at the window looking out; we have to assume and live up to new responsibilities and be ready to 'pay in person'.

Like the tolling of the evening bells that encourage us to bring our day to a fitting close, Pagano repeats to himself and others that we must pay in person.

We parted on 8 September in an office where we were planning a defence of Milan; he went out of one door, I went out of the other. My fate was uneventful. His, you already know.

Active, courageous and intelligent, as ever, Pagano devoted himself to the cause that would grant him freedom as a man and an artist. He was captured twice, and after he had been comprehensively tortured, they took him to one of those camps in Germany where one find no trace of lost friends, comrades or relatives except in the dust of the earth or by raising one's eyes skyward. Thus I conclude the tribute that it was my profound desire to pay to Pagano, but it would be incomplete if it were open to misinterpretation by biased or hurried readers predisposed to belittle his achievement or to exploit his sacrifice.

I am speaking of those architects who, by virtue of never having become members of the party, believed themselves to be absolved of the charge of being reactionary, and who accuse modern architecture of fascism; or of those even more reprehensible types who are skilled in the practice of architecture but remain insensitive to the need for a renewal of society.

Pagano has a story; all of us have, overlapping with or departing from his to varying degrees.

I have spoken of the man and the artist who devoted his life to the laborious construction of his own integrity.

The example holds only for those who have already built within themselves the solid foundations on which, after the storm passes, the ends of a rainbow will rest.

THE EDITORIAL VOICE

Issue nº 204 of December 1944 marked the end of Melchiorre Vega's editorship of *Domus*, with deputy editors Lina Bo Bardi and Carlo Pagani also departing. Just over a year later, in January 1946, the magazine resumed publication under the direction of Rogers. His first act was to replace the old subtitle 'Le arti nella casa' (The Arts in the Home) with the strapline 'La casa dell'uomo' (The House of Man), to mark the distance from previous editorships which had established the magazine as an arbiter of taste for the elite, and to signal his intention to broaden the scope of the publication and reach a wider audience. The text that follows is the first editorial Rogers wrote in his new role. Just three months earlier, *Il Politecnico* – the cross-disciplinary, left-leaning periodical edited by the writer, critic and engaged intellectual, Elio Vittorini – had published an article by Rogers titled 'Una casa per tutti' (A House for Everyone), along with a seminal urban plan for the city of Milan by BBPR – The Piano A.R.[1] The article laid the foundations of Rogers's programme for *Domus*, and formed the basis of several lectures he was to give in Italy and abroad on the subject of reconstruction which, he argued, needed to take into account both the practical problems of housing a displaced population and the more abstract issue of addressing their cultural and emotional needs. It was a question of restoring *la misura umana*, the human dimension, after the inhuman aberrations of fascism and war.

Rogers's editorial team, which remained in place for nineteen consecutive issues, consisted of Marco Zanuso as editor-in-chief, Julia Bertolotti Banfi as editorial assistant and Paolo Chessa, who was responsible for the layout and who, from issue nº 210 onwards, became editor together with the literary writer Nelo Risi. Recalling the context within which she began collaborating with Rogers, Julia Bertolotti Banfi expressed her astonishment that 'in four months, in a destroyed Milan where almost everything was missing, we managed to produce a

1 The Piano A.R. (United Architects Plan) was a plan for the reconstruction of the city of Milan drawn up by a group of Milanese architects associated with CIAM, including Franco Albini, Lodovico Belgiojoso, Piero Bottoni, Ezio Cerutti, Ignazio Gardella, Gabriele Mucchi, Giancarlo Palanti, Enrico Peresutti, Mario Pucci, Aldo Putelli and Ernesto Rogers. It was one of many urban plans worked on by BBPR which included the seminal Valle d'Aosta Plan of 1936 (with Adriano Olivetti), one of the first attempts at regional planning. The Piano A.R., in preparation from early 1944, was entered into a competition organised by the City of Milan in November 1945. It resulted from a critical evaluation of the most advanced plans for other European cities (from the Amsterdam Plan of the 1920s to the 1944 Abercrombie Plan for London) and the application of the urban principles developed by CIAM. For further reading on the Piano A.R., see *Costruzioni Casabella* nº 194 (November 1946) and 'Milan: outline proposals for the replanning and reconstruction', *The Architects' Journal* nº 8 (August 1946).

Previous: Ernesto Rogers (centre) with Walter Gropius (left) and other visitors at the IX Triennale, Milan, Italy, 1951 ©Triennale Milano – Archivi

PROGRAMME: *DOMUS*, THE HOUSE OF MAN

REPRINTED IN *ESPERIENZA DELL'ARCHITETTURA* (TURIN: EINAUDI, 1958)

TRANSLATED IN *LA ARQUITECTURA DE HOY* NO. 14 (1948) AND IN JOAN OCKMAN, ED., *ARCHITECTURE CULTURE 1943-1968* (NEW YORK: RIZZOLI, 1993)

DOMUS NO. 205, JANUARY 1946

magazine of 64 pages. Despite the devastation, there was in all of us, in all Italians, and indeed in all the best Europeans, a desire for renewal. There was a belief that the time was ripe for the realisation of new ideas in architecture and society, along with an extraordinary commitment – to use a word that has unfortunately gone out of fashion. The "house of man" was to be reinvented. Many of us had lost it and lived huddled together under one roof, without class distinctions, or so we thought.'[2]

Each issue of Rogers's *Domus* was divided into two sections. The first was devoted to architecture, offering practical solutions to various housing needs – from the restoration of historic buildings to the prefabrication of housing components, and from furnishings to exhibitions, through to objects and materials. In many ways it echoed the populist tone of the *Manuale dell'architetto*, a professional handbook edited by the Roman architect Mario Ridolfi, published in 1946 and celebrating traditions, local know-how and manual labour. The second part of the magazine sought to explore the relationship between disciplines. Gillo Dorfles contributed articles on art criticism, Nelo Risi wrote on literature, Dino Risi on film, Riccardo Malipiero on music and Guido Ballo on theatre. Each issue also featured a removable insert with reproductions of drawings by artists such as Henri Matisse, Costantino Nivola and Bruno Munari, or construction details by Vico Magistretti, Vito and Gustavo Latis, etc. Although the focus was firmly on the problems of Italian reconstruction and on the Italian proponents of modern architecture, Rogers's *Domus* also published research developed at CIAM, often featuring articles by prominent international figures such as Max Bill, Sigfried Giedion, Alfred Roth, Jane Drew and Alvar Aalto.

2 Julia Bertolotti Banfi (widow of Gianluigi Banfi) had already worked as an editorial assistant at Gio Ponti's *Domus*, from 1936, before starting her collaboration with Rogers, an experience she discusses in 'Esperienze con Rogers', *Quadrante, Domus, Casabella,*' in *Quaderni del Dipartimento di Progettazione dell'Architettura del Politecnico di Milano 15. Ernesto Nathan Rogers: testimonianze e studi*, (Milano: Città Studi, 1993), 19–21. Author's translation.

Every part of the house of man is damaged (if it were a boat, we would say it leaked). A howling wind enters through every crack, through which issue the cries of women and children. We should be running to the rescue with a brick, a beam, a pane of glass, and instead here we are, with a magazine. We do not give bread to the hungry or a raft to the shipwrecked. We bring words.

If we haven't lost our sense of human solidarity, if we are still conscious of our actions, then even this seemingly misplaced offering of words can be justified by its concrete intentions. Anyone who takes a trip through Italy, along Via Aurelia [Apulia] or Via Emilia [Sicily], will see endless disintegration: ruins upon ruins. Of course, the same is true of Provence or Brittany. The same is true for every road in Europe.

Faced with so many disasters our first impulse would be to translate moral sentiment into the precision of economic fact: how many families are homeless? How much material is needed? How much time?

Just think about the fact that winter is coming and how cold these people will be. There is nothing else to think about. What good is beauty to them? Poetry, music, painting, proportions threaten to become nothing more than the empty vessels of our intellectual ambition and egotism: objects of luxury, instruments of sin.
At the home of a friend the other day, listening to a concert as the expansive cadences of the seventeenth century washed over us, I suddenly found myself blushing with inner shame (the kind of shame that informed St Augustine's merciless conscience); doubts assailed me, pressing in like a menacing throng of spectres. What was I doing there?

Yet when the soloist raised his bow from the *viola d'amore* and the last note's echo faded in the applause, I couldn't help clapping along with the rest of the audience (and, I can assure you, these were upright individuals not inclined to waste their lives in idle pursuits). The contrast between art and ethics becomes apparent precisely when we need to address existential questions in a climate of increasingly strict public morality; so in more religious eras, or among those more anxious to assert the immanent values of a society, there are many people who believe - albeit for opposing reasons - that they ought to turn their backs on art.

These people are the ascetics, on the one hand, and the materialists, on the other. Both groups, if they do not actually go so far as to become iconoclasts, end up reducing art purely to a means - an *instrumentum regni* - for achieving a desired end: a realm that denies matter, in the former case, or the spirit, in the latter. Then again, there are those who, with greater presumption than the devout, and less altruism than the humanitarians, rely only on their own selves, cut off from any communion or community, and who toy with art as if it were opium, a prop in their hedonistic world. These are the aesthetes, players without innocence.

Far from the ascetics, but also from the materialists and the aesthetes, and nevertheless recognising that each of these tendencies contains part of the truth, our ideal is found in their midst, at the centre of the triangle.

The truth lies in the relationship between the parts; the words we offer, then, are there, in that relationship. Should we call ourselves functionalists? We want to be among those who are anxiously attempting to re-tie the threads of a synthetic knot where each part is equally necessary for the integrity of the whole.

Why renounce humanity? Or the gods? Why give up on beauty, which often plays the role of intermediary between the two, substituting for virtue? No solution to a problem is complete if it does not address ethics and aesthetics as well as utility.

A house is not a home if it is not warm in the winter, cool in the summer, serene in every season, welcoming the family into spaces that are harmonious. A house is not a home if it does not contain a corner for reading poetry, an alcove, a bathtub, a stove.

This is the house of man.

And a man is not really a man unless he possesses such a house. Does this house exist? Has it ever existed?

The cover of *Domus* nº 205, December January 1946, the first issue edited by Rogers.
Archivio Domus – © Editoriale Domus S.p.A.

They tell me that originally the Greek word *domos*, from which the Latin *domus* comes, meant the most elementary human habitation: an enclosure, that which protects. *Domus* is an ancient and erudite expression, adopted by the Romans (from which modern usage stems) to define the complex of elements that made up the patrician town house.

Domus was, then, not the house of man, but that of a socially privileged family; all the other Latin terms indicate specific constructions rather than a typology responding to the seemingly more abstract but actually much more vital concept of human habitation.

Consider the English, on the other hand: home (I would like to prove, against the conclusions of the philologists, that home and *homo* have the same root). Or why not consider the German *Heim*? The two very beautiful adjectives homely and *heimlich*, which we translate so inadequately as *casalingo* and *domestico*, express the material and spiritual needs of every man in his house. The French is even more telling, with its expressions *chez moi*, *chez toi*, *chez soi*, the constructed elements seemingly taking on the features of the inhabitant.

I want to have a house that resembles me (in a flattering way): a house that resembles my humanity. The extremes of our reasoning can lead us to the utopian or to the commonplace, because if we ask too much we grasp at the unachievable, and if instead we look only at what is immediately around us we run the risk of settling for too little. The house is a problem of limits (like almost every other problem of existence). But the definition of the limits is a problem of culture and the house leads back precisely to it (as do, in fact, the other problems of existence).

If this is the case, words too are construction material. And even a magazine can aspire to that status. The task is to find in our own spirit the state of nature (and to this extent Rousseau may be right), while nevertheless taking the fertile path of experience (which is the generous compensation for lost virginity). There are many useless things that call forth bourgeois vanities, but equally many marvellous things that most people are still not able to enjoy.

A magazine can be a tool, a filter used to establish the criterion of choice.

From what has been said, it is possible to deduce our intentions, i n fact the hopes we set as our goals, which are unattainable by our forces alone.

The idea is to form a taste, a technique and an ethics, as elements of a single function. The purpose is to construct a society. There is no time to lose illustrating odds and ends. Let's all help each other to find harmony between human measure and divine proportion.

In addition to his *Domus* editorials, Rogers also devoted a series of short texts, accompanied by iconic images, to key concepts that he defined as 'problems'. With this series he sought to lay the foundations for a new approach to contemporary architecture.

PROBLEMS

Problemi: il pittoresco

Case e no; ci vien quasi voglia di chiedere a prestito il linguaggio dal nostro amico Vittorini per parlare di questa costruzione che si pone ai margini del mondo sociale come di quello estetico.

Bello e brutto sono termini insufficienti a definire la complessità di un giudizio architettonico; ed è appunto per esemplificare una volta di più la stretta dipendenza tra architettura e società che pubblichiamo la curiosa immagine. Potrebb'essere il rifugio di un cantastorie, forse la locanda di prime notti clandestine.

È innegabile un certo incanto: il gusto del pittoresco può allettarci occasionalmente e ognuno di noi può essere ridotto a sognare una vacanza tra quei sassi.

Ma una immediata riflessione deve condurci alla valutazione più precisa dove l'attributo che avevamo dato per definire la nostra sensazione trova altra classificazione e si confonde con il gusto del mostruoso. Per convincersi come queste siano cose da bandire basti considerare che per un nostro effimero piacere estetico, altri uomini sono costretti miseramente nella realtà della loro esistenza quotidiana a figurare come comparse amorfe.

Questo non è che un esempio, e, per la sua eccezionalità, neppure dei più gravi, ma esso valga per i ghetti, per i « carrugi » e per tutti quegli ambienti più o meno folcloristici i quali purtroppo non affascinano soltanto qualche turista affrettato ma ancora tutti quegli studiosi che non sono capaci di fondare i termini della cultura sopra una più vasta e solida base sociale.

E. N. R.

D. 210 giugno 17

Domus nº 210, June 1946, page 17, Archivio Domus

Problems: The Picturesque
Domus no. 210, June 1946

Houses and not houses: we're tempted to borrow the language of our friend [Elio] Vittorini to talk about this construction caught between the social world and the aesthetic world.[1]

Beautiful and ugly are inadequate terms to reflect the complexity of an architectural judgement, and it is precisely to illustrate, once again, the close dependency between architecture and society that we publish this curious image. It could be a storyteller's shelter or maybe a haven for romantic trysts.

There is undeniably a certain enchantment: the taste for the picturesque can be beguiling, and we can all be reduced to dreaming of a holiday in the midst of those mountains.

But a first impression has to be followed by a more precise evaluation in which the attribute we have used to define our experience finds another meaning and mingles with a taste for the monstrous. To be convinced that these problems are things that should be banished, just consider the fact that for our fleeting aesthetic pleasure other men are wretchedly forced to play the role of amorphous extras in the reality of their everyday existence. This is just one example, and, due to its exceptional character, not even one of the worst, but it can stand for ghettos, *carrugi*[2] and all those more or less folkloric environments that unfortunately fascinate not only the hasty tourist, but still entice all those scholars who appear unable to define culture in terms of a broader, more solid, social base.

1 The opening sentence is a reference to *Uomini e no* (*Men and Non-Men*, 1945), a novel by Italian writer, editor and translator Elio Vittorini. The book describes the ambiguous reality of the underground resistance movement in Milan in 1944 during the waning days of Mussolini's dictatorship, when the Nazis were already in command. Through its violence and foul play, German military rule had suspended the decencies of normal life, leaving the Italian resistance movement no choice but to adopt the same inhuman tactics. When in Nazi Milan, partisans had to do as the Germans did. They become both men and not men.

2 Local word for small alleyways in Genoa.

Problemi: l'ornato

Una piccola ampolla: poco importa sapere che è stata fatta in Persia 3000 anni prima di Cristo, nell'epoca Ouronk della ceramica non dipinta, succeduta all'epoca Obeid della ceramica monocroma e precedente all'epoca Djemet-Nasr della ceramica policroma.
Importa sapere ch'è opera dell'uomo e che racchiude, pur nella semplicità delle forme e degli scopi, uno degli aspetti della sua drammatica esistenza.
La misura (cm. 12), giusto quanto occorre per prendere con due dita, è funzionale; così la proporzione tra il recipiente e il versatoio, perchè ogni goccia si travasi senza sperdersi.
Ma quelle due righe?
Il primitivo artefice non ha saputo resistere alla tentazione dell'ornato e, mentre la sua ragione e lo spirito parevano già soddisfatti dell'oggetto perfettamente compiuto, ecco che i suoi sensi hanno voluto rendersi manifesti insinuando un segno dove compiacersi.
Qui, pertanto, non v'è interferenza, nè conflitto determinato dall'ornamento: l'inutile non altera il necessario e si svolge nel suo legittimo campo d'azione: solo l'osservazione teorica può indicare, per ora, i possibili deviamenti.
Ma in epoche in cui vi sarà meno naturale equilibrio tra ragione e sentimento, quelle due righe diventeranno intrichi incomplessi, volute, rigonfi, foglie, draghi, mostri che di oggetto in oggetto si trasferiranno, come il vizio di una famiglia, da un individuo all'altro, fino a pervertirne il carattere sì da trasformare l'accidentale in sostanziale, sovrapporsi alla funzione e diventare motivo dominante, scopo dell'invenzione. Pensate, per esempio, a certe ampolle dell'ottocento che stillavano rosolio dalla papalina di Pio nono e, allora, la parola di Adolf Loos *ornato è delitto* ci mette a nudo il problema essenziale dell'architetttura.

E. N. R.

D. 211 luglio **17**

Domus nº 211, July 1946, page 19, Archivio Domus © Editoriale Domus S.p.A.

Problems: The ornate
***Domus* no. 211, July 1946**

A small jug: we don't need to know that it was made in Persia some 5,000 years ago, in the Uruk period of unpainted pottery, after the Ubaid era of monochrome pots and before the Jemdet-Nasr era of multi-coloured pottery.

What we need to know is that it is the work of man and that it embodies, even in the simplicity of its forms and purposes, one of the aspects of his dramatic existence.

The size (12 cm), just right to grip with a thumb and one finger, is functional; as is the proportion between the vessel and the spout, so that not a drop is spilled when poured.

But those two stripes?

The primitive potter could not resist the temptation of ornament, and while his reason and spirit seemed to be satisfied by the perfectly completed object, his senses wanted to manifest themselves, inserting a sign in which to take delight.

Here, then, there is no interference, no conflict determined by ornament: the functionless does not alter the functional and is deployed in its legitimate field of action: only theoretical observations could indicate, for now, potential conflicts.
But in eras with less natural balance between reason and sentiment, those two lines will become complex tangles, spirals, swellings, leaves, dragons, monsters that move from object to object, from one individual to another, to the point of perverting its character, transforming the incidental into the substantial, thus overwhelming function and becoming the principal aim, the purpose of the invention.

Consider, for example, the vials of the 1800s in the shape of the skullcap of Pius IX used to pour *rosolio* and the essential problem of architecture, that ornament is crime, according to Adolf Loos, is laid bare.

Problemi: la deformazione

Questa sciagurata figura è di Picasso. Potrebbe chiamarsi: Montecassino, Varsavia, Stalingrado, St. Lô, Coventry, Colonia, Europa o anche Bikini.

È ben difficile che un artista, un grande artista, il quale guardi oggi nei volti dei contemporanei, non ne ritragga orrende immagini: sfruttatori col marchio delle proprie infamie e sfruttati sfregiati dai patimenti, esprimono in un solo urlo la tragedia di chi ha smarrito (o non ha ancora trovato) la parola umana.

Questa figura è una denuncia e solo gl'ipocriti possono sottrarsi dal riconoscere almeno una parte di se stessi nella rappresentazione del comune sfacelo.

Ma anche Picasso in fondo è uno di noi, un dannato, non un giudice e quanto più è sincero tanto più rischia di confondere la sua arte.

Altri artisti, all'opposto, non vogliono essere contaminati dalle contingenze e rifuggono da ogni figurazione del reale.

Mondrian, che è morto poco fa, aveva perfino in orrore gli alberi e si rifugiava nelle supreme sfere della fantasia geometrica.

Così si propone ancora, in forma diversa, il tema di Valéry tra il dionisiaco e l'apollineo che sono i poli entro i quali si dibatte l'umanità quando scava nei propri peccati o quando si astrae nella speranza della virtù.

E. N. R.

D. 212 agosto 23

Domus no 212, August 1946, page 23, Archivio Domus © Editoriale Domus S.p.A.

Problems: Deformation
***Domus* no. 212, August 1946**

This unfortunate figure is by Picasso. It could be called: Montecassino, Warsaw, Stalingrad, Saint-Lô, Coventry, Cologne, Europe or even Bikini.

It is hard today for an artist, a great artist, who looks at the faces of his contemporaries, not to portray them as horrendous images: exploiters - marked by their own infamies, and the exploited scarred by their suffering - express in one single howl the tragedy of those who have lost (or not yet discovered) human expression.

This figure is a protest and only a hypocrite could fail to recognise at least a part of himself in its representation of common ruination. But even Picasso, in the end, is one of us, a condemned soul rather than a judge, and the more sincere he is, the more he runs the risk of confounding his art.

Other artists, instead, do not want to be contaminated by contingencies and avoid any depiction of the real.

Mondrian, who died a short time ago, had a horror of trees and sought shelter in the supreme spheres of geometric fantasy.
So, in a different form, the question posed by Valéry returns, between the Dionysian and the Apollonian, which are the poles between which humanity struggles when it examines its own sins or when it abstracts itself in the hope of virtue.

(da "Petit Musée de la curiosité photographique" ed. "Tel")

Problemi: la tecnica

Non sorridete: qualcuno sorriderà di noi tra qualche anno. E non è neppure il caso d'insuperbire se ormai si va nella stratosfera e, quasi lasciando il suono alle spalle, acciuffiamo la luce.
La tecnica è uno strumento che può rendere più facile e più piacevole la vita, ma, frutto mirabile della ragione, non è tuttavia capace di varcare i limiti della contingenza perchè, ad ogni scoperta, supera o nega le precedenti: essa può collaborare alla risoluzione dei temi spirituali, non può risolverli da sola. Disprezzare la tecnica è assurdo, farsene un mito è da ingenui.
La differenza tra l'ingegnere e l'architetto (in quanto tali) è particolarmente qui: per il primo la tecnica si identifica con i fini della sua opera, per il secondo è soltanto un mezzo del quale egli si serve quando considera la materia di là dai suoi termini caduchi e la trasfigura nel mondo dell'arte. La casa dell'uomo è un problema d'architettura.
L'architettura moderna è ormai sul punto di conciliare il divorzio che ha perdurato durante l'ottocento tra l'ingegnere e l'artista: ispirandosi ai criteri del funzionalismo tenta coscientemente la sintesi tra l'utilità e la bellezza. (Forse il funzionalismo è il frutto di un'epoca che si dibatteva tra il positivismo e l'idealismo).

E. N. R.

Problems: Technique
***Domus* no. 213, September 1946**

Don't laugh: someone will smile about us in a few years' time. And we shouldn't feel superior if we're now able to travel into the stratosphere, almost leaving sound behind, catching up with light.

Technique is a tool that can make life easier and more pleasant, but while it is the admirable fruit of reason, it is still not able to cross the boundaries of contingency, because with each discovery it surpasses or negates those that came before it: it can cooperate on the solving of spiritual themes, but it cannot solve them on its own. To despise technique is absurd, but to regard it as mythical is naïve.

The difference between the engineer and the architect (as such) lies here, in particular: for the former, technique is identified with the goals of his work, while for the latter it is simply a means by which he thinks about elevating physical material to become part of the world of art. The house of man is a problem of architecture.

Modern architecture is now on the verge of patching up the separation between the engineer and the artist that prevailed throughout the nineteenth century; inspired by the criteria of functionalism, it consciously attempts the synthesis of utility and beauty. (Perhaps functionalism is the result of an era that was torn between positivism and idealism.)

(Michèle Morgan in un vestito di *Germaine Lecomte* - da "*Vogue*").

Problemi: la moda

(L'immagine di una donna bella ed elegante presenta almeno due problemi, ma poichè il primo, della bellezza, non può trattarsi tutto pubblicamente nè platonicamente, ci fermiamo al secondo, quello dell'eleganza. E diciamo subito, per di più, che questo è un pretesto per parlare d'altro).

Se all'arte si volessero applicare i ragionamenti di Weininger per ricercare il carattere dei prodotti secondo l'apporto proporzionale degli elementi maschili e femminili si farebbe forse coincidere la moda, che è all'estremo limite del rendimento con l'elemento femminile, e l'estremo della linea della ragione che può chiamarsi tecnica con l'elemento maschile.

L'opera d'arte concreta si realizza nelle zone intermedie, nella congiunzione, il compromesso e il contrasto dialettico di quei valori ciascuno dei quali, da solo, è incapace di creare alcunchè di vitale.

La moda è l'espressione contingente del gusto così come il ritrovato tecnico è un aspetto della ragione, ed è molto difficile che i contemporanei riescano a distinguere la parte caduca da quella durevole.

Un'invenzione della generazione precedente viene considerata vecchia, e decade coinvolta nel gioco dell'esistenza per cui i figli si contrappongono ai padri. Poi, diventa antica e avendo subito il vaglio dei giudizi, riappare. Il male è che le riesumazioni sono a loro volta un fatto di moda, perciò malgrado tutto, la vera risorsa dell'arte è il rischio della invenzione.

E. N. R.

D. 214 ottobre **23**

Domus nº 214, October 1946, page 23, Archivio Domus © Editoriale Domus S.p.A.

Problems: Fashion
***Domus* no. 214, October 1946**

(The image of a beautiful, elegant woman presents us with at least two problems, but since the first, beauty, cannot be fully examined in public, or platonically, we will focus on the second, namely elegance. And, furthermore, we should immediately state that this is a pretext to talk about something else.)

If we want to apply to art the reasoning of [Otto] Weininger - seeking the character of products according to the proportional contribution of male and female elements - we might make fashion, at its extreme limit of performance, coincide with the feminine element, and the extreme of the line of reasoning that can be called 'technique' coincide with the masculine element.

The concrete work of art is created in the zones in between, in uniting compromise and the dialectical contrast of those values each of which, on its own, is incapable of creating anything vital. Fashion is the contingent expression of taste, just as technological invention is an aspect of reason, and it is very unlikely that our contemporaries are able to distinguish the transient part from the lasting part.

An invention of the dating from the previous decade is considered old, and becomes part of the game of life in which sons oppose their fathers. Then it becomes antique and, then, after some discriminating sifting, it reappears. The bad thing is that what is disinterred is itself a matter of fashion, and therefore, in spite of everything, the true resource of art remains the risky business of invention.

Problemi: la retorica

Prima, una chiarificazione per non essere fraintesi: il Prestito della Ricostruzione è una impresa nazionale alla quale diamo incondizionata adesione: la nostra modesta voce si unisce a quella di tutta la stampa per dirvi di sottoscrivere.
Non il Prestito intendiamo criticare, ma i cartelloni. Proprio perchè convinti dell'importanza d'un'opera che s'appella alla responsabile solidarietà di tutti i cittadini, siamo spiacenti di constatare come gli strumenti artistici scelti per convincere psicologicamente il pubblico siano inadeguati e spesso perfino repulsivi.
Accade purtroppo che idee politicamente buone e idee cattive possano vestirsi in quest'epoca di crisi con forme d'arte ugualmente retoriche senza che per questo si sia autorizzati a dedurre superficiali giudizi.
Ciò non toglie che in senso più profondo, se si aspira a una civiltà integra, non si debbano trascurare i valori espressivi atti a rivelare le pieghe più intime.
I popoli non hanno bisogno di retorica e se i politici non s'avvedono che questa è per se stessa un grave male da sradicare, segno è che i rapporti umani sono ancora lontani dalla giusta misura.
Il nostro discorso ritorna sempre dall'estetica all'etica ed è perciò che vogliamo trarre conseguenze generali anche da manifestazioni secondarie.

E. N. R.

28 D. 215 novembre

Domus nº 215, November 1946, page 28, Archivio Domus © Editoriale Domus S.p.A.

Problems: Rhetoric
Domus no. 215, November 1946

First, a clarification to avoid misunderstanding: the Reconstruction Loan is a national undertaking to which we give our unconditional support; our humble voice joins those of all the press in this approval.

We do not intend to criticise the Loan, but the billboards. Precisely because we are convinced of the importance of a work that calls for the responsible solidarity of all citizens, we are dismayed to note that the artistic tools chosen to convince the public psychologically are inadequate and often even repulsive.

Unfortunately, it may be that good political ideas and bad political ideas can be clothed, in this era of crisis, in equally rhetorical art forms, although this does not give us permission to make superficial judgements.

Nonetheless, in the deepest sense, if we aspire to a solid civilisation, we must not overlook the expressive values that reveal its innermost folds.

People do not need rhetoric, and, if politicians fail to realise that this in itself is a great evil which must be expunged, that is a sign that human relations are still far from amounting to what they should be. Our discourse always returns from aesthetics to ethics, inclining us to draw general conclusions even from secondary manifestations.

This issue of *Domus* contains the Italian text of the lecture given by Rogers in Zurich on 3 November 1946 at the invitation of the Schweizerischer Werkbund and, subsequently, at the Casa della Cultura (House of Culture) in Milan on 20 December 1946.

The Casa della Cultura was an association and cultural forum in Milan in which Rogers was deeply involved. His philosophy professor at the Liceo Parini, Antonio Banfi, was one of the founders of the initiative which sought to unite politicians, artists, intellectuals, professionals, humanists and the working classes in the reconstruction effort. In 1931 Banfi was appointed as a professor at the Università Statale in Milan. His lectures became major opportunities for the gathering and exchanging of ideas among the Milanese intelligentsia, including BBPR. Banfi also played an important role in disseminating and promoting the phenomenological approach of Edmund Husserl and the pragmatism of John Dewey (both their voices echo in this seminal piece of writing); he was also important in consolidating what came to be known as the Milan School of Critical Rationalism, a poignant alternative to the idealism of Italian philosopher Benedetto Croce which was prevalent at the time. Not least, he introduced BBPR to one of his students, the philosopher Enzo Paci, who was to become one of Rogers's closest friends and collaborators.

It is in the context of the mission of the Casa della Cultura and the philosophical framework provided by Banfi and Paci that Rogers's famous phrase 'from the spoon to the city' should be understood. Too often I have heard this phrase being used as a metaphor for a kind of *Gesamtkunstwerk* – a total work of art encompassing every aspect of design – rather than as an exhortation to approach the creation of any object necessary to human existence by means of a coherent method that balances 'the needs of the individual and those of the community'. This remained a key issue in the contradictory climate of postwar Italy, and one that is even more relevant today in the face of rapid technological advances and deepening inequalities.

RECONSTRUCTION: FROM THE USEFUL OBJECT TO THE CITY

DOMUS NO. 215, NOVEMBER 1946

A spoon is a spoon, a chair is a chair, a house is a house, a city is a city.

The history of architecture – but I could simply say history – can be seen as a movement of attraction and repulsion between two poles, utility and beauty, as the spirit engages in a dialectical struggle to establish identities like the ones listed above.

Seen from another point of view, there is a push and pull in history between the ideals of freedom and of justice, which determines the dramas in the lives of the individuals and the community. I believe we cannot talk about reconstruction without taking into account these axes, a great cross – or, if you prefer, the cardinal points – superimposed on our every action. Utility and beauty, justice and freedom – these are some of the many names we give to the terms of both ancient dualist dogmas and modern dialectical relativism. And we cannot rebuild, we cannot trace the trajectory of our life, without knowing how to assign a value to the abscissas and ordinates that mark its course.

Allow me, then, to linger a moment over this reasoning. In so doing my wish is not to lead the discussion towards the abstract but rather to set out, as a conscientious architect, the foundations of this modest construction of mine.

Utility and beauty can be considered the indispensable antipolar charges of architectural energy: in themselves, neither the practical principle nor the aesthetic principle is sufficient to give life to architecture.

Therefore we cannot consider as 'architecture' any work that does not in its response harmonise the criteria of both of these. The crude flint of the prehistoric caveman might be just as far removed from the precise solution required as the most finely etched blade of Toledo. That is to say, an exclusively instrumental architecture is just as inadequate as one that focuses on aspects extraneous to its rationale. I would like to point out that in the formulation of this functional aesthetic I am limiting myself to architecture, that is, the field of the applied arts. For the other plastic arts, painting and sculpture, which are not so swayed by practical reasoning, the discussion would certainly be different.

For us architects the difficulty, but also the goal, is to express utility through beauty or, at least, to make beauty useful. I believe that, thought about in this way, architecture can truly be defined as a function: architecture as a function of utility and beauty. And functional architecture is exactly this.

History teaches us that men have often found it more difficult to express a dry practical need than to abandon themselves to fantasy or even adorn themselves with peacock feathers. Likewise, in the field of social relations, they have more often pursued the mirages of individualism than the patient labour of collaboration. The comparison is not as tenuous as it might seem, and now I will try to elucidate the connections.

We will not go so far as to say that Versailles or an inlaid cabinet by the Venetian Brustolon are the Caesars that threaten the foundations of art, but it is certain that both of those masterpieces (and I insist on that term) represent a deviation from the central axis of architecture, just as Caesar was a dangerous deviation from the *misura umana* [the human measure].

What I want to make clear is that I do not wish to trim the wings of imagination, nor to censure genius. I simply want to say that they both have value for our dual consciousness as architects and citizens only if they become functions of a more complete *Weltanschauung* [view of the world].

To establish this coherence requires a titanic effort on the part of the populace; some countries have proceeded along this path, without indulging in dangerous diversions, for centuries and centuries; elsewhere, as in our country, an attempt is now being made to get back on the right track through a gradual reasserting of values.

The aesthetic concept of life, as held, perhaps, by men during the Renaissance (and in a sense by Nietzsche), no longer seems an adequate response to the constructional problems of human existence, because while it can generate marvellous palaces for princes transformed into demigods or glorious monuments to God, it often degenerates into decorativism and cannot resolve the fundamental issue of housing man.

Modern criticism addresses all of the past: [Adolf] Loos has already warned us that ornament is crime, and [Frank Lloyd] Wright – in a rather hasty way, but one that nevertheless contains an element of truth once his polemic tone has been put to one side – dares to point to the dome of St Peter's as a heavy anachronism.

If we then relate these statements, both emanating from the field of art, to the declarations that property is theft, we can see how badly threatened are the foundations on which humankind relies when it has to create objects to support its own existence – everything from the spoon to the city.

Whatever opinion one may hold regarding the rather radical formulation of these principles, we must acknowledge that they have infiltrated our experience and need to be taken into account. Nevertheless, our generation cannot accept them without a serious review, and I believe our task is to give them a humane content more in line with our aspirations and our possibilities.

In reconstructing destroyed cities, people are faced with the dilemma of reconciling the fundamental principles of utility and beauty with those of justice and liberty. While the hierarchy of values might at first glance seem obvious, it turns out to be a question of opinion. A civilisation, a society, also recognises itself by the way in which it establishes an order of precedence for the works of reconstruction: what should be done first? Why this and not that?

I believe it was Wright, again, who coined the paradox: 'Give me the luxuries of life and I will willingly do without the necessities.' But Pittacus, the philosopher of Mytilene, said: 'I like the house where I see nothing superfluous and find all that is necessary.' First: what is superfluous and what is necessary? If you ask someone who is hungry, he will be sure to know the answer, just as someone who is cold will know it.

When the rich man wants to give the poor man that which is superfluous, what does he do? He will break bread in two, and then go home to eat pastries. And if he were to give away the pastries and keep the bread, he would again have given the luxury and kept the necessity; though still the poor man could not claim that he had what was necessary. For those who lack the necessities, luxury is useless; but as soon as we shift these two terms from the limited physiological sphere to the sphere that encompasses the most complex needs of man, the problem gets more complicated, because there are things that might seem indispensable to one person, and less so to the next; thus, for example, a religious individual needs his church just as much as he needs bread.

I do not know if such considerations are a source of concern and debate in Switzerland, where a particular type of civilisation has already established itself on solid, democratic ground, and where a strong economy has made most goods affordable for all classes. But I can say that this is the case in Italy, as I believe it is in France or Holland or Poland. All those countries are almost like the survivor of a shipwreck who, after struggling to reach the shore, simultaneously begs for a shot of cognac, a piece of bread and a cigarette.

In our country, one part of the population has achieved such a refinement of culture that it feels the need for certain objects that have nothing to do with the economic opportunities enjoyed by the masses; as a result, this privileged minority tends to demand works which signal an elevated quality of life (including intellectual life), but which cannot be considered to serve public utility in the broader sense of the term.

Extremists on the right and left evaluate these issues in opposite ways: some justify this approach to reconstruction in the name of absolute liberalism, while others condemn it out of hand, citing principles of egalitarian justice.

So it is clear that in Italy, where the foundations of an ancient humanistic culture do not sustain a solid economic edifice, the terms of reconstruction can seem to be more contradictory than elsewhere. I have attempted to sketch out here some aspects of the useful and the superfluous, which can be seen as the opposite limits of equality and freedom, if we consider each of these concepts separately and therefore in an abstract way.

A practical approach to reconstruction as a whole – from the smallest useful object to the largest urban planning problem – demands that it be regulated by a method that balances individual freedoms and social justice. And many of us believe there can be no other possibility than to establish a National Reconstruction Plan that both indicates the successive timing of works of public interest and defines a vast field of operations for private enterprise.

In spite of the plethora of piecemeal laws enacted along these lines, there is not yet an organic system to frame them, due to the difficult political conditions in our country. This is certainly not the place to list those difficulties; and besides, only a part of the solution lies within our grasp, while the rest depends on the international situation.

Instead, it is worth lingering over certain questions of a more general nature. While remaining within the limits of our competence, as technicians conceiving an object of utility, even a city, our conscience has to address the implications for people of our work. We know we have to supply populations disappropriated by the war with a lot of things as quickly as possible, and these things must meet the needs both of the individual and of the community.

The dialectical opposition of these imperatives is clear, because quantity, besides often being at the expense of quality, is hard to achieve in haste, and variety (to respond to personal tastes) stands in contrast to the uniformity and practical needs of the multitude.

Everyone can understand that the problem would be greatly simplified if it were possible to use a single, albeit carefully studied, model as the basis for providing fifteen million rooms – the number required to fully rebuild Italy's housing stock, according to some estimates.

But can you imagine fifteen million people in fifteen million identical beds? Since the numbers are a reality, and since in any case we must come to terms with the minimum requirement of providing basic housing for three and a half million people whose homes were destroyed in the war, we must find a way to reconcile these opposing imperatives.

From this standpoint, the problem of reconstruction - but we could also say of architecture in general - presents itself in the following terms: what are the elements that satisfy the singular nature of man? And what, by contrast, are the objective characteristics shared by individuals?

We can establish a ratio in which the differentiated numerator represents the individual personality and the common denominator represents the collective dimension. And it is equally clear that we can create typologies by grouping certain categories on the basis of geography or labour or other shared destinies.

The differences and similarities are reflected in the forms of things, from the spoon to the house to the city. Objects of common interest need to be produced in large quantities, while the rest can be limited in number: logically, the former are produced industrially, while the latter can in part be made by artisans.

Once we have applied a kind of electrolysis to separate out what belongs to the individual as opposed to the collective sphere, we will have isolated the elements that go into the house of man. This is the limit of our task as technicians; beyond this, the implementation depends on economic means and political conditions.

I will not repeat here [John] Ruskin's aesthetic concerns regarding the machine, nor the remedies proposed by William Morris on the social plane: these are well known, as is the balanced synthesis - initiated after them by [Henry] van de Velde - between technical and social necessities and no-less-urgent aesthetic needs. At this point, what is important is to establish a method that will allow us to develop our work in future.

Things, like human beings, reveal the limits of their own virtues: standardisation solves the problems of mass production, but may fail on the human plane, where in certain circumstances we feel the need to preserve personality.

If, for example, we examine a dwelling and distinguish between the elements that respond to objective physiological functions and those that relate to more intellectual or spiritual needs, we can conceive of two distinct sets of architectural elements: on the one hand the kitchen, the bath, the bed, etc., whose measurements are determined by the physical dimensions of the human body, and on the other the expressions of individual activities. Two nuclei thus emerge, of which the first can be seen as a machine composed of unchanging elements, albeit with some variations in its assembly, while the other may have a more varied appearance, depending on the composition of its constituent parts.

The objects found in the home tend equally towards these two opposing poles: on one hand there are the machines, on the other art objects as free manifestations of the infinite needs of the spirit. If properly guided, industry can address all spheres, but it is clear that for the moment at least it operates within those areas where mass production is required to meet practical needs; it also remains debatable whether one can replicate *ad infinitum* a work of art, while it is generally accepted that it is possible to repeat a useful object.

Having said that, it is worth pointing out that both industrially produced goods and the individual works of the artisan need to have a unitary conception of the functional relationship between utility and beauty.

Therefore in modern society increasing value is placed on the figure of the architect and of the other members of the great orchestra who are called on to translate every formal representation of existence, from the spoon to the city, into poetic song.

We all sense that the crisis of civilisation - and its resolution - is shaping our destiny, demanding our response as men, workers, artists. And therefore we know that the form of the house of man tomorrow will depend on the perfecting of our knowledge, our craft, our art.

Man - we are reminded by [Alexis] Carrel - is at the centre of the universe, between the atom and the stars: the problem of the house of man is at the centre of our existence and, in the specific field of our technical expertise, it is the fulcrum between the smallest useful objects and the largest urban complexes (community centres and national plans).

The task of our era seems to be to regain an awareness of *la misura umana*, the human dimension: this will provide the yardstick by which to establish all other relationships.

Perhaps functionalism is an attempt at synthesis between the idealism and the materialism that have sundered the culture of an entire century, but I certainly do not want to enter the minefield of philosophy here.

Remaining within the sphere of our technical expertise, we can gain further confirmation of the renewal of the relations between man and object if we look at issues of production from an economic and social viewpoint.

I would like to make it clear that I do not believe that intellectual or spiritual activities can be generically subordinated to economic laws, but it is natural that those laws should be taken into account in the making of architecture, where the various motifs of existence are closely intertwined.

Are not the heavy stones of the pyramids a symbol of the exploitation of slaves? Brick, too, would prove the ideal material for construction characterised by slowness of production and low wages. As we now perfect new means of construction we are preparing to discard the brick, once the basic module determined by the size of the human hand. We are seeking the new module in the greatest common divisor that, with the help of the machine, will allow us to create architectural organisms that respect individual personality while accommodating the variations required by humanity.

Accordingly, techniques of standardisation and prefabrication will not just respond to present contingencies but will allow for future adaptations. The costs of construction will be reduced, not by exploiting the labour of one part of mankind, but by taking advantage of technological progress. At the same time, a new aesthetic is opening up fresh horizons to be explored by the artist's imagination.

It should be understood that two potential pitfalls present themselves in choosing a new module: it could still be too small and therefore unsuited to present requirements – just like brick; conversely, it could be too large, limiting the range of possible combinations. The first error springs from an indiscriminate freedom, the second from a rigidly egalitarian principle. Both have an impact on utility and beauty.

So our reasoning, which began with general considerations, is anchored by and unfolds from the observation of the particular: the nucleus of construction.

I could have gone into other arguments, or cited some figures regarding Italian reconstruction. However, I have preferred to address the theme in general terms in the hope that theory is not an abstraction, but a modest contribution to the practical solution of problems.

We may, in professional practice, be forced to make compromises every day, but we should nevertheless avoid becoming too caught up in contingencies, nor should we get into the habit of accepting compromises as the norm.

Reality today is some way off from what we aspire to, but if we make a mistake when fastening the first button, those hopes will forever be frustrated.

The technicians engaged today in the study of the master plans for Milan or Genoa, or in the renovation of the mediaeval districts of Florence, are repeatedly torn between the difficulties faced by Italian society, which is alternately too rich or too poor, and their ideals, which lie beyond these issues. So, here as elsewhere, architects are forced to promulgate their ideas with words that at times seem to be at odds with their own works, because the works cannot take shape around ideal themes, but must cope with concrete facts. We would run the risk of being mere visionaries if we did not have faith that such matters of the spirit are in themselves a reality that is simply waiting for the right moment to manifest itself in three dimensions.

If we consider the progress of functional architecture we can say that our faith has not been in vain; and if we observe that even the official world, driven by necessity, is today beginning to embrace new ideas to correct flawed positions, we have the proof that our work as artists, critics and technicians has fallen on fallow ground. The seed that is already sprouting is becoming an integral part of our future.

Less than a year into his editorship, in the face of a new, fast-growing conservatism, Rogers wrote an editorial to defend his strategy of selecting works for publication – works which were often 'by young people whose immaturity and even mediocrity we can undoubtedly recognise'. *Tendenza* (meaning tendency or trend) was the term adopted by Rogers to describe the concept that informed his approach to the continuation of the modern project. He made room in *Domus* for all those experimentations which, however crude or dubious, kept the modern movement alive by challenging its established methods as well as its aesthetic, social and political drivers. Contrary to the idea of an *avant-garde* presenting a cohesive cultural front or a movement, Rogers's *tendenza* pointed to a looser strategy, underpinned by a cultural and artistic sensibility, a strategy more attuned to the changing nature of modern culture and society. Throughout his career he regularly had to clarify and defend this position, as testified by subsequent editorials written for *Casabella* such as 'Continuity' (*Casabella Continuità* nº 199, December 1953–January 1954, see page 183); 'Orthodoxy of Heterodoxy' (*Casabella Continuità* nº 216, October–December 1957, see page 215); 'The Evolution of Architecture: Reply to the Keeper of the Frigidaires' (*Casabella Continuità* nº 228, June 1959, see page 225); and 'Architects without an Oedipus complex' (*Casabella Continuità* nº 289, July 1964).[1]

1 It is worth noting that towards the end of the 1950s, *Casabella* became the centre of political dissidence in Italy, and Rogers himself was the reference point for what came to be known as *La Tendenza* (borrowing a term used by Rogers himself and echoing the theories of Antonio Gramsci): the Italian architectural movement that rose to eminence in the 1970s, led by Aldo Rossi and several other of Rogers's young collaborators at *Casabella*.

IN PRAISE OF *TENDENZA*

DOMUS NO. 216, DECEMBER 1946

They say we have one-track minds, that we wear blinkers and fail to notice or gather the swathes of beautiful flowers by the wayside, then crown ourselves with garlands of withered boughs: they say we are presumptuous.

We, on the other hand, nurture the illusion that we are coherent, that we are following a *tendenza* (tendency) with the aim of creating a style.

And we seek consolation in Baudelaire:

As for criticism worthy of that name, I hope the philosophers will understand what I am about to say: to be just, that is to say, to justify its existence, criticism should be partial, passionate and political, in other words, written from an exclusive point of view, but one that also opens up the widest horizons.

This definition is scarcely paradoxical if we understand that it does not amount to praise of the arbitrary, but is a recommendation that it is the responsibility of the critic to act as a guide with an opinion and not just as a passive channel between artist and audience.

Coerenza (coherence), *tendenza* and style are not synonyms, but three aspects of the historical process that determines the artistic phenomenon.

An artist needs *coerenza* in order to form his own harmonious relationships with the world of morals; everything he does springs from this baseline. *Tendenza* is the deliberate translation of those acts within a well-defined intellectual furrow. Style is the formal expression of *coerenza* and *tendenza*.

Therefore, we believe it is not only legitimate but a matter of duty for us to declare our sympathies, to investigate elective affinities and force the doors wide open so as to reveal *more horizons*.[2] *Tendenza* consists precisely in taking responsibility for pointing out

2 This is a reference to Goethe's book *Wahlverwandschaften*, published in 1809 and translated as both *Elective Affinities* and *Kindred by Choice*. The term 'elective affinities' was borrowed from chemistry (where it describes exothermic chemical reactions, or chemical reactions in which one ion would displace another) and used as a metaphor for human passions, which Goethe believed were governed or regulated by laws of chemical affinity.

the horizons that offer only a glimmer of light, and for turning our backs on dioramas of papier-mâché and illusory sets even when they appear so much more spacious than those small windows. For these reasons we often welcome works by young people, for all that we may recognise their immaturity and even mediocrity, as long as they are on the side of the barricades where *criticism* (and therefore action too) is *deemed right*; we stubbornly ignore products that may be more mature and perfect in themselves but are made by those who, in our view, dance to the tune of a dying or already dead world.

We do not set ourselves up as judges, assuming the vantage point of the infallible and impartial Almighty, but we do try to conduct subjective analyses from the more modest niche to which our human condition has assigned us, where partiality can aspire to universality only if it is transformed into faith.

Like any faith, this too is subject to the trials of doubt and temptation.

How often, for example, do we find paleochristian works in books, side by side with the more mature products of Roman or Hellenistic art? They may both be very beautiful; they may even represent the same subject.

You can be sure that there were differences of opinion between the artists who made all of those works and that they denied the value of one another's work.

Are *tendenza* and *coerenza*, therefore, only ephemeral causes of discord between contemporaries that the centuries may then overlook, leaving them behind and erasing them?

Such reasoning leaves us perplexed because it seems to condemn, among other things, the concept of the avant-garde on which rest so many of our normal aspirations as discoverers of new horizons.

And it cannot be denied that if we were to settle for a purely idealistic critical position, we would have to say that things are fine, and that plenty of cooks can make the broth in the capacious kitchen of art.

A historical perspective does seem, though, to be necessary to inform a critique, which is incomplete if it fails to observe phenomena from all sides; in the same way a critique cannot settle for presenting the past without substance, and when it considers the present and the future, it is all the more important for our passions to be taken into account.

After all, it is not difficult to identify with the disputes of the past and to consider them as *faits accomplis* while having an awareness of eventual outcomes. We can certainly agree that on the aesthetic plane every object has its own value, but we must not overlook what derives from it and the horizon that may thereby reveal itself, a new scene in the unfolding drama of humanity.

Our sympathies are captured by the paleochristian artist who translated the artistic language of those who went before him into a way of speaking - stammering, perhaps - that was utterly poetic and conveyed the original message.

On a par in terms of aesthetic achievement, shouldn't we award him another point for this divining of future forms? Bear in mind that in saying *future* we make a judgement that is favourable not only to the successful artist, but also to the mediocre and immature artists with the *tendenza* that dares to probe unexplored horizons. And, while granting them high marks, at least against a historical background, we are effectively inflicting a complete thrashing on the mediocrities, who are mostly conservatives.

In conclusion, a *tendenza* is a modest act that inserts the activity of the individual into the culture of his time and leads him to see himself as, more than anything else, an element in society, which thrives on the work of each of us and thus creates history and its representation in styles.

In this colourful account of the 1947 CIAM congress in Britain at Bridgewater, Rogers outlines his thoughts on prefabrication, a topic he had started to explore in 1944.[1] On one hand, he saw prefabrication as a tool for developing architecture's social agenda; on the other, he feared it as a potential encroachment on his and, more broadly, society's freedom of choice. To illustrate his point, Rogers describes the amusing and rather challenging experience of a 'beautiful Indian woman' during a visit to a prefabricated housing factory in England. The Indian woman was in fact Minnette de Silva (1918–98), an internationally acclaimed architect, regarded as the pioneer of modern architecture in Sri Lanka and the first Asian representative to CIAM.[2]

1 Ernesto N. Rogers, 'Problemi di metodo (La prefabbricazione)', *Bollettino del centro studi per l'edilizia* nº 1 (June 1944). Written during Rogers's exile in Switzerland, the text began to reflect on the issue of reconstruction and to question the general aversion to taking advantage of the new technology of prefabricated construction and the reasons behind the gap between technical progress and the generally slow uptake of technology in the construction sector.

2 De Silva was also a Fellow of the Sri Lanka Institute of Architects, the first Asian woman to be elected an Associate of the Royal Institute of British Architects (RIBA) in 1948 and one of the founding members of the journal *Marg*. Late in life, she was awarded the SLIA Gold Medal for her contribution to architecture, particularly her pioneering work in developing a regional modernism for the tropics.

PARABLE

DOMUS NO. 222, SEPTEMBER 1947

England (whatever people may say) is a country where serious work is being done: if you can, go there and you will observe this to be true.

During a recent trip for the CIAM congress I had the good fortune to see some interesting built works which have allowed me – in their positive and negative aspects – to test the implications of certain theories in practice.

Up there (where the black market is a rarity), even the wealthiest men may not have more than one new suit a year, yet every demobbed soldier is kitted out from head to toe in civilian clothes. Luxury is banned and great sacrifices are made to distribute the necessities of life. The construction industry is approached in the same manner.

Here, in our country (and I beat my own breast as I speak), a large part of the construction effort is devoted to the privileged at the expense of the homeless, who are packed into schoolrooms. There – in the traditional cradle of free enterprise – a strict plan is in place to redistribute production in accordance with defined social aims. Everywhere, experts have understood that if the problem of reconstruction is to be tackled with resolve – that is to say, rapidly and comprehensively – there must first be a thoroughgoing reform of the methods of production, from the artistic concept to the industrial phase: prefabrication. In England, far more than elsewhere, such ideas have had a practical impact. And certain war industries, transformed for peacetime, have shifted their focus to construction.

During the congress we took a trip to Bristol to visit a large manufacturer of prefabricated housing and another – no less large – factory producing aeroplanes. We comprised 70 architects in all, including a very pretty Indian colleague.

This combination of elements provides the pretext for this article. And now I will tell you why.

The aeroplanes and the houses are made of aluminium (not the Indian woman, no, by Jove). The houses are small, minimal units,

CIAM 6 Bridgwater, England, 1947. The group photograph was taken during an afternoon trip to Bristol Aeroplane Company's temporary aluminium housing factory. Ernesto Rogers is in the upper left corner and Minette de Silva is in the front row in the middle © Architectural Press Archive / RIBA Collections

while the aeroplane hangar is so large that one of our group was prompted to exclaim: 'In this country I'd rather be an aeroplane than a person!'

The remarks above contain a critical observation that I would immediately like to draw your attention to, as a taster for my conclusions.

In the housing factory production is carried out on an assembly line: I won't go into technical details, because I'd like to focus for a moment on the human problem that arises from these diligent efforts.

Before us lay the load-bearing aluminium frames, the formwork for the poured concrete elements, the layers of insulation: little by little, as they travelled through the various departments, the form of the houses developed. Here was the skeleton, then the flesh, then the skin of the house. In the central factory hall, the vital organs were worked on – the kitchen-bathroom unit. Next the walls were welded together to make one room, then another, then the roof on top; a touch of green on the drainpipe, the window frames and the door, a creamy yellow on all the rest, and the house was done. Raised on four wheels and drawn by a tractor, it set off for its destination, perhaps ending up alongside its siblings in the midst of the charming meadows of Somerset or, further afield, in the smoke-filled streets of a Welsh mining town.

Such houses will be an integral part of the landscape, of urban planning, of life. And herein lies the problem.

They're all the same? Yes, every last one of them.

As we moved through department after department, I stayed close to the beautiful Indian woman, watching her and watching the houses as well.

She was wearing an amaranth silk sari that wrapped her body and passed with a sweeping gesture over her head: 'without pins' – she told me – 'without stitches'.

The houses were all the same, inexpressive, one after the other, while - almost without uttering a word -our gentle companion continued to express her feelings, her opinions, repeatedly adjusting the drape of her garment, now tightening it as she wrapped it around her arm, now leaving it loose, like a sail offered to the wind to carry her away.

Le Corbusier, watching her, confided to me: '*Et nous prétendons leurs apprendre la civilisation...*' [and we think we can teach them about civilisation ...], a parenthesis in the extended discourse of a man who has been the lifelong prophet of machines and undoubtedly the human response of an artist confronted by the serial application of what he had preached and finding it soulless. When we reached the hangar the Indian lady asked to go up into the plane: in her vestal's robe she did indeed seem like the best person to endow the aircraft's maiden voyage with good fortune. But on the steep steps the folds wrapped around her knees hindered her progress. It was the revenge of the machine. So were the prefabricated houses imperfect with respect to the human needs represented by the Indian woman? Or was the Indian woman imperfect in relation to the aeroplane, the symbol of technical progress?

While the aeroplane is simply a means to make life easier, more convenient, more practical, the house is identified with the very aim of existence as the place where the individual strives to find harmony within the family, and the family within society. It is the dual task of the modern architect both to guarantee precious freedom to the many aspects of the individual human, as exemplified by the Indian lady, and to grasp the marvellous ingenuity suggested by, say, the aeroplane. In this sense, prefabrication, like any other advanced technical system, is a skilled complement to our inventive scope, and is commendable only if understood in this way.

(Of course, there is nothing we could do without, but if the impoverishment of our times forced us to choose, we would certainly be inclined to give up the aeroplane rather than the beautiful lady from India).

In this last *Domus* editorial, penned after his dismissal, Rogers expresses his frustration at having failed to reach more than an elite readership through the pages of an expensive magazine which, despite his efforts, was still acting 'as an arbiter of taste'.

Difficulties in sales and a changed political situation, which seriously challenged many of the cultural and political projects pursued by exponents of secular and progressive culture, led to the magazine being entrusted once again to Gio Ponti, its founder and original editor. Ponti also seems to have played an important role in the events that led to the rebirth of *Casabella*, which had ceased publication in 1944. Aware of the usefulness of a confrontation with an alternative cultural project to define a coherent and clear editorial line for his own magazine, Ponti had agreed to take over the direction of *Domus* on condition that Rogers was entrusted with *Casabella*.

Following his dismissal, Rogers took a break from editing and practising. He entered a period of enforced silence and intense teaching, reflection and the consolidation of international connections in the field of modern architecture. Between 1947 and 1948, he spent a year in Argentina in the dual role of advisor to the Buenos Aires Urban Plan and professor at the new faculty of architecture in Tucumán, where he was also charged with promoting the organisation of a South American CIAM group. It was in this context that he met the Argentine painter, designer and thinker Tomás Maldonado (1922–2018), who would go on to direct the Hochschule für Gestaltung in Ulm, Germany, between 1964 and 1966, before founding the Faculty of Design at the Politecnico di Milano.

FAREWELL

REPRINTED IN *ESPERIENZA DELL'ARCHITETTURA* (TURIN: EINAUDI, 1958)

DOMUS NO. 223-224-225, OCTOBER-DECEMBER 1947

A magazine is like a field that has to be tilled, ploughed and sown: the harvest is at first a long way off, beyond the grey of winter and the spring hailstorms, beyond the pilfering crows; patient labour places its faith in the future.

We have cared anxiously for this *Domus*, the house of man, entrusted to us after the Liberation, helping it back to life after the tempest, this creature salvaged from the wreckage. As we adopted it, we sensed that it was not just ours, but that it belongs to all those who believe in a given architecture and the ability of architecture to contribute to the renewal of a society, allowing matter to be reunited - and identified - with the spirit, and utility with beauty. A symbol in spite of the sceptics, an act of faith in spite of the cynics: a work of mediation between the public and the most cognisant avant-gardes. A banner, a pledge, a promise.

We were aware of the difficulty of the task, but, just like the farmer, we assumed it would be work stretching over many seasons. After the Liberation, there was such an intensity of commitment to progress that everyone encouraged us in our struggle: at rare moments in history ideals seem so close to realisation that they awaken the interest of those who would not usually be capable of appreciating them, except as tools enabling them to achieve their own material ends. Our program was to speak with a voice so clear that it could not be suspected - when extreme positions were being defended - of conventionalism or acquiescence (echoing more uncertain voices) or of demagogy.

Intolerant of being confined to a single province, crossing boundaries, we have seen our task as making known the researches of the most energetic Italian artists, who gather together and let us know about what is being developed elsewhere with similar aims.

A magazine promulgating *tendenza*, tendency, admittedly - and we have repeatedly taken responsibility for this circumscription in the belief that the particularity of a viewpoint, far from negating a universal principle - renders it evident by establishing the coordinates of a more precise reasoning where one's own opinions and those of others, clearly defined, are presented to enable more honest comprehension.

Due, especially, to this need for *coerenza*, coherence, we have attempted to pose questions regarding the problems specific to architecture in the shared light of other modern cultural problems; we are convinced that, as in the realm of physical experience, a flame in the spiritual field benefits from the warmth of other flames and conveys its own warmth to them. To speak of a poet or of a sculptor when discussing the issues of our art is not, as some have alleged, straying away from the subject, rather it is developing variations on a theme.

We have therefore willingly accepted being labelled as humanists and have taken this as a sign of valour, much like being welcomed into an order of knights having demonstrated - through a particular art or craft - that we are at one with the vastness of the human spirit.

Human beings and humanists, thus both social and political: a programme - you see - that is ambitious, presumptuous, persistent, and does not seek approval from those circles that cultivate dandies. What kind of audience could we expect?

A magazine printed with some care, like ours at Editoriale Domus, is necessarily expensive and it cannot be published, initially at least, if those in a position to buy it don't understand it: that is one challenge.

We knew that we could, with ease, find our way into the homes of fairly privileged people, but it cannot be true that for all those people we need to lower ourselves to engaging in compromise, adulation or even falsehood.

An ambiguous economic structure in a society undoubtedly has dramatic cultural repercussions, and it is not always possible to find a common interest among individuals; technical and aesthetic developments - the theoretical discourse of architecture, for example - have progressed greatly, while the social means for people to take advantage of these remain primitive. Material interests frequently diverge from spiritual interests, so that among people living in the same era no true contemporary condition, no *coerenza* exists. The task of a genuinely useful magazine must be to gather up and join the threads according to the most rigorous selective criterion possible.

The problems are so challenging that they are seldom resolved, even when one sets out with the best of intentions; moreover, life itself forces upon us so much adulteration that there is really no need to deliberately add more contamination for fear of seeming too pure.

We have such lofty ideas about art and architecture; the mere thought of the Olympian summit takes our breath away: we would be truly mad to think that we had even caught a glimpse of it, let alone reached it.

At times though, someone shows us a way up: a Le Corbusier, a Gropius, an Aalto, a Neutra, etc., says to us, Come on up, you are on the right path - '*une des plus belles revues du monde*' (one of the truly good and ingenious periodicals of the world). And we catch sight along the way of many whom we consider among the finest, scaling the rocks above us: [Max] Bill, [Alfred] Roth, [Josep Lluis] Sert, [James] Richards, [Alfred Burgess] Read, Edwin Maxwell Fry, [Helena] Syrkus, [Sigfried] Giedion, [Cornelis] van Eesteren, the people at the Museum of Modern Art, the most authoritative magazines, the friends of the CIAM, MSA, APAO, writers, painters, sculptors, critics, in Italy and in every part of the world.

Thus encouraged, we hoped we could improve: eliminating our shortcomings, at least to some extent - imperfections of which we are well aware in spite of the praise we have received.

Two years have passed - too little time for our land to change from growing sunflowers to producing grapes or olives.

We regret abandoning our efforts and we say this openly, since we believe in our ideas and wish to continue to pursue our commitment to them. Arrivederci.

Casabella had been out of print since 1946.[1] Market conditions, too unfavourable in 1946 for *Costruzioni Casabella* to continue, had now improved enough for the publisher to consider reviving its most prestigious title. Postwar reconstruction, carried out without any real consultation with modern architects, was perceived by many as a missed opportunity largely in the hands of speculative investors. Against this background, Rogers's cultural project, previously considered inappropriate for *Domus*, could play an important part in the relaunch of *Casabella*.

The new editorial staff of *Casabella*, which like its predecessors was housed in two rooms at 15, Via Monte di Pietà in Milan, comprised Rogers, who was concerned with the relationship of modern architecture with history, Marco Zanuso, who focused on technology and innovative building systems, and Giancarlo De Carlo, who offered a critique of the anonymous modernist formalism (known as International Style) that was becoming dominant in Europe and the USA. They were supported by the recently graduated Vittorio Gregotti, who initially took charge of the layout, and Julia Bertolotti Banfi (formerly with Rogers at *Domus*), who worked full-time as the publication's editorial assistant.

Unlike most Italian and international journals, typically geared towards boosting the profession, Rogers's *Casabella* offered itself as a lively forum for debate on topics surrounding architecture and society. It quickly became the most dedicated journal of *tendenza* in the world, with perhaps only *The Architectural Review* and the newly founded *Architectural Design* showing a similar commitment to promoting critical and interdisciplinary discourse. In line with this goal, as announced in this first editorial, Rogers consistently published works by young and established voices alike so long as he recognised in them 'the first stirrings of a break with hardened preconceptions'.

The first issue of *Casabella* was indicative of this editorial line, previously tried out by Rogers at *Domus*. Alongside a welcome text by Walter Gropius and a contribution by Marco Zanuso on Jean Prouvé's prefabrication systems, it featured two unorthodox and strongly contrasting works by Mario Ridolfi and Ignazio Gardella. These were

1 Edited by Pagano and Persico from 1933, *Costruzioni Casabella* had been closed down by the fascist government at the end of 1943. The magazine resumed publication in March 1946 under the editorship of Franco Albini and Giancarlo Palanti, who was also the editor-in-chief, while editorial work was carried out by Anna Castelli Ferrieri, a recent graduate from the Politecnico di Milano. However, only three monographic issues of this new series saw the light of day, two of which were just 20 pages long and contained very few advertisements. A copy cost 200 lire, a sum that in Italy three years earlier had been the equivalent of an annual subscription. Economic difficulties led to suspension of the publication at the end of 1946.

CONTINUITY

TRANSLATED AND REPRINTED IN JOAN OCKMAN, ED., *ARCHITECTURE CULTURE 1943-1968* (NEW YORK: RIZZOLI, 1993)

A TRANSLATED EXTRACT ALSO APPEARS IN HARRY FRANCIS MALLGRAVE, ED., *ARCHITECTURAL THEORY* VOL. 2: 1871-2005 (OXFORD: BLACKWELL, 2006)

CASABELLA CONTINUITÀ NO. 199, DECEMBER 1953-JANUARY 1954

the 'barbarous and robust' neorealist residential towers on Viale Etiopia (Rome, 1948–1954) by Ridolfi and Gardella's more refined Housing for Borsalino employees (Alessandria, 1948–1952). As De Carlo writes in the same issue, despite their very different appearances, the two schemes 'converge from their extremes to represent the most original and fertile aspect of contemporary Italian architecture. They are the first results of the tension that in recent years has freed architectural discourse from abstract dogmatism and opened it up to profound research into reality.'

The structure of the first issue, with a few exceptions, was to remain unchanged over the next few years of the magazine. The work of a foreign architect – among them, Sven Markelius, Arne Jacobsen and Alvar Aalto, with particular attention paid to the masters of modernism, Frank Lloyd Wright, Gropius, Le Corbusier and Mies van der Rohe – would appear flanked by that of one or more Italian architects. These treatments were followed by theoretical contributions on urbanism, historical essays, reviews and articles on topical issues. Almost every issue contained detachable plates with technical details, an idea taken from Pagano's *Casabella*, as well as drawings by nineteenth- and twentieth-century masters such as Alessandro Antonelli, Raimondo D'Aronco, Gustave Eiffel, Erich Mendelsohn and Louis Sullivan. Designers and critics who had already written during Pagano's editorship, such as Giulio Carlo Argan, Pier Luigi Nervi and Mario Labò, also contributed to Rogers's *Casabella*. Among the new contributors was the philosopher Enzo Paci, a close friend of Rogers who also took part in the editorial meetings, in a way playing the role of the 'critical conscience' of the magazine, as in the case of a planned issue on 'tradition' that, although fully developed, was never published.

He who has seen present things has seen all, both everything which has taken place from all eternity and everything which will be for time without end; for all things are of one kin and of one form.
—Marcus Aurelius, Meditations, Book 6, XXXVII

Casabella might seem a banal title to encapsulate the programme of a magazine with such ambitions, were it not for its history, which has nourished it with an energy that has transformed its very substance. The tensions arising from its contents have drifted into the name, which now vibrates with the force of a symbol: *Casabella* is the magazine guided by Giuseppe Pagano and Edoardo Persico through years of darkness towards the ever-postponed goal of definitions, discoveries, inventions, fantasies.

We have gathered the fruits from seeds sown by them.

But times have changed: Pagano and Persico, were we lucky enough to welcome them into our midst now, would certainly not be the same as they were over a decade ago.

Setting aside the scale of their achievement, which compels us to be courageous, we too are different from our friends - indeed, every individual will stand out from the rest if he sincerely asserts his own irreducible personality.

What remains, what unites us all, is the principle of *coerenza*, of congruance with the historical moment of which we are part. It is through this *coerenza* that we attempt to establish our originality, just as they Persico and Pagano asserted theirs in the face of the events that shaped their actions as artists and critics.

We too love architecture, not as an abstract idea, but as an act that fully expresses our will to live, because we are among those who still believe in the unity of existence or, or rather, in the fundamental responsibility of each artist in relation to his work.

We believe in the fertile cycle of 'man-architecture-man' and want to represent its dramatic unfolding - its crises, its few but indispensable certainties and its many and even more necessary doubts. Accordingly, we think that being alive means, above all, accepting the effort of daily renewal and rejecting established positions; it means enduring anxiety that comes close to anguish in the perpetual struggle to enlarge the field of human 'sympathy'.

The sign, the motto of our way of feeling, lies in the word *continuità*, continuity, that now appears above the old [single word] title both as a reminder of the commitment we have made and as an expression of our humility in accepting this legacy and our presumptuous hope that we will be equal to the task.

'*Continuità*' is much more than a mere addition to the *Casabella* masthead; it signifies historical awareness, an awareness of a deep-running tradition or *tendenza*, tendency, which, for Pagano and Persico, as for us, is expressed in the eternal struggle of the creative spirit against any sort of formalism, past or present.

Dynamic continuation and not passive copying: not mannerism, not dogmatism, but rather research that is free of preconceptions and consistent in its methods. We will consider as 'ours' only works and ideas that have been thoroughly worked out; on the other hand, we will also draw attention (perhaps especially) to those works in which we can recognise the first stirrings of a break with hardened preconceptions, new signs of boldness, intuitions, desires, hopes.

We are neither idolaters nor iconoclasts: we love both the masters of today and those of the past, recognising, with great appreciation, how we have been nourished by their example, but we refuse to give up that most jealously guarded of our possessions: a free-ranging, critical mind.

Therefore, starting with this issue of *Casabella*, we have gathered contributions, not only from the major exponents of architectural thought but also indicative work from younger, talented individuals who are less confident and mature, all of them nevertheless able to arouse passions. To our way of thinking, both groups represent necessary moments of progress, like the diastole and systole that circulate blood in a living organism – continuity.

Rejecting every cliché but also every form of equivocation, our focus is necessarily on those expressions which seem to manifest

The cover of *Casabella Continuità* nº 199, December 1953–January 1954, the first issue edited by Ernesto Rogers and designed by Vittorio Gregotti © Mondadori Portfolio / Electa / Marco Covi

that yearning for freedom - on those works of architecture (that is, of art) which symbolise the sublime effect of the historical process ...

The universal nature of culture: continuity in time; continuity in space.

A work of architecture not genuinely rooted in tradition is not a truly modern work, and yet ancient buildings have meaning today only to the extent that they resonate through our voices. By avoiding the conventional limitations of chronology, and of a no less abstract idealism, we are able to examine the phenomenon of architecture in its historical concreteness. But where are the boundaries of the Earth? If the dead and the living coexist in our spirit, where are the boundaries between living men?

We are against the imperialism of imposed and poorly absorbed ideologies; against the anodyne cosmopolitanism of the latest academic varnishing, more insidious than mildew; against the chauvinism of the nostalgia-bound or the retrograde revolutionaries; against demagogic folklorism. We are for a truly international language, one based on mutual comprehension, to which each of us can bring both our inner freedom and the cultural perspective characteristic of the region in which we operate.

Do you remember that chorus by Bertolt Brecht? Let's repeat it here:

It is very important to understand each other clearly.
Many say yes and yet do not agree.
Many are not asked and many appear agree.
As such, it is very important to understand each other clearly.[2]

Reopening the pages of *Casabella* after this long silence (interrupted only by the three issues that have appeared since the war), we wish to devote them to debating vital issues, because we know that things are built as much with impassioned discussion and an honest exchange of opinions as they are with tangible materials. To once more relate problems of quantity to the binding sanction of quality, helping to ensure that quality progressively becomes quantity: that is the ethical basis of our aesthetics, which

2 From *Der Neinsager* (He Said No), a 1930 *Lehrstück* (didactic drama) by the German dramatist Berthold Brecht.

we want to pursue by restoring the original synthesis of craft and art – techne.

A task of this kind can be attempted only through the conscious efforts of all those concerned with architecture (whether as producers, artists, industrialists, artisans or as consumers), and therefore we address ourselves to all of them: Italian and foreign readers, our many old friends as well as the new ones we hope to meet, students, requesting that they help us to give substance to our programme.

In the following editorial, Rogers summarised much of his thinking on the relationship between a building and its environment, outlining his ambiguous theory of *preesistenze ambientali*, pre-existing conditions. This was a design method based on a rigorous analysis of reality (although it remains unclear how such analysis was to be conducted) that Rogers saw as an antidote to formalisms of all kinds: from classicism to the abstract dogmatism of the International Style, through to the neo-folklorism of projects such as the Tiburtino district of Rome and the village of La Martella near Matera.[1]

As Ezio Bonfanti and Marco Porta have pointed out, what Rogers starts to elaborate at this time is the idea that 'all architectural interventions are "conditioned", that is, they are inserted into a larger human project, to the point that every project is, in a sense, a work of restoration. One that isolates two elements, the existing and the newly made, which acquire meaning in relation to each other.'[2] It is no coincidence that, at this time BBPR was working on two seminal projects in the historic centre of Milan: the Torre Velasca (1950–58) and the restoration of the Castello Sforzesco (1947–56), which had been severely damaged during the war and was to be adapted to accommodate the city's art collection. Both new builds and restorations are confronted by the relationship between invention and contextualisation.

Rogers's editorial on *preesistenze ambientali* was accompanied by articles on the works of Louis Sullivan, a founding father of the modern movement, and Paul Rudolph, who was of the new generation. The issue also featured an essay by Sibyl Moholy-Nagy on native architecture in North America, while contemporary Italian architecture was represented by the Olivetti headquarters in Milan, designed by Annibale Fiocchi, Marcello Nizzoli, Gian Antonio Bernasconi and the Villa Bernabò Brea residential complex in Genoa by Luigi Carlo Daneri, Giulio Zappa e Luciano Grossi Bianchi.

The section in this issue dedicated to education featured the work of a discontented group of students from the Politecnico di Milano, ironically and provocatively nicknamed by De Carlo the '*giovani delle colonne*' [the young columns guys], among them Silvano Tintori, Guido Canella and Aldo Rossi. Protesting the adopting of a 'mannerist'

1 The growing influence of the '*giovani delle colonne*' on the editorial stance of *Casabella* sparked a number of controversies both within and outside the magazine.

2 See Ezio Bonfanti & Marco Porta, *Città, museo e architettura: il Gruppo BBPR nella cultura architettonica italiana 1932-1970* (Milan: Hoepli, 2013): 46; first edition, Florence: Vallecchi, 1973.

PREESISTENZE AMBIENTALI AND ISSUES OF CONTEMPORARY BUILDING PRACTICE

TRANSLATED AND REPRINTED IN JOAN OCKMAN, ED., *ARCHITECTURE CULTURE*, 1943–1968

CASABELLA CONTINUITÀ NO. 204, FEBRUARY–MARCH 1955

rationalist language by some teachers at the Politecnico, this informal group of students found the popular and civic expressions of neoclassical architecture far more 'progressive' and politically committed than the formalist abstraction of the modern movement, which, according to them, had lost sight of its original social and moral imperatives. In response, their research started to explore the work of architects who, between the eighteenth and the early twentieth centuries had reinvented the classical tradition to express the ideals of the emerging bourgeois class, allowing it to assert itself against the old aristocracy. This group saw in the work of figures such as Étienne-Louis Boullée, Alessandro Antonelli, Giovanni Antolini, Camillo Boito, Peter Behrens, Hannes Meyer and Adolf Loos a blueprint for an alternative to the rapidly advancing postwar capitalist city, a version capable of embodying socialist ideals. De Carlo, who criticised the *giovani delle colonne* for their retrograde attitude and for treating history as a reservoir of languages from which they could freely borrow, was in turn scorned by Rogers who wrote in the same issue (nº 204), 'There is freedom of opinion in the editorial office of *Casabella*. Personally, I don't entirely agree with De Carlo's point of view ... young people have the ability to choose between good and evil in and out of school, so one must hold them responsible for their nostalgic attitudes.' The episode marked the beginning of a rift that would soon bring change to *Casabella's* editorial team as well as to its lines of enquiry.

To move forward there are at least two steps contemporary architecture can take that are consistent with its own theoretical premises. One has to do with a more precise definition of its practical means, as part of a refinement of the techniques that are designed to translate its figurative language into physical reality. The other involves a more profound development of this language, with the aim of making it increasingly responsive to the cultural values into which the new forms have historically been inserted. In the article 'Pretesti per una critica non formalistica' (Pretexts for a non-formalistic criticism), in Casabella, no. 200, I have outlined several premises that in my view form a necessary basis for assessing a given work of architecture in a way that is not abstract or schematic, but rather takes into account the contextual (as well as historical) conditions in which it arises.

For example, I said that a critique could be accused of formalism if, in evaluating a posteriori the significance of a construction in Brazil, it fails to respond to the fact that the building exists in Brazil. Similarly, an architect could be accused of formalism if he does not absorb into his work, a priori, the specific givens and character of the context.

Straightaway a more general problem becomes apparent: since every work of architecture is, by definition, a work of art, and every work of art is, by definition, an original act, what limits must the artist observe if he is to ensure that his work does not - so to speak - go beyond the margins of the real but is organically inserted into the given spatial temporal situation? The battle between conservatives and innovators always revolves around the practical definition of this theoretical dilemma. And the confusion arises not only because of the particular inclinations of each side (to be more or less creative), but also because frequently neither one nor the other really understands the terms of the controversy.

Many who consider themselves innovators make the mistake - just like so-called conservatives - of starting with formal prejudices, believing that the new and the old are opposed, failing to realise that they represent the dialectical continuity of the historical process. Both limit themselves to the idolatry of certain styles frozen in fixed appearances and deprived of their true essence.

Claiming to build in a predetermined 'modern style' is just as absurd as enforcing a repetition of past styles.

Anyone who approaches a creative problem today has to relate their own thinking to an objective reality that, in each instance, presents itself for their subjective interpretation. For this reason, they will not design a construction in Milan that is the same as the one they would develop for Brazil. In fact, on every street in Milan they will attempt to construct a building that is appropriate for that specific location.

Precisely because the method of approaching the problems is the same, it follows that the solution will be different in each case. And it is not enough to examine the project solely in terms of its practical functioning; we are also required to identify, accurately and responsibly, the other givens that define its specific nature. A construction in Milan will be different depending on whether it is to be used for offices or for housing - which is only natural - but it will also vary according to whether it is on one terrain rather than another, near certain existing constructions rather than others. An artist's style is indelibly expressed in the way he brings together and characterises the various technical aspects of his creation, among them all the forces that are already at work in the field in which he operates.

The ambiente, the setting, is part of these pre-existing forces, and it would be misguided to ignore its influence.

The first architectural manifestations of the modern movement demonstrated a polemical concern with the invention of a figurative language that could be set against traditional styles. They were limited to isolating architectural phenomena and aimed at an objectivity of expression that would represent each artistic product within the autonomous limits of its own individual existence. Even Frank Lloyd Wright and Le Corbusier, though sensitive to the promptings of the 'natural environment' (the first trying to blend his works into it, according to a romantic taste; the second opposing it, in keeping with a classical conception), had for a long time neither the opportunity nor the desire to explore possible links with a 'cultural environment'.

Even their urban designs, in which they extended their zone of influence, were indifferent or even drastically opposed to existing historical reality.

Proceeding as we are in broad, schematic outlines, we can say that the problem of historical continuity (that is, of the conscious historicisation of modern phenomena with respect to those manifested in the past and nevertheless still present in our lives today) is a relatively recent addition to architectural thought: examples in the evolution of the two aforementioned masters, for example, are the [unrealised] Masieri house by Lloyd Wright in Venice, and the architectural complex in the Punjab by Le Corbusier. In both cases, specific attempts have been made in the artistic endeavour to adapt to the respective cultural traditions.
An appeal to national culture today – putting aside the machinations of reactionary nationalists or folklore-obsessed demagogues – presumes that architecture should be rooted in and nourished by the deepest strata of tradition. A complex, varied contemporary reality needs to be integrated with the immense patrimony of inherited experience.

If we admit, with appropriate humility, that we are nevertheless operating in the orbit of the methodological processes initiated by Gropius, it is easy to see that a vast evolution is possible by staying on the path already followed, still taking the original assumptions into consideration and even carrying those principles to their ultimate conclusion. The slogan of Gropius – 'in addition to, not instead of' – can be deployed empirically to widen the horizons of research and to embrace the resulting coerenza (coherence). The functional relationship between utility and beauty which forms the basis of our aesthetic values, while previously limited to almost tautologically expressing the world within the boundaries of a given architectural organism, may now radiate and expand, extending its influence to contexts where the cultural interaction becomes more intense, more sensitive, more dramatic – substantially more human. The notion of the maison de l'homme evolves beyond the abstract and indiscriminate scheme of the ideal man: it goes deeper – taking on a sense of the dramatic vicissitudes of human history, and wider – in recognising the distinct characteristics of modern society (and, therefore, also relating to the working classes) that are only now discovering the potential for flourishing. La maison de l'homme which was originally formulated as a generic house, for anyone, is now a house for each individual.

The insertion of these new contents inevitably has an effect on the appearance of the artefacts, because the forms spring from them in their physical representation.

Lamentably, certain weak artists have struggled to reconfigure the sensibilities they propose to express and have resorted to the language of the old discourses (of vernacular or refined architecture). But it is also the case that the best artists have tried to find original ways in which to communicate their poetic intentions.

It is as difficult to specify a detailed method for analysing the problems and prospective solutions as it is, conversely, to confine reasoning to bland generalisations: for this reason it is appropriate to outline briefy some questions regarding method in order to frame our initial query concerning the relationship between invention and ambientamento - considering something in relation to its setting.

One might object that every invention already implicitly contains its own particular interpretation of the ambiente (positive or negative), but it should be recognised that it is possible to identify different moments, different emphases in the creative process allowing us to pick out different attitudes based on a deepening awareness of the specific problem.

Considering ambiente means considering history. Since more profound exploration of the significance of history provokes one of the most characteristic arguments in present-day philosophical thought, architectural thought cannot fail to be influenced in its turn (however gradually). In considering the past and the present in terms of the inherent intentions that characterise them, we observe the increasing dominance of two notions that might at first glance seem contradictory yet are actually perfectly in tune.

The first is that the events of the past find their own rationale in the consistent texture of the original acts that have determined them; secondly, the present, in its turn, is an original creation. Rather than causing history to fall away, however, there is a unifying effect and a sense of continuity in which the past projects itself onto present events, and these events connect back, rooting themselves in what came before.

Being modern simply means sensing contemporary existence in the context of the whole of history, and thus to have a sense of responsibility for one's own actions, not limited to an egotistical manifestation, but as a collaboration in which our contribution adds to and enriches a perennial actuality of all possible formal combinations within a system of universal relations.

When constructing a building in an environment already characterised by the works of other artists, one must respect those artists by contributing one's own energy to sustain and perpetuate their vitality.

This can be achieved only through a creative act, but this act cannot be gratuitous. Unlike the early masters of the modern movement, who thought of themselves almost as Adam, free of original sin - didn't they even refuse to allow any antique furniture at all inside their buildings, so absorbed in the polemic were they? - we now know that we have to reconcile ourselves with multiple generations of forebears. Each step we take is like that of a mountain climber roped to the rest of his team. Whether we build in an urban or a natural landscape, we will attempt to interpret its particular character and practical imperatives; in both, our intuitive act will reach complete fulfilment only if it is a personal interpretation of objective givens. The copying of traditional forms will obviously be out of the question, but equally, the design of an architecture that only responds to our taste and contemporary techniques with abstraction will not adequately express these new sensibilities.

Forms must convincingly document the subtlest ethical aspirations, both of the collective and of the individual, perpetuating an age-old conversation.

And our language has to be capable of responding to the questions of the present time, directly and without reticence. To incorporate the necessities of life into culture and - reciprocally - to insert culture into everyday life: this is the task of the architect; to build a single reality through synthesising the two, while recognising that the observance of the objective givens plays an indispensable part in this.

The influence of objective givens in the process of architectural synthesis is vital as it forms a basis for analysing and elucidating phenomena that would otherwise merely be observed and re-stated, reduced to an almost naturalistic view, as if they were mere biological manifestations. This is the second important step to be taken.

Operating polemically, the early masters of the modern movement, insufficiently aware of the historical cultural influences inherent in their doctrine, often tended to use technique as a symbol rather than as a necessary means of clarifying (giving a physical form to) their expressive language. With the exception, perhaps, of Auguste Perret, who set himself the goal of solving the practical problems of correct construction, very few took the time to consider this fundamental quality; thus even when its poetic motifs have been based on a rationale, the resulting architecture has not been capable of resolving these premises in built form.

For many years we have nurtured a dislike of eaves and cornices in the belief that only a flat roof would suit our designs; the vertical window seemed likewise unsuited to expressing our intentions. All this, if it was justified within the terms of a bold updating of the figurative language of architecture - and the same justification could also extend to the idiosyncratic attitude towards antique furnishings - would lead the weakest among us into the trap of formalistic aestheticism.

Such historical pretexts, going back to the polemical birth of modern architecture, continue to have a bearing on the actions of contemporary architects - even the youngest find it hard to free themselves entirely of this legacy.

Reactions to the cultural and practical conditions of our forebears tend to be exaggerated and one-sided. Some, believing they can improve on what their predecessors achieved, turn to forms deriving from national, regional and vernacular traditions, without adaptation, and fall into slavish imitation or caricature; others, preoccupied by the technical shortcomings they identify, think like technocrats, under the misapprehension that they can resolve the dialectical synthesis of architecture simply by concentrating on one aspect of this vital drama.

Nevertheless, critics can justifiably look with interest at both camps, if history does not simply mirror exemplary and well-balanced achievements, but is also the chronicle of honest attempts. It should be understood that the two steps involved in moving forward that we have looked at separately in the interests of clarity, cannot be separated when it comes to judging the architectural phenomenon, which is only fully realised when it arrives at a synthesis.

To achieve such a synthesis - and in particular to evaluate the ambiente without compromising the practical solutions dictated by the novelty of the subject matter - is so difficult that it could be considered a miracle, something sublime and extremely rare. However, it is only once has been achieved that the resulting work merits the name of architecture, which is neither sculpture nor machine.

The rift between Rogers and Giancarlo De Carlo, which had begun with issue nº 204, eventually led to De Carlo's resignation as *Casabella's* editor-in-chief, and, from issue nº 214 (February–March 1957), he was replaced by Vittorio Gregotti. De Carlo had become increasingly uneasy with Rogers's editorial line. He resented Rogers's insistence on featuring the work of the precursors of the modern movement, in particular Louis Sullivan, Henry van de Velde, Auguste Perret, Peter Behrens and unorthodox works by Le Corbusier[1]. This widening of focus, passed on to Rogers's younger collaborators, had ignited the rediscovery of architectural culture at the turn of the nineteenth and twentieth centuries, promoted in particular by Gregotti, Aldo Rossi and Guido Canella.

After De Carlo's departure, this historical bent became even more apparent. Issue nº 215 (April–May 1957) sparked a heated debate. The issue featured Mario Ridolfi's most recent works, along with an extensive revisiting of the Tiburtino district of Rome, with texts by Lodovico Quaroni, Carlo Aymonino and Federico Gorio. Criticism and perplexity, however, were directed above all at the works of Gabetti & Isola, in particular the Bottega d'Erasmo and the Turin Stock Exchange, realised with Giorgio Raineri. The provocative effect of these works was reinforced by Rossi's essay on Stephan Tschudi Madsen and his writing on Art Nouveau, Guido Canella's text on the Amsterdam School and Pierre Dalloz's essay on the reconstruction of Le Havre under the direction of Perret.

Echoing objections raised by De Carlo, Rogers, in this rather ambiguous opening editorial to issue nº 215, distanced himself from Gabetti & Isola and Rainieri and warned against the free appropriation of vocabularies from history by, for instance, repeating the figurative language of Art Nouveau (which in Italy took the name 'Stile Liberty'). On the other hand, Rogers supported the report signed by some of the '*giovani delle colonne*', including Canella, Rossi and Silvano Tintori, together with Gae Aulenti and Gregotti, in which the young people proposed a new programme for *Casabella*, from which the centrality given to the historical problems emerged even more strongly.[2]

1 De Carlo criticised the decision to feature Le Corbusier's Chapel at Ronchamp, France, in issue nº 205 (September–October 1955), which provoked a lively discussion taking the form of epistolary exchanges between Rogers, Giulio Carlo Argan and De Carlo in subsequent issues of *Casabella*.

2 This is particularly true in the case of Aldo Rossi, as noted by Pier Vittorio Aureli in *The Project of Autonomy: Politics and Architecture Within and Against Capitalism* (New York: The Temple Hoyne Buell Center for the Study of American Architecture at Columbia University and Princeton Architectural Press, 2008): 56.

CONTINUITY OR CRISIS?

TRANSLATED AND REPRINTED IN *ITALIAN QUARTERLY* (LOS ANGELES: UNIVERSITY OF CALIFORNIA, 1959)

CASABELLA CONTINUITÀ NO. 215, APRIL-MAY 1957

Without setting out to make an assessment, I would like to address several questions that seem particularly timely in terms of the architecture of today because they provoke heated discussion among young professionals and students whose opinions should be carefully monitored as indicators of a more widespread mood in sensitive areas of culture. Can architecture develop the premises of the modern movement or is it changing its course?

Here is the problem: continuity or crisis?

Clearly doubt in itself is no proof of weakness, since it is actually the driving force of any intellectual or moral action. But we need to clearly define the horns of the dilemma; otherwise doubt deteriorates into confusion. The rethinking and updating of architecture in the present situation are rich in indubitably positive ferment that can lead to concrete outcomes.

But apart from the respect that is deserved by any honest opinion, and the psychological interest that can be stimulated by individual movements, I feel I should point to the danger of regression or dead ends for the architectural process when the individual unconsciously tends - due to personal limits - to generalise from his own bewilderment rather than formulating a critique with calm objectivity: is an impasse caused by these limits or is it truly the sign that the direction of thought taken thus far has terminally exhausted its historical trajectory?

Looking at history as a process, one could say that it is perpetually characterised by continuity or crisis, depending upon whether one wants to accentuate continuing or emerging factors; but for a more precise understanding of the discourse, it is best to clarify the philological interpretation of the terms I am using: the concept of continuity implies mutation within the order of a tradition. Crisis is the rupture - the revolution - that is, the moment of discontinuity caused by the influence of new factors (not encountered previously except as opposites of the factors that trigger, by contrast, the urgent need for substantial innovation).

To take stock of the present situation (and future possibilities) we have to delve into the motivations of the modern movement distinguishing between those that emerged as reactions to contingencies and are therefore of limited duration and those that may last longer because they relate to the essence of the movement.

Nor can the architectural phenomenon be considered in isolation, because it involves contributions and influences from all the other sectors of knowledge, which in turn have recently lived through their own dramatic developments: we have to identify our position while taking part in this multi-faceted movement, without demeaning its natural aspirations by limiting them (and ourselves) to the confines of academic schemes.

The polemical drive that prompted the first proponents of the modern movement to advance their actions in the spirit of a crusade in opposition to the environment in which they found themselves, along with their extravagant declarations and manifestos, no longer exists: but who can forget that the flat roof, for example, was deemed indispensable in any claim to modernity?

The justification for the tactical break that had to be made in the wake of that opposition is no longer valid, and therefore the terms for distinguishing between progressives and reactionaries have shifted; the struggle is no longer between traditionalists (slavish imitators of traditional styles) and avant-garde artists, who in any case are all concentrating on the drive towards innovation, because there are now good actors and bad actors in both camps: it is no longer enough to be generically modern – one has to articulate the meaning of that modernity.

For me this is obvious, and I have been repeating it for decades. But the great misunderstanding arises when people persist in considering the 'style' of the modern movement in terms of figurative manifestations rather than the expressions of a method that has attempted to establish new and clearer relationships between content and form in the phenomenology of an always open historical-pragmatic process, which, since it excludes any apriorism in the determining of those relationships, cannot be judged schematically.

Any deeper investigation or widening of the architectural experience that incorporates the foundations of the method referred to above has to be seen as the result of a normal evolution, whether or not the resulting forms resemble those of previous examples.

It can of course be objected that from nuance to nuance – as happens in the organic system – here too, though they both hail from the same seed, the tadpole becomes a frog and at a certain point its name changes as it has metamorphosed both intrinsically and extrinsically; the Gothic becomes the Renaissance which becomes the Baroque; the modern movement morphs into another movement; continuity runs its course, and there is a crisis. But has this crisis actually come to pass? Has architecture truly strayed from a given orbit?

After this introduction outlining the problem methodologically, the answer clearly depends on the evaluation one wishes to make of reality. In my view, there is no crisis, because if we consider the works of the most sensitive artists and pay attention to critiques made of them, the most valid and profound of these depend more or less consciously on the tenets of the modern movement itself and demand, if they are to be judged, the use of the criterion applied hitherto.

If, for example, you try to investigate the meaning of the works put forward by some of these more anxious young people and pressure them into admitting that their works are valid only if they accept that they have been driven by matters of taste (and not justified by any relationship to the objective given aspects of the brief), they rebel and try to prove to you that the forms they have come up with embody (on a more highly evolved level) those practical and moral values that were cited as the mainstays of the modern movement. They repudiate both the principle of art for art's sake and the idea of an intimistic architecture springing from an individual's internal monologue reflecting personal torments and consequent choices. And, if anything, they will speak of the pursuit of a more generally rooted language that draws its lifeblood from the deeper layers of tradition. Who can deny the urgent need for such research as well for a greater knowledge of cultural roots and habits?

But here we come up against the sympathy for the neoclassical, for the late nineteenth century and Liberty style, and values that are not easy to square with an escape from the intellectualism that these same authors have rejected in the modern movement; this is precisely because while it is still both possible and timely to recover certain of the elements left afloat in the historical process, one must intercept those aspects of them that are not fully developed, taking care not to resort to banal forms which are merely a revival of tastes gone by and are unsuited to the expression of the needs of contemporary society.

How is it possible to reconcile an approach based on taste without checking it against a declared intention to extend the architectural experience, and without quantifying the models?

In its early stages, the modern movement had to reject or even battle against the cultural movements of history, running the risk of confusing - in an equivocal nominalism - the essential values of the tradition with the figurative language through which those values gradually found expression.

Deeper investigation of historical knowledge has served to establish a more precise relationship between the contents and forms of artistic phenomenology, allowing us to place the products of art in the era when they first appeared, and, as a result, to define the coordinates of our actions in relation both to those moments and to our own time: respect for the past, authentic expressions of the past imply respect for pertinent expressions of the present. Any inferiority complex regarding the past has been overcome, because we no longer feel that we must work in opposition to it; rather, if anything, we are continuing with it, invigorated by it as part of the entirety of our culture.

In particular, certain artistic manifestations at the beginning of the [twentieth] century, which had provoked polemical responses from the pioneers of the modern movement, take on a new light with the benefit of a historical perspective, and their specific character can be considered without there being an obligation to contest them in order to assert the autonomy of our own work.

In this regard, the growing interest in Liberty style is indicative, on one hand in terms of its positive revival where there has been a complete assimilation of it, and on the other, where certain obvious literal and nostalgic references are concerned, which contribute nothing of substance to the issues confronting contemporary architectural discourse.

In the reassessment of Liberty style (as of any historical-artistic manifestation, in fact), there are several approaches, some of which validate and others which invalidate the operations of a modern architect: the former, which is a legitimate approach for historians who do not have direct responsibility for artistic creation, is to evaluate Liberty style in its cultural reality, for what it was, identifying relationships and elucidating them; the other is to repeat the style's figurative language or, in any case, to draw from it motifs for today's designs. The latter is an anti-historical approach, both because it does not attempt to understand the forms in the terms that gave rise to them in their time, and because it does not account for the fact that our epoch, addressing other themes, necessarily calls for different figurative motifs: this way of seeing is characteristic of those who rely on taste and probably fall back on formalism.

To be frank, it seems to me that the construction by the group from Turin published in this issue, while it is an attempt to make useful recuperations, falls foul of this misunderstanding.

Finally, there is the approach through which it is possible to recover reclaim certain values, such as refinement of materials, elegance, a lack of preconceptions, visual acuity, the most detailed, varied and rich analysis of language: possibilities, all of them, that have remained unexpressed in the necessarily more cautious artistic manifestations of the modern movement, but which are not at all in conflict with a more subtle elucidation of its intrinsic positions. Furthermore, it is clear that while the interest in Liberty style certainly does not prevent us from comparing its objects to ours, as is possible with any antique object, we cannot indulge in imitation without failing in our duties towards our contemporaries, who expect us to update our historical legacy in keeping with their practical and spiritual needs.

It is an illusion to believe that the growing need for images to embody communicable contents can be fulfilled by accepting the figures of the past, because through them the best we can do is satisfy our need for memories; what we cannot create in this way are symbols of our existence now.

Even if we were to accept the dismal hypothesis that it is impossible to invent new images, would we ever be able just to dust off, *sic et simpliciter*, those recently consigned to the attic? The modern movement – having, in some haste, confused technique and artistic expression and so believing that the architecture of today could be limited to the use of reinforced concrete and iron – has attempted to historicise the practical means beyond a modernistic technocracy, allowing us to draw on all possible means of construction. Now, however, we must take care not to reverse the process by identifying the technical methods used in the past (which remain valid) exclusively with the forms of the past, which are undoubtedly unsuited to representations we may wish to make. One further step needs to be taken, however, namely that while recognizing the fact that technique is a tool subject to the will of the artist, we must be aware that it also represents the cultural acquisitions of a society and that, as a result, it implicitly contains the possibility of a common vocabulary.

To be put into practice, the process of architecture demands that the activity reflect the energies of two equally essential poles; because it is certainly not predetermined forms or particular materials that characterise contemporary style, but the method deployed in order to achieve a formal solution with appropriate materials. However, should the result no longer be a synthesised expression of utility and beauty (which are ethically inseparable), were it, for example, to be derived from just one of those, we would be obliged to acknowledge that the principles of the modern movement were in crisis and to accept a new definition as a result. Nevertheless, if we are to speak of a crisis (in a constructive way) we need at the very least to demonstrate sufficient *coerenza*, consistency of thought, to point to new aims, unless what we mean by crisis is reaction (including, of course, to ethical and social matters), unless we believe that confusion is already, in itself, a sufficiently useful crisis to guarantee progress. This latter argument, however, would be decidedly discouraging for those who are seriously tormented by conscience.

The problems of *continuità*, of tradition, of the insertion of new works into *preesistenze ambientali* (pre-existing conditions), of finding the most expressive vocabulary and the quantification (including technical) of qualitative values are all correlated by means of a methodological sequence. They start from a concept of space-time that may be summed up by these sentences of [José] Ortega y Gasset (please note, use of this quotation does not necessarily imply acceptance of his doctrine in its entirety): '...the isolated individual is an abstraction. The life of an eminent individual consists precisely in a condensed characterisation arising from a mass of people. Heroes can therefore not be separated from the masses. This is an essential dualism in the historical process...'
To get back to the question, to talk about crisis it is necessary, therefore, to replace the sequence of terms deriving from the postulates of the modern movement with an equally coherent one, which as well as indicating an indeterminate taste can lead to the solution of issues of wider interest. If a crisis is coming, then come it must; in the meantime, let us be content with avoiding easy diversions and wasting energy, and try to make the best of the legacy we have inherited.

Only those who cannot see the range of the as-yet-unexplored horizons of the modern movement and the dramatic character intrinsic to the method we have deployed for the most thorough-going investigations can think that by speaking of continuity I am attempting to smooth over the tensions, pouring oil on troubled waters out of some misguided quietism.

In any case, what is urgent is to move beyond the confusion.

Issue nº 216 took the form of an epistolary exchange between Rogers and the Milanese architect Eugenio Gentili, a frequent contributor to *Casabella*. Condemning the content of issue nº 215, Gentili confronted Rogers, accusing him of a dangerous departure from the canons of the modern movement. Focusing his attack on the magazine's editorial line, Gentili expressed his dissatisfaction with the pages dedicated to Auguste Perret's reconstruction of Le Havre, the Amsterdam School, and the Tiburtino housing complex in Rome, but above all with the attention paid to the architecture of Gabetti & Isola, which he dismissed as a 'breed of monstrous fruit' for its 'excessive stylistic and decadent indulgence', predicting that *Casabella* nº 215 would mark the official birth of neoliberty.[1]

1 The term 'neoliberty' had been coined by Paolo Portoghesi in a famous article titled 'Dal neo-realismo al neoliberty', *Comunità* nº 65 (1958): 69–79.

ORTHODOXY OF HETERODOXY

CASABELLA CONTINUITÀ NO. 216, OCTOBER-DECEMBER 1957

Dear Eugenio,

I'd like to thank you for allowing me to publish your letter, because it opens up the possibility of a discussion that goes beyond the limits of a private dialogue.

The last issue of *Casabella* no. 215, triggered controversy, and you are not the only one to speak out, as many criticisms have reached me, similar to yours or on the opposing side. Don't imagine that I think having opponents on two sides implies that I occupy the correct middle ground: if anything, it obliges me to fight on two fronts, against those who accuse me of having conceded too much to tendencies considered heterodox, and against the others who refuse to recognise any historically established trends, and therefore insist on removing any constraints on the formulation of judgement. Were I to be simply satisfied by the controversy caused by a gesture, I might be pleased with issue no. 215 of *Casabella*, since after the issue on the Chapelle de Ronchamp [no. 205] few others have provoked so much discussion. But of course, that is not my aim. I am not looking for external effects - scandal - but for dialogue in which an initial word is followed by other, more constructive words, a stone placed to receive others, so that little by little an edifice is constructed.

If the stone we have attempted to place is damaged, it would be no consolation to me if friends or enemies alike gathered around it. Therefore I would like to show that in spite of its inevitable shortcomings, issue no. 215 of *Casabella* is in line with its predecessors - not only those under my direction, but the entire run of the magazine.

Therefore I would like to reiterate that a magazine is not a book, and certainly not holy scripture; it has to be judged as a whole sequence of issues, not by singling out one issue in isolation.

Allow me to respond to your letter by making some general observations, rather than picking over it point by point. A modern architecture journal - you say - is one that 'approaches the problems of our time with the means of our time'. All well and good. That even seems fairly obvious - we could perhaps say that it should act as a tool of *actualità,* actuality, or at least of actualisation. But the debate starts here.

Actualità is a matter of choices made between the phenomena of contemporary experience (posing the first challenge). Actualisation is bringing to contemporary awareness certain manifestations from the past selected by us (a challenge similar to the first) or encouraging the exploration of problems currently in their early stages, seeking their solution; here the capacity for choice has to be joined with that of prophecy, increasing the level of difficulty. As long as the coverage provided by the magazine is limited to the small number of contemporary masterpieces the risk is quite limited, though it does still depend on our judgement. But because, generally, the coverage focuses on imperfect works, the risk increases because the way in which it is judged may be based either on acceptance of the overall formulation of a work that has not been sufficiently elaborated- the better option - or on the consideration of some detail, regarded as exciting enough to be noted in the sphere of cultural sensibility.

These problems increase in complexity when, instead of considering each individual case on its own merits, we try to frame it in a historical system, with the light and shadows thus cast depending on the critical viewpoint from which one sets out to examine that case.

For me, the order of reference is the modern movement which - unlike you - I wouldn't know how to separate, unless by an effort of abstraction, from the context of the architectural reality that identifies it. But on the other hand, as I have said many times, any formal interpretation of this architecture is not valid, because formally accepting Gropius would mean rejecting Le Corbusier, and the language of Aalto would exclude that of Mies van der Rohe, and so on.

In my view, only a methodological evaluation of the phenomena is viable; this permits unitary discourse across a very wide horizon, which while it embraces the valid manifestations that have arisen thus far, also opens out into a coherent vision for future investigations. It follows that it is of course legitimate for us as artists to prefer a given sector according to our individual temperaments. But to ignore even one sector, as critics, means arbitrarily skewing the historical process. The job of a magazine is to take part in the dialectic between the inevitable subjectivity of adjudicating, while also objectively highlighting cultural ferment.

I deny that there is a crisis but I recognise, not least because I am involved in it, that we are in a period of critical re-evaluation of architectural problems, which consists above all in reclaiming many values set aside during the period when polemical reaction was at its height. At this time, the precursors, in order to add force to their reasoning, proceeded more or less consciously through simplification, which it was just as logical to apply to their theoretical formulations as it was to the physical design of forms. Many young people (and many of their elders) speak of crisis (and believe they are operating in an atmosphere of crisis) because, out of impatience, arrogance or simple lack of control, they do not attempt to bring their experience back into the sphere of the methodology that would give the works greater and more lasting meaning.

But our task - and this is not just in the context of *Casabella* - is to look with sympathy, attention or at least with generosity at the signs of this ferment, and I would even go so far as to say that we have to try to be even more tolerant when we feel that we cannot approve of certain impulses. After all, we are surrounded by danger, the followers of hearsay are legion, and structuralist formalism, plasticism and spatialism seem no less damaging than the eventual imitators of Liberty style or any other stylistic revival. What counts - while we must still insist on diversity - is agreement on a method that allows us to quantify qualitative values; otherwise we will lose ourselves in the fulmination that the neo-Liberty or pseudo-functionalist positions threaten to foist upon us.

Since we do not believe in dogma and cannot therefore provide any guarantee of a priori judgement within a critical paradigm, we must run the risk of our Gropius-like maieutic: freedom generates freedom, and the effort to understand the thinking of others prevents us from falling into quietism as long as we conserve the ability to distinguish between the weeds, parasites and poisonous toadstools that sprout in our neighbour's garden, and the seedlings - including the most fragile of them.

Why rip up everything in a single fistful? The earth would be so monotonous were we to sow it with only a single crop. Am I going to have to resort to paraphrasing Mao Tse-tung to remind you that 'all flowers have a right to blossom'?

While I was boasting to my student, L.S., about teaching people to think freely, I also complained about the use made of that freedom by many of his classmates, who take advantage of it as soon as they are able to argue against me, and he said: 'You have to completely accept the consequences of your pedagogy: after all, if you taught us to steal, even the best of us would attempt to steal the watch you carry in your pocket.'

I learned something from this very intelligent observation: to evaluate the relationships between me and those with whom I am discussing things with greater courage. I am not saying that I do not suffer when, after I've made an effort to clarify an opinion, it is challenged by the very people who are closest to me; but then I find the strength to regain my composure, to avoid being overwhelmed by the convictions of others while still not betraying my own, and to put myself dans la peau des autres, as though inside their mental (psychological as much as logical) processes. Of course, I demand of them not merely sufficient good faith, but also the ability to follow the trajectories of their thoughts and sentiments coherently to their conclusions.

The amplification of our inner world is even more necessary when we engage in discussions to evaluate the contradictory artistic manifestations we are witnessing. And the exercise is even more daunting when we must attempt to view the actual horizon while being immersed in the waves ourselves, since we know for certain that the actor and the viewer are dramatically united in the act of judgement.

This is the difficult task I take on as the editor of a magazine, while actively continuing to work as an architect.

Were I to confine *Casabella* simply to my own beliefs, it would mean limiting the field to my personal preferences (or even to my experiences as an artist) without leaving any gaps through which influences not congenial to me, or that I happen not to like, might slip: the magazine would thus be reduced almost to documenting self-criticism in order to avoid falling into the even greater tyrannical arrogance of unilateral opinions deprived of debate and the energy of opposition.

Nevertheless, a magazine - so as not to become agnostic or swayed by every breath of wind - demands that someone, namely its editor, take the helm, accepting responsibility for his decisions, and providing bearings for the reader. This is the task my editorials are meant to fulfil (if you will allow me to assume that someone reads them).

But should I, therefore, hold forth paternalistically on every page? Always front and centre with my yes and my no, my reservations? At times, I know that far too optimistically (or with exaggerated expectations) I rely on the goodwill and memory of readers, and I think that no-one who has known me thus far, as a critic and an artist, would wish to attribute to me thoughts that contradict those arising from my past actions; so they should know that I do not agree with the work of the young architects from Turin, which I admittedly thought I had criticised with sufficient severity in the last article, where I drew attention to its slightness (amounting as it did to little more than some anxious attempts at research). They should also know that although I recognise its historical meaning, my objections regarding the Tiburtino district are the same as those that I have expressed regarding La Martella (after all, the authors themselves have implicitly acknowledged those criticisms in the texts that accompany the illustrations). And that for the Amsterdam School, although the contents change, the rationale regarding Liberty style still, by inference, applies, and so on.

Casabella has sometimes been accused of not paying enough attention to marginal phenomena, thus avoiding controversial themes. (And I'd have something to say about the article on [Willem Marinus] Dudok in the current issue.)

But now you and others come along and cry 'Sacrilege!' because you reckon that too many pages in issue no. 215 have been devoted to historical studies featuring documents that are not sufficiently edifying. Yet these voices are those of the very young people about whom you seemed to care about so deeply.

It is very easy for me to defend their intelligence and concomitant critical commitment, although at times their immaturity does reveal itself. Nor should you regard it as paradoxical if I tell you that I am more inclined to include them, even though they present things with which I do not agree, than to close myself off in an orthodoxy, cloistered in the archives which might seem superficially more congenial to me but where I know I would end up gathering dust. As for [Auguste] Perret, I feel obliged to refer to the booklet I wrote about him, in which I believe I established the ambit of my critical perspectives from the start: 'Perret is a typical protagonist of the contemporary cultural drama, in which the intentions and the works of a single author can clash in the dialectical process of his existence, to the point that we are left perplexed and dissatisfied...'

And, to the stupendous interior of the church, this great work of his old age that, itself, would fully justify the publication of Perret's Le Havre, we have to add the entire urban project, which, though it does not achieve complete poetic expression – beyond being an exercise in a rigorous method of construction – still remains one of the few examples of coerenza, coherence of thought, amidst the chaos of European reconstruction.[2]

Although there may be disagreement between us, this does not lead to serious moral questioning.

What also, in my opinion, counts in the case of Perret or [Mario] Ridolfi or any other outstanding personality are the less successful works – as in Ridolfi's Via Marco Polo [Rome]. I admit that I should been more explicit in my disapproval regarding this work, and, once again, I have understood that it is not enough to think that an opinion can be taken for granted, and that we are clear only when we are explicit.

2 During World War II, the city centre of Le Havre was completely devastated by bombing. The reconstruction project – which included the church of Saint Joseph, referred to here by Rogers – was entrusted to the architectural office of Auguste Perret, giving him the opportunity to re-imagine the city with an almost blank slate and to apply the principles of modular construction and prefabrication. His reconstruction of the city is now a World Heritage Site noted for its exceptional urban planning and architecture.

Dear Eugenio, when I asked you - as I ask everyone I admire - to express your longstanding and ever-enthusiastic affection for *Casabella* by making a concrete contribution in writing, you asked me to provide you with some guarantees regarding the orientation of the magazine. Well, I cannot guarantee that we will never make mistakes, but you can rest assured that the magazine will always be an active forum for freedom, as demonstrated by the full publication of this letter of yours, which was certainly not one expressing agreement.

Not only in my name, but also in that of *Casabella*, I return the favour of your expressions of friendship in the hope that you will soon respond to our cordial invitation.

The exchange between Eugenio Gentili Tedeschi and Rogers (*Casabella* nº 216) was just one episode in a wave of growing dissatisfaction concerning the content of the magazine. Within a few years, the local storm over *Casabella*'s support for unorthodox views on modern architecture had spread beyond the confines of Italian print culture. Following an animated debate between *Casabella* (nº 217, 1957 and nº 220, 1958) and *L'Architecture d'aujourd'hui* (nº 73 and nº 77, 1958), in 1959, the British critic Reyner Banham, writing in *The Architectural Review* (nº 747 of April 1959), added fuel to the controversy when he pejoratively labelled as 'neoliberty' a wide range of expressive experimentation in postwar Italian architecture (lumping together the works of BBPR, Gae Aulenti, Vittorio Gregotti, Lodovico Meneghetti, Giotto Stoppino, Roberto Gabetti and Aldo Rossi), all of which he saw as evidence of architectural revivalism and, as such, of an 'infantile regression' from the modern project. For Banham, Rogers, 'the hero figure of European architecture in the late 1940s and early 1950s', had played a major role in the formation of these attitudes, both as editor of *Casabella* and as a member of BBPR, and he had recently completed the Torre Velasca and the restoration of the Castello Sforzesco in Milan.

In *Editoriali dell'architettura*, where Rogers's uncharacteristically harsh response to Banham is reprinted, the text is prefaced by the following note: 'The esteem in which I hold Mr Banham did not prevent me from attacking him on his own ground, because he had imprudently deduced extreme consequences from unfounded premises.' And indeed, Banham's diatribe, although calling Rogers directly to account, was not so much in response to something written by him, but rather a critique of some of the works he had published and of a particular article by Rossi called 'Il passato e il presente nella nuova architettura' (Past and Present in the New Architecture) in *Casabella Continuità* nº 219, May 1958, which was footnoted and cited throughout the text, and which, in Rogers's view, was grossly misrepresented by Banham as an exhortation to turn back to the turn-of-the-century bourgeois building tradition while abandoning the achievements of the modern movement.

THE EVOLUTION OF ARCHITECTURE: REPLY TO THE KEEPER OF THE FRIGIDAIRES

CASABELLA CONTINUITÀ NO. 228, JUNE 1959

REPRINTED IN *EDITORIALI DELL'ARCHITETTURA* (TURIN: EINAUDI, 1968)

TRANSLATED AND REPRINTED IN JOAN OCKMAN, ED., *ARCHITECTURE CULTURE 1943–1968* (NEW YORK: RIZZOLI, 1993)

There are some sensations you can't seem to shake off, like certain smells that are connected, as Proust says, with certain thoughts. Reading Mr Banham's article in *The Architectural Review* I am unable to ward off the image of the amusing but decadent Victorian-style 'pub' reconstructed in the basement of that magazine's offices, with its display cases of 'stuffed fishes' and other customary trifles. Here we have a way of recovering history through the artefacts of a particular society, of absorbing the flavour of that society through a meticulous indulgence in even its most obscure, dusty and even objectionable representations.

It is likely that this 'pub' simply indicates the flipside of a cultural position to which the magazine has committed itself with matchless intelligence and rigour, but it is clear that, as with all fiercely fought campaigns, some critical values are bound to be compromised before its aims are completely defined.

It would be uncharitable to suggest that the whole action should be condemned on account of these or other possible errors, or to say that the editors seem to have entirely overlooked much more important challenges in the formation of a contemporary architectural consciousness.

The Architectural Review and *Casabella* are, from a cultural viewpoint, the most engaged magazines in the world, the most audacious and, as a result, the most exposed to criticism. Whether or not one agrees with some of the stands they take, no one can deny that they have made a valid contribution - through their critical discoveries, in-depth research and proposals - to a key issue in today's architectural discourse, namely, how to break up the schemas of modernist formalism.

I wish that those who talked about us and about Italian architecture would use a language that was equally respectful, not playing fast and loose with the facts or being satisfied with improvised and, in any case, superficial and hasty pronouncements. It is disappointing, then, that a magazine that we respect to the extent of having even published an essay about it (Matilde Baffa, 'L'architettura al vaglio di una rivista inglese', *Casabella* no. 220), has seen fit to publish an editorial such as Mr Banham's 'Neoliberty: The Italian Retreat from Modern Architecture'.

An editorial cannot be judged in the same way as other articles, since it customarily expresses the views of those in charge, giving an official stamp to the convictions of the publication.

Evidently Mr Banham, forgetting the context in which he is operating, thinks he can accuse those who have considered 'the remaining monuments of Art Nouveau in a degree of detail that bespeaks more than historical interest. Works of [Antoni] Gaudí, [Louis] Sullivan, [Raimondo] D'Aronco, [Victor] Horta and the Vienna School, in particular, have been described and illustrated even to the extent of original drawings and colour-blocks of their exteriors, supported by texts that were far less expository or explanatory, than they were eulogistic or rhetorical.' If the articles are rhetorical, we are at fault, as we would be if, for example, we had written what appeared in Bruno Zevi's editorial for *L'Architettura* no. 37 (November 1958):

Rationalism, as a proposition, set alight by the prodigious metamorphosis of [Le Corbusier's] Ronchamp, here commits subtle, virtuous, extenuated suicide; at the age of 72, Mies van der Rohe has ended the game. One needs to start here when judging the various problems of contemporary language relating to architecture: the leaning towards the Liberty style, the formalism of the Milanese school, the complicated research of [Carlo] Scarpa, the brutalism of [Marcello] D'Olivo, the clever empiricism of [Ignazio] Gardella in Venice. Cues, attempts and experiments, all open to discussion but vital, real, indicative of the possibility of a new beginning for modern architecture. Having paid due respect to Mies in the gleaming mausoleum of rationalism, we go out drinking with these friends who are less perfect and respectable, at times hedonists and troublemakers, but who at least have the courage to continue a tradition that until yesterday was that of Mies, the tradition of anti-conformity.

For us, by contrast, the modern movement is not dead at all: our modernity lies in moving forward in the tradition of the masters (including Wright, of course). But, to our credit, we have been sensitive to the beauty (and not just as a record) of certain works that up to now have not been sufficiently appreciated. And it is also to our credit that we have offered a historical framework and contemporary meaning for certain values that were left in limbo while other battles were waged.

Mr Banham imagines that he has found (probably in the dusty drawers of those Victorian cabinets) the magic key with which to open the sluice gates of history and direct its course towards his own personal nursery of lampreys, ready to suck your blood.

It seems that for him it is easier to justify using an old Ford, rather than a horse, because the Ford arrived after the industrial revolution, while the horse obviously came before it. Such an inference can be made based on the conventional stance of the article as a whole, where he states that, in the matter of imitation, those architects who look back to De Stijl are more acceptable than those inspired by the Liberty style, because that 'at least revives forms created since the watershed' between our era and the past. In other words, it is better to steal five lire than ten. I have repeated many times that 'formalism is any use of unassimilated forms: ancient, contemporary, erudite or spontaneous' (*Casabella* no. 202). On the other hand, it is useful for an artist to make a critical, considered review of historical tradition, provided he does not accept precedents in a mechanical manner. For Mr Banham, however, the determinism of forms according to an abstract line of development seems to override a concept of history.

Hence his habit of handing out absolutions and excommunications that can only mummify reality.

No less objectionable is his system of raising some poor person so high as to make him stumble, only then to cast him down so low as to render him unrecognisable.

And while I am willing to take on board any criticism, in line with the principle of freedom of expression, I am not at all inclined to put up with accusations that are contradictory in how they evaluate - or even how they report - the facts; a much more precise level of information and more accurate citation would be required. Personally, I am not flattered to be designated the 'hero-figure of European architecture in the late 'forties and early 'fifties' if I am then also considered to be one of those responsible (along with

Belgiojoso and Peresutti) for having curated the Italian section of the 1958 Furniture Exhibition in London (with works by Albini and other excellent colleagues) which 'seemed to be little more than a hymn of praise to the Milanese *borghese* taste at its queasiest and most cowardly'.

I am responding because the article - despite its weaknesses, and certainly because of the authority of the magazine that published it - has caused something of an uproar here, because of the rather presumptuous tone in which Italian affairs were addressed. I am responding because I am the villain of the piece, and my two associates are named along with me; and because it is necessary to disentangle the discussion from a prejudice attached to a name, that of neoliberty, which, in keeping with the extemporaneous classifications typical of Banham, is used to lump together architects of various ages, responsibilities and *tendenza*; and, finally, because - if we were to accept an extension of the name - we would have to include in it all those who attempt to escape from conformism and formalism. The silence regarding a Gardella, a Ridolfi, a Michelucci, an Albini, a Samonà, say, sows further confusion in the already great confusion characterising Banham's pronouncements. I am responding because I do not want to be accused of occupying positions we have not taken. Finally, I am responding because by refuting the statements of others, I hope to make it clear that I do not indulge in the attitude of *'tout va très bien Madame la Marquise'*[1]; on the contrary I am no less concerned than Mr Banham about a certain dangerous trend in Italian architecture, which it is my responsibility to analyse as an artist, critic and teacher.

Mr Banham claims he is disappointed because, in the aftermath of the war, he had placed such great hopes in us (us Milanese, above all), even creating a myth by which to position us.

But who is it that embodies these 'illusions'? Two Roman architects, it seems: [Luigi] Moretti and [Luigi] Vagnetti. Especially the former. Mr Banham then correctly anticipates that we will reject his

1 The chorus of a popular 1936 song by Ray Ventura – 'Everything is fine Madame la Marquise' – which became a proverbial catchphrase to express an attitude of blindness in the face of a difficult situation coupled with a clumsy attempt to gloss over reality.

interpretation. In fact, it is clear that this adroit but capricious formalism not only fails to reflect the ends we were supposed to reach, but also denies the theoretical and above all moral premises of our struggle, which rejects aestheticism and intellectual games.

As for the works of the young architects, of Aulenti, the Novara group of Gregotti, Meneghetti and Stoppino, as well as Gabetti and [Aimaro] Isola, it is not true that *Casabella* has published them 'with evident editorial approval'; while it is obvious that nothing appears in this magazine without my approval, I have been open in my critique of these works, limiting myself to seeing them as a manifestation of a *tendenza*, as meaningful examples of work by certain young people intelligent enough to react to modernist formalism.

If we then want to accuse them of letting themselves be guided, after an initially correct impulse, by a negative polemic over and above an equally necessary action of positive reinterpretation, this would correspond precisely to the thinking I expressed in *Casabella* no. 215 ('Continuity or Crisis?').

But that is not what Mr Banham is asserting, as can be seen from an imprecise and unfaithful summary of the article by Aldo Rossi, 'Il passato e il presente nella nuova architettura' [The Past and the Present in the New Architecture], in which Rossi criticises his own friends on precisely those points, with clarity and honesty, while Banham makes him look like a kind of demagogue of the bourgeois spirit.

After all, in the very same issue of *Casabella* (no. 219), Aldo Rossi, in a critique of the book by Hans Sedlmayr opposing modern art - 'Una critica che respingiamo' [Criticism that we repudiate] - and voicing a position widely shared among young people in Italy, emphasises the difference between reactionary and progressive critiques of the modern movement: 'The rejection of the values of the modern world necessarily implies a new barbarism, since *in any case* today it is not possible to ignore how much the modern world has characterised the Europe of recent years... In essence, the motive of decisive dissent is still this: that this type of criticism does not point to a prospect of development,

Gabetti & Isola's Bottega d'Erasmo, Turin, Italy, 1956–1957, detail of the facade © Archivio Gabetti & Isola an alternative within modern culture, but presents itself as a negation of modern culture.'[2]

Every alternative or development we have supported has always been *within modern culture*, and this is why our task is laborious and difficult. Why hasn't Banham, that self-styled expert on things Italian, tried to read better and more rather than insisting on his all-too-hackneyed definitions of the 'Milanese' and the 'Turinese'?

Nor are Gabetti and Isola and the others in the same category, because while the definition of neoliberty might apply to the 'Bottega d'Erasmo' (and to other works by other young architects that crop up here and there in Italy), it can be applied only in a uselessly distorted way to the various groups that look back not so much to Liberty style as to Dutch expressionism (in the case of Aulenti) or the eclecticism of Boito and [Hendrik Petrus] Berlage (for Gregotti and his associates). As for the works of the Cooperativa architetti e ingegneri of Reggio Emilia, they are not neoliberty at all and could almost be taken as examples of what Banham calls 'current architecture'.

Nor are [Luigi] Figini and [Gino] Pollini neoliberty; this is obvious, even when they indulge in naturalistic thinking. Were it not so polemical in its tone, I might find the alarm sounded by Banham useful, to some extent, but the small amount of validity, on which we might easily agree, that can be gleaned from his observations winds up being tainted by the twists and turns of his discourse, so much so that the general accusation levelled at the most recent manifestations goes beyond the modern movement, and beyond Italy, revealing an impervious incomprehension of so many fundamental events such as to call into play the wider possibility of development of international history as a whole. If we are to heed Banham, in modern Italian architecture, it was 'the backstage influence of [Filippo] Marinetti (whom [Alberto] Sartoris once acknowledged in print as a patron of the movement) … [that] was most likely to be felt'.

But what does it matter to us if Sartoris says this? One whose gaze

2 Hans Sedlmayr, *Art in Crisis: The Lost Center*, trans. Brian Battershaw (Chicago: Henry Regnery, 1958); originally published as Hans Sedlmayr, *Verlust der Mitte: Die bildende Kunst des 19. und 20. Jahrhunderts als Symptom und Symbol der Zeit* (Salzburg: Müller, 1948).

is not so keen misrepresents everything he sees: 'the "modern" was practised as a style since it could not be practised as a total discipline – as the literally hollow formalism of [Giuseppe] Terragni's Casa del Fascio at Como brilliantly demonstrates.' Doesn't Banham recognise the relationship between form and content? Has he no knowledge of Terragni's struggles to give an (unfortunately misconceived) content and moral form to his work? And why did [Giuseppe] Pagano, [Gianluigi] Banfi and [Giorgio] Labò have to die, if not because, as artists, they could not help but be opposed to the rules of the dictatorship?

Banham should have recognised, with greater subtlety, what has been repeatedly observed by writers in our country, namely the continuous dramatic struggle of culture in general against the contingencies of Italian society (before, during and after fascism); from this he would have to infer the difficulty of identifying art with life: the dialectical relationship, the relentless duel of love, the conquests, the misunderstandings, the rebuffs, the redemptions. Then he could have intuited one of the most interesting aspects of our history: precisely that Italian architecture – in its authentic examples – is a moral act and, at least implicitly, an instrument of political struggle, alternating between success and failure, like the entire political history of Italian progressive tendencies, though certainly not to be scorned or condemned for this.

After the war of liberation and the extraordinary period of partisan struggle, it seemed that the world, Europe, Italy could rise again to a definitively better life, and we nurtured hopes, imagining that they represented reality when we should have realised they were new utopias. Since then, all of Italian society – that which is progressive and aware – breathlessly struggles to avoid being stranded by officialdom. And the fact that there exists an architecture at times more laden with sentiment than with reason is due not to a retreat on the part of architects – quite the reverse! It is a struggle against the tide. One has only to observe what happens in municipal offices, in the offices of the ministries, and to watch how the small band of those who believe in art have to grit their teeth as they try to blast a path through the barricades.

It is no coincidence that Ridolfi, Gardella, Bbpr, Albini, Samonà,

Michelucci and [Luigi] Piccinato, who are among the most strenuous defenders of modernity, no longer do what they once did, and it is for precisely this reason that they are consistent; has Banham ever wondered about this? It is impossible to imagine that these people, and many others, have all suddenly become irresponsible to the point of renouncing the victories that have been won with such effort.

Their strength has been their understanding of the modern movement as a 'continuous revolution', meaning continuous development of the principle of adherence to the changing contents of life.

The thematic gradually became richer, and as a consequence its exigencies more subtle. Formal issues, therefore, became more difficult as they attempted to encompass an ever greater number of propositions: the widening of the architectural problematic and the immediate effects of critical thought; the historicist revision of all historical periods, and especially those closest in time, which had been distorted through the normal opposition caused by the dialectical traffic between generations.

A better understanding of Liberty style also emerged (and why not?); here there were still energies to collect and to channel. The fact that Liberty style should be considered not only in terms of its historical definition as a precursor of modernity, but also in terms of its values, corresponds, after all, to a very necessary awareness that, as a student, I touched on in a paper written for my degree.

What is so frightening about it?

There can be no doubt that we need to look back on the experiences of the past (all of them), without getting trapped by them, of course, as unfortunately happens to some – and I am the first to recognise that.

This complex process of revision, though slow and elaborate, has been misunderstood by those unprepared for it, for whom it has come as a shock; though we have to acknowledge, in any case, that it may have made even the finest minds overlook some cultural components (like that of technology) that have received greater attention at other times. But progress is the result of choices and suspending judgement, which at any moment may err through being incomplete; in addition, progress is achieved at the cost of mistakes, but I am convinced that some of the risks taken by Italian architecture give rise to a greater awareness, despite the arrogant goading of Mr Banham who acts as the 'keeper of the Frigidaires' and believes, furthermore, that 'the revolution in the home began with electric cookers, vacuum cleaners, the telephone, the gramophone and all the other mechanised aids to gracious living that are still invading the home, and have permanently altered the nature of domestic life and the meaning of domestic architecture'. While we're at it, I would also add the blender, which could be used to make a nice cocktail from the other revolutions which, in his view, have their 'milestones' in the 'Manifesto of Futurism, the European discovery of Frank Lloyd Wright, Adolf Loos's Ornament and Crime, Hermann Muthesius's lecture to the Werkbund Congress 1911, the achievement of wholly cubist painting, and so forth'. But it could still do with a touch more salt.

I am convinced that the whole experience has been useful. So useful that Italian architectural criticism and production have, in spite of everything, taken steps forward that have yet to be attempted in many other countries.

These will certainly lead others, perhaps in a different direction, according to particular cultural and economic conditions, but I do not believe that our experience, that of a proven historical awareness, of the necessary usefulness of culture in the order of space and time – of the relationship between new works and the preesistenze ambientali, pre-existing conditions – is of little value or can be written off in such a superficial way.

Be that as it may, let's not presume to be the only ones moving ahead. Much more luminous examples have been provided by the masters: Le Corbusier has created Chandigarh which echoes to the sound of all India, Gropius the embassy in Athens, immersed in Greek history, Mies a 'monument' with the skyscraper on Park Avenue in New York; and Wright, towards the end of his life, designed works that, while highly consistent in spirit, do not keep to the letter of declarations he had previously made.

No one has stood still. For the masters themselves we might paradoxically apply Nietzsche's aphorism: 'One repays a teacher badly if one remains nothing but a pupil.'

This is true in our context, and all the more so for those of us who do not like to get bogged down in slavish dogmatism.

If everything that departs from academic modernism or does not, out of ill-advised escapism, resort to the bravado of formalism is neoliberty, then we would find ourselves in large and good company. But if neoliberty is a tendenza, a tendency, to replicate Liberty style itself, then what we are talking about would frame the small painting whose figures are represented, in Italy, by a few young architects who are – I hope – sufficiently aware to avoid believing that they amount to the sum of all Italian architecture. And we can also hope that they will soon become aware of some of the useless equivocation to which they have fallen victim.

To conclude, I would like to invite Mr Banham, who I believe is more familiar with English than he is with Italian, to ignore the lame interpretation of Marinetti, a fascist 'revolutionary' who died wearing a felucca on his head,[3] and instead to read *The Poetry of Architecture* by John Ruskin, who was a great Englishman: 'We shall consider the architecture of nations as it is influenced by their feelings and manners, as it is connected with the scenery in which it is found, and with the skies under which it was erected.'

There he will find some starting points for the evolution of architecture.

3 The *felucca* was the two-pronged hat worn by the intellectuals of the Reale Accademia d'Italia (Royal Academy of Italy), the cultural institution that brought together the great and the good of the Italian intelligentsia during fascism. Founded by royal decree in 1926 and active from 1929, the Italian Academy was supported by Giovanni Gentile (the so-called 'philosopher of fascism'); its task was to promote and coordinate the Italian intellectual movement in the fields of science, literature and the arts. Its members – all Italians, all men, not a single Jew – were chosen by Mussolini himself, and its president was a member of the Fascist Grand Council. The members of the Academy received a large salary, wore a gala outfit with gold and silver embroidery and the *felucca* and enjoyed the title of 'Excellency'. Among them was Filippo Thomaso Marinetti, who acted as literary secretary, together with figures such as Marcello Piacentini, Guglielmo Marconi, Giuseppe D'Annunzio, Luigi Pirandello and Adolfo Wildt.

Under new leadership, and with a new name – Group for the Research of Social and Visual Inter-relationships – CIAM held its final conference in September 1959 in Otterlo, at the Kröller-Müller Museum. Team 10 – a newly formed group of discontented younger members – had set the agenda and dominated the proceedings. Unlike previous iterations of the CIAM, this meeting was planned as a working congress. The letter of invitation asked each participant to come with a project that best expressed their understanding of the role of the architect urbanist and their thoughts on how the architect might harmonise the relationships between people and their environment. Each presentation was to be followed by a critical discussion and evaluation. The aim of the congress, as stated in the letter of invitation, was 'to establish whether there is a real affinity of thought between the participants, not only in the spoken word, but more profoundly at the level of plastic invention through the communication of direct building ideas', and thus to assess the future viability of the organisation.

The atmosphere was heated during each of the presentations, but particularly during Rogers's account of BBPR's Torre Velasca, which was attacked by Team 10 members Jaap Bakema, Alison and Peter Smithson, who saw it as a dangerous model for imitation. The previous debate, devoted to the discussion of the London Road Study designed by the Smithsons, had already seen the British cross swords with Rogers. The Smithsons accused him of historicism, Rogers criticised them for their indifference to place. 'You access streets only as directions [paths] ...', Rogers commented, 'If you destroy the context of Soho, why bother conserving the directions [...] I really don't know what will remain of the character of London in the future.'

What follows is the transcript of Rogers's presentation and his response to the criticism of Team 10 as reported in *CIAM '59 in Otterlo*, the publication compiled by Oscar Newman at the behest of Bakema. This publication was considered by some who attended the meeting to be an inaccurate account of the event, including Alison Smithson, who complained that her comment describing the Torre Velasca as having been 'dropped like a pudding over Milan' had been edited out of the proceedings.[1]

1 Alison Smithson, 'L'incidente di Otterlo', in *Quaderni del Dipartimento di Progettazione dell'Architettura del Politecnico di Milano 15. Ernesto Nathan Rogers: testimonianze e studi* (Milan: Città Studi, 1993): 37–38.

PRESENTATION OF THE TORRE VELASCA AT CIAM '59

CIAM '59 IN OTTERLO: GROUP FOR THE RESEARCH OF SOCIAL AND VISUAL INTER-RELATIONSHIPS (LONDON: ALEC TIRANTI, 1961)

The building bylaws in Milan do not allow any building to be higher than the [Madonnina], which tops the Duomo at about 106 metres high. Our building is approximately 100 metres high and within that height limitation.

The general shape of the building is the result of a very rational design approach. We were required to design a building which was to be occupied partially by offices and partially by dwellings. Our studies of the space distribution requirements for the offices and dwellings led us to conclude that more space was obviously required by the dwellings per floor than by the offices. We therefore increased the floor area of the apartments and expressed this in the façade. We put the apartments above the offices so that they might have better access to the sky, the cleaner air and in particular the splendid view. Putting the offices below was a logical consequence.

In describing this building, I am mixing the rational and the expressionistic, because they must really be mentioned together. There were people who criticised this building, saying that it was an imitation of the towers of the Middle Ages. I don't mind if it is, but I must say, it is only a casual coincidence resulting from needs which are, for different reasons, similar to those of the Middle Ages. During the Middle Ages it became necessary to conquer the sky because the space within the fortified walls of the city was limited; as a consequence, any new expansion, once all ground was accounted for, had to be upwards. With the increasing population the mediaeval city found it necessary to widen its streets. In order to maintain a suitably large living area, the upper floors of dwellings were cantilevered over the streets below. It can be seen then that it is only by coincidence that our building is similar to a mediaeval tower; a similarity which arose from the same needs, but to fulfil different purposes.

The floors of our building are distributed as follows: there are two floors underground devoted to a garage for 400 cars; the first eighteen floors above the ground are for offices (four of these eighteen being provided with shower facilities, kitchenettes and other amenities); the eighteenth floor is a service-floor containing the machinery for the pumps and other things the people in the

Rogers (left) with Jacob Bakema at CIAM 11 in Otterlo, Netherlands, 1949 © Bakema, J.B. Archief / Het Nieuwe Instituut

building require; the next eight floors are devoted to apartments, the last two of which are penthouses with roof garden facilities. In the design of any building there are three things to be considered: how the building meets the ground, how it meets the sky and the variation of the body (how it goes around the corner). In our building the contact with the ground is smoothly indicated by the structure. Its contact with the sky is satisfactorily concluded - it is not an infinite building; it is a building with a definition - the roof is its natural conclusion - a kind of hat on the building. To give continuity to the volume, the corners are cut, so that the movement is smooth and continuous. The diagonal corner itself forms a window which gives continuity to the inside volume as well.

The structure of the building is concrete, although our original conception of it was in steel. The building was studied for many years and underwent many changes, but our general conception of the space distribution remained the same. The construction system and, consequently, the rhythm of the system, was changed because the structure in steel in Italy would have been too expensive: 30 per cent more expensive.

The panels between the columns are prefabricated elements. They are within the limits of our economy and our building technology in Italy. We have used windows of more or less standard production and the panels, to which we devoted special study, are of reconstructed stone (*Kunststein*). The panels form a certain rhythm of a simple composition. In between the panels of precast stone are prefabricated concrete clips which are used in fixing the panels in place. The construction, though the result of a rather complicated study, is a very simple one. During our study of the different floor plans, we concluded that it was impossible to know who the occupants would be. We decided to devise a flexible system which would allow the interchanging of the voids and the panels in the facade. The structure is in concrete but is not a cantilever system; it is continuous from the foundation to the roof. The structure needs containment where we have the extension on the 18th floor, so we have provided those tensors you see there, which run right through the building. I think that is about all I can say technically. There are of course many other things I could mention but I think it is important to speak technically, because technique requires precise decisions. And not only theoretical ones, whereas aesthetics can be either communicative or not.

We have used two main colours in the building. These harmonise with the two principal colours to be found in the buildings of Milan: the colour of the bricks which were used in the buildings of the Middle Ages and the colour of the stone used during the neoclassical period. Another reason for our using the pink stone is that it harmonises with the pink 'Andova' marble which was used in the construction of the Duomo. Of course, this is only a kind of a sympathetic reaction: no more than a kind of 're-paint *d'automne*', as the painter said. It is not a result of a sentimental approach. It is a technical approach to vision. The technical expression is accented by our indicating the structure in a quite different colour. We hate those things you see all over Italy: the bright, contrasting colours. Therefore, we tried to do something else, and made it very simple. We nevertheless feared we might be misunderstood. The structure is expressed as it is because we think that the articulation of the structure is one of the good qualities of modern architecture.

The main entrance is in the form of a pavilion set in front of the main building, with facilities for offices above. There are two reasons for our having done this: firstly, it was necessary to provide a space for offices of a big surface area and this allowed us to give them a corresponding increase in height, and secondly, it served to create an intermediate dimensional relationship between a person entering the building and the main tower - it gives a human scale to the building.

In conclusion I would like to say that when I speak about the past and tradition, and when I speak about the building's life being connected with the past, it is not intended that this be an imitation of the forms of the past. If this building by chance of circumstances has taken the shape that reminds you of the past, that is not the main point of the problem, and I do not care about the form it has taken. Our main purpose was to give this building the intimate value of our culture - the essence of history -, we were never given to imitating the shapes and forms of the past, only understanding what has happened before us. This building is a skyscraper in the very centre of Milan, 500 metres from the Cathedral. It is at Milan's very historical centre, and we found it necessary that our building breathe the atmosphere of the place and even intensify it.

The attitude of the fathers of modern architecture was anti-historical. But this was an attitude which was born of a great revolution, and it was necessary that the first premise of our culture be a new attitude to history. But this is now no longer necessary

Peter Smithson responded by accusing Rogers of having created a 'bad model' which 'contains the possibility of other people doing similar things in a worse way'. Unlike masters such as Le Corbusier and Mies van der Rohe, whose written and design work provide 'an answer to the problem as it is and have the generalising aspect of all problems of such a nature in such a time', Smithson sees 'a certain element of irresponsibility in this building [...] because there are things that can be so easily distorted and become not only ethically wrong but also aesthetically wrong'. To which Rogers promptly responded:

There is one main difficulty that I see and that is that you think in English. Now that is not my way of thinking. But I will try to answer. You said that our acts are mainly moral acts, and of course they are because what we are doing cannot be hidden. That may be a superficial attitude because morality is something much more intricate than to grow out of the immediate value of simple moral or immoral acts. However, our acts are objects and very important objects in the very call of life. Therefore, what we do can be for the good or for the bad. And we have a great responsibility for doing what we do. With all that, I fully agree. But there are two kinds of morality. One is the personal morality of the artist and that is the consistency of his thinking and actions - to do what he really thinks is right; to express himself consistently and with complete awareness - that is, I think, the first act of morality. We know that this is a new attitude in the history of art - the way in which many modern artists very often refuse to do a work, or refuse to do a building, to accept a client, or a kind of society.

We have accepted this job with full moral responsibility, and I do not feel at all guilty for it. The second aspect of morality lies in the way of doing a thing; in the way of realising how to do your job, and what your object is – the intimate morality of your object. To me the intimate morality of an architecture is the clarity and sincerity of the structure and the awareness of the use of the many things required in the putting up of a building – that is the morality of the object. There are many other things which come into the morality of a work of art: we must never do something which is offensive; our work must be beautiful, and then beauty is moral again. But we can go on discussing morality for a long time and not come to any agreement. Now the question of models. Palladio wrote: 'Everybody who has looked upon my work or read my books will easily be able to resolve the problems of architecture as well as of beauty, utility and enjoyment.' For Palladio, the idea of plans and schemes was the idea of giving a model. He was prepared to give models – even to be copied. His personality was so strong that for two or three centuries after he lived, the society not having changed, the techniques not having changed, it was possible to follow him. But I do not think that we can do that today. I think that the only architect of the present who has had this same effect is Mies van der Rohe. For he is the only architect who is really modern in the sense that Palladio was in his time. He who copies Le Corbusier or Gropius is an imbecile. For all their products are absolutely personal. You cannot learn from Le Corbusier or from Gropius.

There is much to be learnt from these people but you cannot learn the lesson of form. I think that the fundamentals of modern architecture came from Gropius, he taught us the methods but not the models in the sense of forms. Therefore, what you can take here from our building is the concept, if you like it, or simply leave it if you don't like it. But if you take the forms you are a weak person. Similarly, if you take the forms from Le Corbusier you are again nothing more than Le Corbusier, because the value of Le Corbusier is not in his shapes but in their fundamental moral, and aesthetic thought.

It fell to Peter Smithson and Jaap Bakema to provide concluding remarks. Smithson returned to the question of models, saying that the Torre Velasca 'doesn't demonstrate a method of arriving at a building, but actually represents a formal plastic vocabulary. [...] It seems that the programme led to the definition of the basic parts of the building, and from then on the tower was designed within a self-contained formal system.' And he concludes by suggesting that the tower 'does not live in the same world as the artefacts of our time, because the plastic language it speaks belongs to another time.' To which Bakema added that the Velasca failed to represent the ideals of modern life, choosing to respond to the mediaeval fabric rather than celebrate the car as an expression of contemporary society.

Rogers's editorial provides an account and commentary of CIAM'59 elsewhere, and the meetings that had determined the end of the organisation. Rogers, whose work and research had, albeit unintentionally, contributed to the progressive crisis of CIAM, laments the loss of 'international thinking' and therefore of the ability to judge architecture on the basis of a shared understanding of concepts such as 'modern', 'past' and 'tradition'.

As Rogers explains, the crisis had its roots in CIAM 9 at Aix-en-Provence in July 1953 and arose from conflicts between the generations. These led to the formation of Team 10 and had intensified by August 1956 at CIAM 10 in Dubrovnik. Rogers was part of the Public Relations Commission, charged with moving between monitoring the various commissions of the congress and reporting directly to the president. Later discussions on how to continue CIAM's mission included the suggestion that 'a group of 30' be formed, composed of Josep Lluís Sert, Walter Gropius, Sigfried Giedion and Jacqueline Tyrwhitt, with Jaap Bakema as president, Rogers as vice-president, Pierre André Emery as secretary-general and Alfred Roth as treasurer.[1] The group decided to rename CIAM 'Research Group for Social and Visual Relations' and planned the subsequent and final CIAM congress for September 1959 at the Kröller-Müller Museum in Otterlo, a building designed by Henry van de Velde. It was here that Rogers gave his explosive presentation of BBPR's Torre Velasca, Giancarlo De Carlo presented his house at Matera, Ignazio Gardella the Olivetti dining hall at Ivrea and Vico Magistretti his villa at Arenzano. They were all harshly criticised as having failed to express a contemporary aesthetic and functionality, which prompted Rogers to respond with this editorial, followed by several illustrated pages, detailing the Torre Velasca, whose design stages are well documented, along with other achievements of the BBPR studio: Casa Lurani in Milan and the building in Corso Francia in Turin. All of this is prefaced by an important article, significantly titled 'Clarification' which aimed to demonstrate how works of very different appearance can be the products of the same design method.

1 Eric Mumford, *The CIAM Discourse on Urbanism, 1928–1960* (Cambridge, Mass.: The MIT Press, 2000): 258.

CIAM AT THE MUSEUM

ALSO PUBLISHED IN *EDITORIALI DELL'ARCHITETTURA* (TURIN: EINAUDI, 1968)

CASABELLA CONTINUITÀ NO. 232, OCTOBER 1959

It might be out of place here to tell the story of CIAM which, in general terms, is well known, and in its particulars would require another book, to which we should devote our undivided attention as soon as possible. For the moment, let's consider the final act.

I'd like to clear up straightaway the matter of the title: museums are architectural organisms intended to conserve the documents of historical experience, not objects that are dead, now and for ever, but objects that, although they are no longer part of the active cycle of life, are still worth being displayed and studied.

The last CIAM congress took place at the Kröller-Müller Museum in Otterlo, Holland; it marked the definitive end of this glorious institution, an active force for three decades of the modern movement.

A more suitable place could not have been found to mark the end of a perfect parabola that began in 1928 at the La Sarraz Castle near Lausanne.

The Kröller-Müller Museum is a masterly work by Henry van de Velde, the great patriarch of modern architects, who designed it in 1930, when he was already well along in years. It is a straightforward construction with just one level formed from a chain of simple, vital and affecting parallelepipeds that wind through an immense park that is one of the most beautiful imaginable.

The collection of dozens and dozens of works by Van Gogh, accompanied by paintings by Cézanne, Seurat, Renoir, Picasso and Mondrian, and excellent sculptures, is displayed in an exemplary way amidst vases of flowers - masterpieces of gentility and care that seem to echo the perfection of the architectural container and the things conserved therein. This ambiance made it possible to find the courage to admit, without giving way to pessimism, that CIAM was fatally spent while the few surviving older participants had some regrets - as is always the case when one looks back at paths laboriously taken and the illusion of destinations not always reached - the great beauty surrounding us had a restorative value, a reminder of the reality of art, as well as a reverence for it, that was useful for an exercise in self-critique and for promoting a dynamic belief in the potentiality of future works.

After the CIAM congress held in Dubrovnik in 1956, the organisation had been virtually dismantled, and a coordinating committee was appointed (eight members and the secretary J.B. Bakema) with the aim of deciding whether it might be possible for some of the core aims to be transferred from the old institution to a new one, but in such a way as to update them and make them responsive to the current needs of architecture.

Like any revolutionary intellectual movement that is little known until it emerges into the public domain, CIAM became the victim of its own success: as its influence spread, so the clarity of its message was lost. It quickly became apparent that it would no longer be possible to take an *a priori* position against a single adversary, something that had been easy to adopt by the founders of CIAM, who, in spite of their different backgrounds and temperaments, were able to join forces, rejecting the academic architecture of traditional styles. It was a position invested with enormous dynamism, which was exactly what gave CIAM its constructive and pedagogical value.

The only way to attempt the formation of another association was to proceed in an empirical manner and, if possible, to discover a sense of shared intention. The Committee invited, on an individual basis, about 50 architects from 20 nations, asking them to bring with them documentation of a significant work useful for discussion.

Acceptances arrived in encouraging numbers, making it possible to plan meetings in Otterlo for one week in September. The exhibition of works submitted by participants, shown on panels in several rooms made available by the museum, dealt with a wide range of topics of interest, from the most complex studies in urban planning to the most modest architectural organisms. More important, however, was that, leaving aside the value of the individual contributions, the way in which participants judged both their own work and that of others was substantially different. This was due to the fact that the notion of modernity and of the past or tradition, in other words, a historical awareness, and, ultimately, the evaluation of reality, all lost the cultural significance that had been easy to communicate

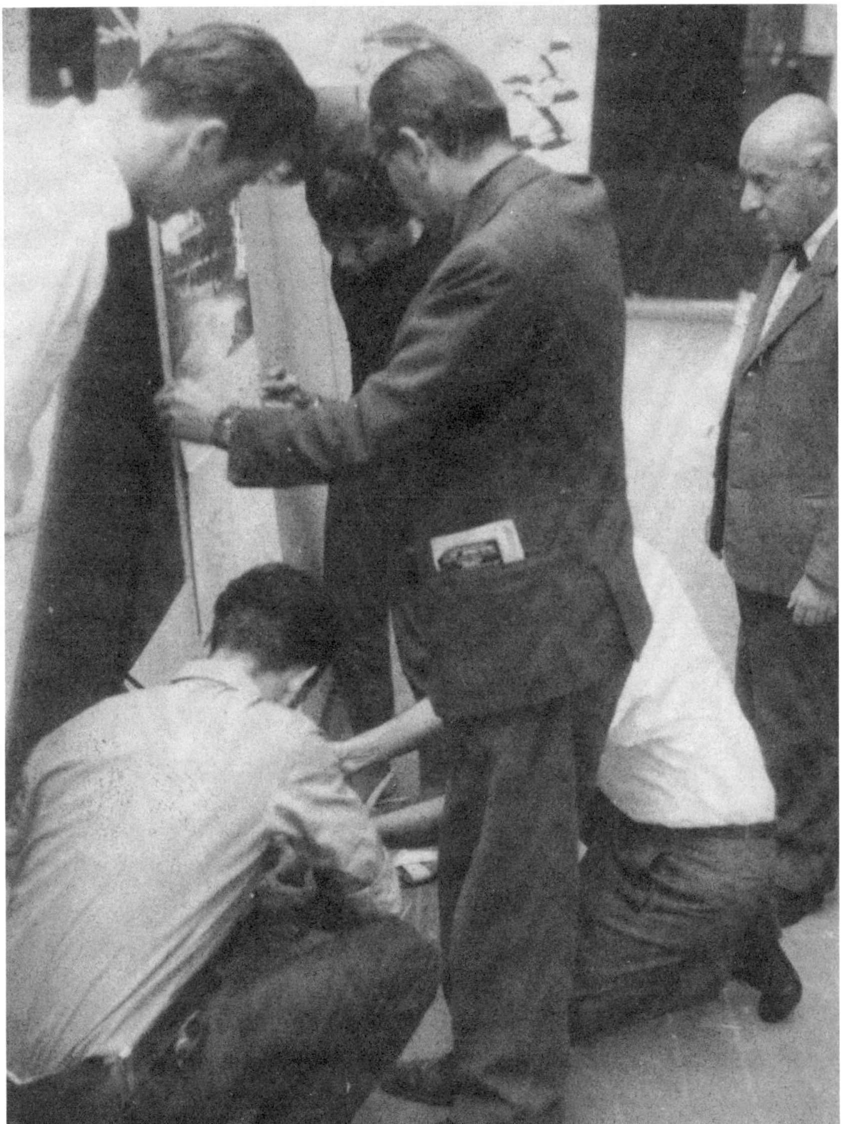

Rogers (standing on the right) at CIAM II in Otterlo, Netherlands, 1949 © Bakema, J.B. Archief / Het Nieuwe Instituut

without the need to make a declaration of faith or to dwell on subtle explanations.

This gradually became evident as the authors illustrated their own works and others began to discuss them by raising fundamental objections. It was the Italians - Giancarlo De Carlo, Ignazio Gardella, Vico Magistretti and the undersigned (although attending individually we were thought of as a group) - who were the most obvious source of controversy; and it is curious that this was the result of our challenging attitude regarding individuals whose national cultures might have had much deeper roots from which rebellion might spring.

It is significant that in this international debate we occupied common positions as it shows that in Italy today there is a shared commitment (one shared, also, by many absent colleagues): to achieve an architecture more closely connected to our lives, that is, a tendency to a more modern position.

The works we illustrated - De Carlo's house at Matera, the Olivetti dining hall by Gardella, Magistretti's villa at Arenzano, and the Torre Velasca by BBPR, with very different appearances due to the diversity of their purposes and the personalities of their makers - all set out to go beyond the abstract schematics of the 'modern' language and thus to bring to architecture a new degree of modernity.

I will frankly add that, by contrast, the works of our adversary friends (who with equal sincerity rebuke us for using a language not suited to the times) seemed to us to be trapped in formal language which makes it hard to discern signs of the concern with novelty so consistently expressed by them - albeit, no doubt, in good faith. The closest to us, though far away in terms of form, was Kenzo Tange, who illustrated his city hall in Tokyo and the Kagawa prefecture facility; in these works, his new contribution has been combined with the Japanese tradition. By saying this, I do not intend to compare the results, but to indicate the parallel nature of the content, the meaning pursued along compatible lines. It is also clear, above all, that while in his work, too, technical means may not have been exploited to their full current potential (as in certain reinforced concrete structures influenced by traditions of working with wood, for example), he is never reduced, as in many other cases, to sapping his own potential and thus blocking progressive development.

I had not seen for some time a CIAM congress that was so impassioned as a consequence of the tension between ideas tugging towards distant polarities, but neither had I witnessed a meeting at which ideological and temperamental differences could not at least attempt a provisional synthesis from which to unleash a new dynamic of common effort.

The definitive end of CIAM is due, above all, to this inability to accept the dialectical contradictions that provoked upheaval during the good times in the history of the congresses.

Maybe it will still be possible - as many of us hope - to resume encounters again, but they will be new and productive only for those who have the chance to participate in person, as at Otterlo, where the exchange of ideas certainly did provide those present with clarification. If a gathering of this sort does take place, it will not be a *congrès de travail* (work congress) like those that produced the studies for *Existenzminimum* or the Athens Charter, and so many other precious tools that were disseminated beyond the limited circle of CIAM's members, invigorating architectural culture all over the world.[2]

Maybe it is now time to lay out the accumulated experiences of the most recent generation; these phenomena need to be put into a historical context and a critical assessment arrived at regarding what is positive and what is negative. This summing-up can be undertaken only through teamwork among like-minded people. Those who have been part of CIAM can be proud of having belonged to a community of people who have collaborated for years on a monument that truly deserves to be placed in an

2 These are references to the second and fourth CIAM's. The former took place in Frankfurt-am-Main in 1929 and focused international attention on the attempts to define the minimum habitable dwelling for urban populations (the *Wohnung für das Existenzminimum*); the latter, in 1933, which took place on a boat that sailed from Marseille to Athens, produced the Charter of Athens: an urban planning document based on theories developed by Le Corbusier and other CIAM members, which had a considerable influence on much of the urban design work carried out by architects in Europe and beyond after World War II.

imaginary museum containing works that embody the intelligence and morality with which they were conceived.

The CIAM congresses articulated the greatest commitment and solidarity in modern architecture: a commitment that is even more valid and necessary today if we do not want to give up on the debate and the pursuit of a progressive architecture.

We should certainly not define what this architecture should be like, *a priori*, and a formal description would lead to fatal errors. But, on the other hand, giving up on renewal, giving up on research through which to evolve would mean betraying precisely those ideas that have given historical substance to the modern movement.

This is the sense in which I speak of *continuità*, continuity. And there will be much to draw on and actively to transform in the years to come, because no young, talented individual can overlook, in their practice, the fertile reality constituted by the experience of CIAM for everyone.

With the double issue 294–295 dedicated to the 'Problems of the USA', Rogers ended his editorship of *Casabella*. While Vittorio Gregotti's involvement in the magazine had been progressively diminishing over the last few years, his contributions reduced to a few sporadic articles, other editors – Aldo Rossi, Francesco Tintori and Luciano Semerani – were gaining more and more control over the editorial line. Likewise Rogers's interventions had been limited to his editorials, which were less and less related to the content of the issues and focused almost exclusively on the problems of education, reflecting the fact that, since 1962, he had been entrusted with the course in architectural composition at the Politecnico di Milano. He was to stay in this role, 'drunk on his devotion to the school', to quote Guido Canella, until 1968.

An earlier issue of *Casabella*, nº 287 in May 1964, was devoted entirely to education and the reform of architecture schools. It collected, among other things, the testimonies of the students who had taken part in the occupation of architecture faculties in 1963. This issue must have aroused the publisher's concern as it caused more than a little embarrassment in certain Milanese financial and economic circles; so too did the issue devoted to the Soviet Union (nº 262, April 1962). In addition to disquiet regarding the editorial direction of *Casabella*, the first signs of the illness that would, in 1969, lead to Rogers's death, were beginning to become evident. The publisher feared a loss of control in the management of the magazine, which, in the absence of Rogers, would be left entirely in the hands of younger, left-wing editors. This is likely to have hastened the decision to replace Rogers with a new editor, Gian Antonio Bernasconi.

DISCONTINUITY OR CONTINUITY?

REPRINTED IN *ESPERIENZA DELL'ARCHITETTURA* (TURIN: EINAUDI, 1958)

CASABELLA CONTINUITÀ NO. 294-295, DECEMBER 1964-JANUARY 1965

Yes, this is the last issue of *Casabella Continuità* that I will oversee with the collaboration of the present editorial staff, who are my valued friends.

Though this may not be the right moment for an assessment, I cannot help but recall the most significant positions we have adopted over this period.

We have truly travelled a long way in eleven years. Since December 1953 we have published almost 100 issues (including the monographs, which count as books), developing and thematically addressing the premises outlined in my first editorial, 'Continuità'. Equally, new stimuli have arisen over time, not with the invention of abstract theories but by critical engagement with the reality that has gradually revealed itself.

In representing the dramatic unfolding of this fertile 'man-architecture -man' cycle, we have communicated - as I proposed - 'its crises, its few but indispensable certainties and its many and even more necessary doubts'. And I believe that we have kept faith with that approach, because we have continued to reject 'every cliché but also every form of agnosticism', focusing on those works where we felt we could glimpse that 'yearning for freedom, those products of architecture (that is, of art) which symbolise the sublime effect of the historical process'.

And, to conclude my quotations from the time of our debut, the greatest effort has always been made to 'once more relate problems of quantity to the binding sanction of quality, helping to ensure that quality progressively becomes quantity: this is the ethical basis of our aesthetics, which we would pursue by restoring the craft and the art to their original synthesis: to *techne.*'

Many and various trials have been necessary to test and then establish appropriate viewpoints from which to question the universal character of the culture (continuity in time and continuity in space) that we are examining.

I hope I don't sound like an old commander who, when bidding farewell to his regiment, comes across as rather pathetic, his tears giving the lie to the courageous demeanour that won him the respect of friends and enemies alike. I only wish to recall some of our experiments, not as proof of their complete success, but more to acknowledge their effectiveness, which in certain cases is not unrelated to other priorities.

We began with the inspiration of the pedagogical system of Gropius, based on the image of a growing tree: starting from the seed, already incorporating potential, its trunk expand in ever wider circles. In a similar manner, moving from a consideration of works that exemplify certain architectural phenomena (both by proven masters and by immature but nonetheless promising architects), we have increasingly extended our field of inquiry to urban planning, or more specifically to the design of towns. In recent months we have paid particularly close attention to the latter, since we are convinced that far from being beyond the competence of an architect, this is the most natural and necessary terrain for development, the place where theoretical and creative work become one. Scientific research gives meaning to the image; its opposite, mere formalism, holds no interest for us.

The collaboration of Julia Bertolotti Banfi, Gae Aulenti, Francesco Tentori, Aldo Rossi – of [Guido] Canella, [Luciano] Semerani, [Carlo] Aymonino, [Paolo] Ceccarelli, [Manfredo] Tafuri and many others – has been exemplary. Just consider the commentaries on plans for the business and commercial centre of Turin, for Tel Aviv, and on the challenges faced by Tokyo, Hamburg, Boston, Vienna, Helsinki, Berlin, Philadelphia or San Francisco.

Nor do I think it is presumptuous to take pride in *Casabella*'s contributions to the historiography of the USSR, France, England and the USA, with truly original discoveries not only of documents but of the critical connections between works that for the most part have not previously been seen in relation to each other. The monographs on Van de Velde, Loos and Behrens have not only enriched writings in Italian, they have also contributed to the world's appreciation of these masters, as has been widely acknowledged. By temperament and conviction, we could not fail to take a firm stand in many cases where the debate extended beyond the specialists to the public arena. The proposed Frank Lloyd Wright building in Venice was a case in point, but perhaps the most pressing question concerns architectural education in Italy, a subject on which we still have a great deal to say, even now. I would like to think that my editorials at the beginning of each issue have been of some use in relation to the investigation of the theory of architecture, of *preesistenze ambientali* (pre-existing conditions), the utopia of reality, the evolution of the modern movement, the concept of tradition. Nor do I think it was pointless for me to enter the fray to debate social and political issues, convinced that you must first of all be a man, then a citizen and then an architect, in order to achieve the moral unity, the inalienable synthesis of man-citizen-architect.

It was to attempt this synthesis that I have been editor of *Casabella Continuità* for eleven years. At times I have been misunderstood – for example, when I was accused of being responsible for the introduction of neo-Liberty into Italy – perhaps because I was insufficiently clear or perhaps owing to the specious attitudes of a few readers. In any case, I pride myself on also having published articles I disagree with – perhaps I should have emphasised that more – because I believe that in a democratically run magazine the editor should not be a dictator. I know that for many people it is harder to deal with success (it goes to their heads) than with misfortune: I enjoyed directing *Casabella Continuità* and I hope I have done so with sufficient balance; I will not despair at its loss, but I am not so proud as to fail to be moved by praise or disapproval, and I flatter myself that the former has been more frequent than the latter.

This also shows that it is indeed the case that I have put 'impassioned effort' into this magazine as I have endeavoured to live up to the legacy of Pagano and Persico. That is why I ambitiously added *Continuità* to the name *Casabella*. It is also true that the magazine has 'achieved exceptional prestige around the world'; the credit for this must be shared with the staff, who are just as committed in their own free and individual ways.

The group that will take our place appears to have a programme quite similar to ours.

If that really is the case, I will be happy to see further *continuity* in the magazine to which we have devoted so many years of work; although, given that, one might also logically wonder why such a change was necessary.

If the programme is different, on the other hand, this *continuity* will definitely come to an end; the reader will be the judge of that, and of the consequences thereof.

Without further ado, I extend my regards to the publisher and my thanks to the staff and contributors, the members of the editorial committee and the research centre, and our readers.

To say that we are sorry to leave this magazine is an understatement, because it would be more to the point to express our disappointment. We will try to move on with new work so that it is clear to everyone that we still believe in the usefulness of battling over ideals in the field of architecture, in its deepest human, political and social content while taking an anti-fascist, democratic and progressive stance.

THE VOICES OF THE GENERATIONS

This is a very sweet letter, with strong premonitory overtones, written by Ernesto to a newly born Richard Rogers (1933–2021). Born and raised in Florence, Richard was the son of one of Ernesto's cousins. At the outbreak of World War II, Richard's family moved to England, where, subsequently, under Ernesto's influence, he decided to enrol in the architecture department of the Architectural Association, graduating in 1959 and then working at the BBPR studio in Milan before completing a master's degree at Yale University and going on to become one of the most influential architects of our time.

Previous: Franco Albini, Piero Bottoni, Gianluigi Banfi, Ernesto Rogers, Gio Ponti, Marco Zanuso (left to right) at the Casa della Cultura, Milan, 1950s © Fondazione Franco Albini

DEAR DANI

LETTER TO A NEWBORN RICHARD ROGERS, 1933

Dear Dani,
A new breath has stirred the air and the scent of a new soul has blended with the perfume of flowers. A new chain of love wraps the Earth.

I don't know your name so I have called you Dani, son of Dada and Nino, and I will call you this forever, the name that has awakened this love in my heart.

Dani, beautiful baby, this is life. Do you like it?

See? That is the sun, that blue is the sky, that is a rose, that is a donkey, these are men. This is me, Ernesto called Ernestino, second cousin, and I am an architect.

In general, I am likeable. I am not handsome, but I live to give back to the world, making an effort to invent beautiful things.

I am an artist: deceiving myself. Perhaps you too are an artist, and when you grow up you will work hard to keep your soul as big as it is today: this gift from God.

See? This is life; you don't know, but then nobody knows if you like cherries, and we will have to wait four or five years before we can answer this question.

See? All men when they are born possess the truth, they are God's sons; and when they grow up, they lose it a bit along the way, and then they are forced to make enormous efforts to understand many things that you, a baby, can understand perfectly.

Live. Life is beautiful, life is curious. Many get confused: they spend their lives eavesdropping from behind the door, but not you; break down the door, listen to the voice within, the world is you.

One day we will meet and we will become friends.

Dani, Good Morning, and thank your parents for their Love which brought you to life. Best wishes!

Kiss,
Ernesto

This is the original transcript of a speech given by Rogers at the Architectural Association (AA) in London during the 1949–50 academic year. In the summer of 1949, Rogers chaired the Education Commission at CIAM 7 in Bergamo. According to one of the delegates, AA student Andrew Derbyshire, Rogers made a 'magnificent effort' in marshalling a polyglot agglomeration – fifteen members from the USA, Italy, Switzerland, Belgium, Austria, Holland, England and Norway – with the aim of coming to some sort of resolution on the future of architectural education[1]. Shortly afterwards, seeking to implement the principles developed by the Education Commission, the first CIAM summer school was held at the AA between 8 August and 2 September 1949, with Rogers invited as a juror. So successful was Rogers's stay that the then director Robert Furneaux Jordan made an informal exchange agreement with him whereby a succession of AA students would each spend a term based at BBPR's Milan studio, while the BBPR partners would, in turn, come to the AA as visiting lecturers.

Francesco Gnecchi-Ruscone, who was an assistant at the AA during these years, recounts that '... the extraordinary vitality of this school, so unstructured and full of seemingly scattered activities, had both fascinated and puzzled [Ernesto]. It must also be said that at that time most of the students had been at war or mobilised for seven or eight years, they were often in their thirties, and the relationship between teacher and student was therefore one of adult equals, dependent not so much on prestige as on credibility, which had to be earned.'[2] What Rogers distilled from his encounter with the AA students was a certain 'pre-existing atmosphere' of dissent. On various occasions, when describing these exchanges, he affectionately referred to these rebellious and obstinate students as the 'I don't agree' gang, whose motto, as Rogers put it, provides the fundamental key to the 'anti-conformist spirit of the modern movement'.

1 Speaking at the AA on the same occasion Derbyshire recalled 'Dr Rogers' magnificent efforts at four o'clock in the morning to get this polyglot and, by that time, worn out and irritable crew to understand and agree with one another. [...] The report which the Commission eventually produced outlined a philosophical approach to the education of the architect, and went on to recommend certain essential points in school training, such as practical work on site, office, factory; the need for teaching staff to be practising architects; group-designing among students in the school and with those from other faculties; and the need to study the history of architecture, not in isolation from the rest of the curriculum, but in direct relationship to the immediate problems of design.' For the full transcript see *AA Journal* 1949–1950: 124–127.

2 Francesco Gnecchi-Ruscone, 'Un'amicizia nella scuola e nella vita', *Quaderni del Dipartimento di Progettazione dell'Architettura del Politecnico di Milano 15. Ernesto Nathan Rogers: testimonianze e studi* (Milan: Città Studi, 1993): 15–16. Author's translation.

THE 'I DON'T AGREE' GANG

AA JOURNAL 1949-1950

I regard it as a great honour to be invited here to this School, to your Association and to this meeting, and I should like very much to be able to thank you precisely and sincerely, but I am afraid that if I am to be precise I have to write what I want to say, and I am not able to write in English, so that I can only be sincere.

My approach to the AA is rather like a musical crescendo with variations. My first contact was in Bergamo, with two very brilliant students of the School – so brilliant that any school in the world would be very proud, I think, to have them as ambassadors at such a meeting as the CIAM congress. My second approach was in September, when I was here on a different job and had the great pleasure of meeting Mr Jordan, our Principal, the conductor of the orchestra, and then finally I was able to hear the whole orchestra of students and the chorus of the AA.

At Bergamo I worked in very close contact with your students there. We worked sometimes until the early hours of the morning, as Mr Derbyshire has told you, and sometimes we were very tired. They always came to see me after our meetings, and I was a little afraid at first of these young men; they had a very strange and for us romantic appearance. The physical contrast between long hair and my own condition was rather strong, and the first time I asked them what they thought of our work they replied 'We don't agree.' The second time, which I think was about two o'clock in the morning, when I asked Mr Derbyshire what he thought, he said to me, 'I don't agree.' Yet a third time I asked their opinion, questioning Mr Turner, the other student, and again he answered, 'I don't agree.' I think that 'We don't agree' is a very beautiful motto for this School: it means, 'We don't agree, because we should like to do better.' This is the idea which we should all have, that we want to do better, and I should like to make use of this motto myself.

I don't agree that there are necessarily differences between different generations, when someone like Andrew Derbyshire is able to put before us the new problems which he perceives and describes with such poetic intelligence. I don't agree that there is a difference between the past and modern life, if someone like Ian Colquhoun can translate into modern architectural terms his appreciation of ancient culture. I don't agree that there exists an

Rogers's drawing, London, 1949 © Fondo Peressutti / IUAV Archivio Progetti

iron curtain between nations, when a man like Hugh Morris is able to go to Czechoslovakia and bring back so clear and honest an account of the country that we are able to judge for ourselves whether we like it or not.

The AA School has not only very good eyes and ears but a very clear voice, and I am happy to second this vote of thanks.

‘Who are you?’ was the rhetorical question addressed to young people as well as being the emblematic title of Rogers’s opening lecture at the first post-war CIAM summer school in Venice in 1952; his response was, ‘you are the heirs to this history of struggle’ and ‘you can decide if you are a new shoot sprouting in the ancient woods of architecture, or else a branch springing from the trunk of the two or three previous generations.’ In this text, he defined the theme of *continuità*, continuity, with the work and ideals of previous generations within which he situated his own pedagogical approach and, later, the cultural strategies of *Casabella*, which he would soon be called upon to lead.

WHO ARE YOU?

VENEZIA ARCHITETTURA, NOVEMBER 1953

So many superfluous lectures, and now this too? What justification could I have for asking for still more of your attention?

Well, the previous speakers have made a valid contribution to your education by sharing their thoughts on various aspects of architecture that you yourselves will have observed, although not actively shaped.

But now I would like to talk about you, and more precisely about the part you have played - and will play - as protagonists. I've been lucky enough to see some of the world. I've got to know many people like you, both inside and outside academia - including a number of you who are here today - so please allow me to offer my point of view.

You will excuse some inevitable generalisation, I hope, as this is an issue that needs to be discussed in generational terms rather than our lingering over individual personalities. So I'm addressing all of you students - men and women - who are around 20 to 30 years old. And when I'm talking about you, I'm evidently essentially referring to your qualities as architects, which should incorporate all other human qualities.

I should make it clear that when I say the architect should be representative of the person, I certainly do not want to suggest that the architect comes before the person - that would be absurd, ethically - but rather that being an architect reveals and justifies our human condition by giving it direct expression, by making it socially tangible.

Not everyone has to be an architect - clearly, logically - yet I firmly believe that an architect cannot be judged independently of his human values. Therefore, if I do not speak of other values that you hold, they should be considered implicit in what I am about to say. I will speak to you in all earnestness, to establish parity between those who are being judged and those who are taking it upon themselves to do the judging, a parity that makes it possible for us all to judge one another. The aim of my critiquing is to enable a conversation on the level of general self-evaluation. All of this becomes possible if what I have repeatedly said in public - at the cost of alienating people of more than one generation – is true, that today there is no old guard and no youth among us modern architects.

In considering the events of this century we should recognise that the modern movement asserted itself as a continuous revolution – a revolution that, while being very dramatic in terms of its inner dialectic does not provoke rifts between the three generations it encompasses.

We are all on the same side of the barricades, albeit with weapons of different potential.

The composition of CIAM itself reflects this harmonious coexistence of contrasts and provides relatively convincing proof of my thesis that an association like ours could not have arisen in any epoch other than our own, or for any other kind of architecture. It favours the possibilities of understanding, collaboration and exchange, and overcomes the boundaries that divide nations as well as generations. Masters and artists alike have contributed to laying the groundwork for a common culture that is vaster and deeper than the capacities of any one individual. On the other hand, having progressed beyond the positions of traditional styles, there are endless instances in which the individual architect can – and must – supply an original solution, shaped according to individual temperament.

The field of architecture is consciously homogeneous yet has perhaps never been as varied as it is now. The agnostic cosmopolitanism of academics of all stripes is countered by an architecture that, at every moment and in every place, poetically exalts reality. Unity of method and diversity of language: these two inescapable concepts are for me the bases of today's architectural thought, setting out the direction of its development in the educational sector and, as a consequence, the relationship between the generations, embodied in the training of the individual. Our system aspires to cultivate free spirits which are nevertheless able to adhere to the rigour of a method: only in this way will we manage to spread and perfect a style without falling into the trope of formal imitation.

This declaration of principles is crucial today, since we have nurtured the necessary critical means and depth of historical knowledge that will enable us to venture even further into the realms of the imagination.

The dialectical tension between generations (and, it should be clear, between individuals), far from being a source of weakness, takes on new meaning if the youngest, rather than opposing the eldest, join forces with them to take architecture forward. Young people can accept this position of serious and effective struggle if the older generation, in turn, knows how to set aside personal ambitions and forgo any attempt to impose, with the authority conferred by a white beard, preconceptions disguised as axioms.

It is possible to have a vibrant school when those who were born earlier are willing, as they teach those born later, to learn alongside them. This is also how to achieve a continuity of direction outside the school, keeping alive this productive exchange, a sense of everyone having a role in the same play.

So, to reaffirm the premise of this discussion, while I said I do not believe in an opposition between the present generations, I can still be cognisant of differences in age and use the words 'old' and 'young'.

Yet you would have to be living on a different planet not to notice that, as things presently stand, young people today are restless and often disgruntled: this is true in Italy, France, Argentina, Chile, Peru, the USA, Scandinavia, Holland, Switzerland - everywhere I have been - and I could mention members of other nationalities that I've met in Italy.

If you make an effort to help young people, challenging them with questions about architecture, awakening their intuitive faculties, setting them on the path of analysis and thus impelling them to take charge, you may be rewarded with their respect and their friendship, but their rebellion will not necessarily be quelled. In fact, this teaching method often leads to discouragement and anxiety. Rebellion, doubt and dissatisfaction are often signs of fertile vitality: in the face of this phenomenon, the older generation needs to act like patient farmers, trying not to trample on the seedlings, while young people need to accept some helpful pruning from those with more experience. Critique and self-critique blend in mutual sympathy, that is, in an understanding of how to suffer together. I have always admired a brilliant group of English students at the Architectural Association School of Architecture in London, a group I have had the privilege to count among my students. They are the most rebellious, the most obstinate and even the most presumptuous students I have ever met, so I affectionately call them the 'I don't agree' gang. I have learned a lot from these English friends of mine, so much so that sometimes, well... *I don't agree* with them either.

The motto 'I don't agree' is the only possible guide to understanding the nonconformist essence of the spirit of modernism, so I would like it to become the slogan of all those who try their hand at modern architecture – that way they will always be prepared (and this should not seem like a paradox) to continue in the spirit of previous generations. 'I don't agree' is the motto of systematic doubt, the dialectical basis of scientific thought, but it is valid only if seen as a means, not as an end in itself. Otherwise, it is a closed figure – like that of the serpent that bites its own tail and poisons itself. So we have to be careful. And when we study, say, Thales Theorem, we have to apply the system of the dialectic *ad absurdum* to reach the objective conclusion he has suggested to us – even if, my friends, this means admitting that the generations who came before you were right all along.

But why do young people rebel; why are they dissatisfied? I believe there are three main reasons: the first, *felix culpa*, lies in youth itself: in its expansive energy, its natural explosions – those of a volcanic land, convulsing with its own inner fire. The second reason lies in a historical superstructure, usually identified with the Oedipus complex, that is, a feeling of inferiority in relation to the older and already established generation and the concomitant irrational dissent felt towards it. The third reason lies in a rational awareness of the real shortcomings young people observe in the world they have inherited from their fathers. (Naturally the first two reasons often influence the objectivity of the third.)

Where the first reason for rebellion is concerned, I would hope that none of the older generation, however advanced in years, would hold the youth of young people against them, that they will have the presence of mind to remember their own happy youthful excesses. But I would like to point out the danger that arises when certain young people - and there are quite a few of them around today - do not accept their condition (the advantages and corresponding disadvantages) and believe that they can overcome their discomfort by disguising themselves as older people, like little boys smoking paper cigarettes, or little girls nursing their dolls.

It is our duty to take responsibility for our condition and to cope with the demands imposed by it. Although part of the problem of youth lies with teachers, many of the issues have to be resolved by young people themselves. Otherwise existence would be sterile.

As far the Oedipus complex is concerned, like every such disorder it can be cured if we take heed of the forces that are at work within us. In the specific case of your generation of architects, I hope that my brief introduction defining modern architecture as a method shows how fathers and sons can work together in harmony.
But there is another basis for harmony, a philosophical one, that can also be deduced from the opinions so elegantly expressed in Professor Argan's lecture. For did he not say that it is only during this century [the twentieth century] that urbanism has emerged into general consciousness? In critical terms, this is also true of architecture.

And if that is the case, we may deduce that we cannot operate outside this general consciousness when we express our individuality and that, moreover, by operating consciously we can work as a team, with a common rational system guiding our instinct, intuition and inspiration. Whereas in the past, *quand les cathédrales* étaient *blanches*,[1] teams would coalesce around shared sentiment, nowadays they are formed on the basis of shared thinking.
All those alive in spirit can walk together - fortunately there is as

1 This is a reference to Le Corbusier's book *Quand les cathédrales étaient blanches, voyage au pays des timides* (Paris: Pion, 1937), translation: *When the Cathedrals Were White* (New York: McGraw-Hill, 1964), in which he compares 1930s America with Europe in ancient times, when social and technological changes went hand-in-hand, and monumental buildings (now bleached white by sunlight) were the most cutting-edge of their time.

yet no bureaucratic requirement for us all to have to hand documents evidencing our physical age so as to keep a check on the age of our spirit.

So now we can address the more objective complaints that are directed at the older generation by young architects today. Am I hoping we will get together to sing the refrain '*tout va très bien, Madame la Marquise*', or '*tout va très bien, Madame l'Architecture*'? ['everything is fine, Madame la Marquise', or, everything is fine, Madame Architecture].[2] No, heaven forbid. Let's try instead to examine the issues confronting us and find out whether the older generation can empathise with the positions taken by the young. This could be framed as a question regarding how to proceed, the essence of which, I believe, could be distilled as follows. Some of you say, 'First let's stage the revolution, and the renewal of architecture will inevitably follow.' Others insist on a different point: 'We must only take on work that is entirely in tune with our innermost convictions - no military barracks, for example.' And then you have the chorus: 'No prisons, no palaces, nothing we would not want to build for our children.'

Putting aside my own personal opinions, my immediate impulse is to declare that I have the greatest sympathy for both of these positions - the first is extrovert in nature, putting the emphasis on a political-social agenda for architecture, the second more introverted, arising from moral scruples. I also sincerely believe that these theses are defined so generically that they are just as difficult to disprove as they are to defend.

Personally, I am always sensitive to the charm, or rather the torment, of these states of mind (especially the latter) because the practice of our profession puts me - indeed places all of us - in daily opposition to them.

I therefore do not wish to critique the above-mentioned theses in a way that would belittle their generous moral impetus; nonetheless, I feel it is vital to note that, in my view, neither of these positions

2 Rogers plays on the refrain from a once-proverbial French popular comic 1936 song by Ray Ventura, which, as it unfolds, demonstrates an attitude of clumsy denial in the face of a desperate situation.

addresses the concrete reality of the drama of architecture. The first misses the target by aiming short, looking at the phenomenon of architecture only within the narrow limits of its tactical and practical consequences, without fully perceiving the regenerative value of its qualities as a work of art. (And if one does not believe in these foundations of the profession, how is it possible to practise architecture at all, I wonder?) The second thesis misses the mark because it overshoots, finding its target in some mirage of society, but missing the beating heart of architecture.

The generations before yours shared a deep conviction that the new aesthetics brings with it a certain set of ethics, whereby their every work must represent the indivisible synthesis of utility and beauty. (For what else does 'functional architecture' mean if not true structures for true people?)

Perhaps we laboured too much under the illusion that exemplary architecture could instigate social renewal. Such aspirations have suffered many setbacks – that cannot be denied – yet it also remains true that individual works, whatever their purpose, use or users, have sought to represent this ideal symbolically. It was for this ideal, fighting as partisans in the Resistance, that the Italian architects Pagano and Banfi lost their lives, as did the student Giorgio Labò and many other friends who are the true martyrs of our faith. I am certain that each of you thinks of them with gratitude: they also died for you.

The ideological morality of the rational, the honest and the poetic can be found in the work of architects who have refused all compromise. Frank Lloyd Wright may design houses almost exclusively for wealthy, privileged people, but in the attempt to actually build them he has suffered for years, running up debts and even ending up in prison.

Le Corbusier, at the age of 64, is only now starting to reap some financial rewards, but while he was building that masterpiece known as the Unité d'habitation in Marseille he was threatened by a number of reactionaries, who sued him for 20 million francs in the name of protecting the French landscape.

Gropius, who is 70, is obliged to go on seeking work, because his academic pension is very small.

These are the masters. As for our finances ... the least said the better; we can all speak of ongoing daily struggles.

Who are you? You are the heirs to this history of struggle.

And there is still much to be done.

So, your dissatisfaction is justified, though it seems to me there is less justification for your rebellion or for the pessimism of those of you who believe we have to start all over again, from scratch.
The deep political chasm that splits humanity in two has direct repercussions in architecture and threatens to cloud our judgement regarding the synthesis that has already been so clearly identified and ably attempted.

Quality and quantity have become a dilemma.

To give a simplified, generic example: you could frame this as the choice between building a large number of houses that are generally pretty ugly or building houses for only a few, some of which are very beautiful.

Quantity vs quality, a false dilemma.

Quantity does not figure in the assessment of art, and that which is not art is not architecture. Architecture can also exist in isolation, as a single work, so long as it fully achieves the synthesis between utility and beauty - that is a principle I have no intention of abandoning, but I will immediately add that the isolated work of architecture needs to do more than stand up to artistic evaluation if it is to satisfy all those other needs that loom - so large! - in our conscience.

To establish harmony between artist and the human being, recognising the inalienable needs of art even under the pressure of moral imperatives: this is your task. Yours? As a matter of fact, why shouldn't this be a task for all of us, in accordance with the (admittedly varied) terms dictated by our individual consciences?

So, then, who are you?

I will leave the answer to you. You can decide if you are a new shoot sprouting in the ancient woods of architecture, or else a branch springing from the trunk of the two or three previous generations, solid enough to have withstood many storms, yet still capable of producing the sap of new life. If you accept this latter hypothesis, the objective dispute between you and us has only a chronological meaning, as I postulated at the start and have attempted to demonstrate throughout my talk.

Aside from the historical reasons I have put forward, I have been encouraged to continue this thesis by the fact that after the heroic age of the masters, the generation to which I belong has already shown itself to possess that constructive humility I am recommending to you.

This text (which also appeared in *Der Bau* nº 4, 1958) was initially written for a series of lectures given by Rogers in 1955 at various universities in the USA on the occasion of his appointment as Honorary Fellow of the American Institute of Architects, and subsequently at the Zentralvereinigung der Architekten in Vienna in 1958. The editorial introduces an issue of *Casabella* focused on the theme of tradition and partly dedicated to the masters Frank Lloyd Wright (whose Price Tower is documented) and Eliel Saarinen, along with works by Louis Sullivan, Hendrik Petrus Berlage and Henry van de Velde, followed by a reflection on Finnish architecture and by Giuseppe Samonà's analysis of BBPR's restoration of the Castello Sforzesco in Milan.

In *Architettura, misura e grandezza dell'uomo*, where an Italian version of this text is reprinted, the editor Serena Maffioletti includes a note by Rogers, which she found in the BBPR archives and which indicates the circumstances in which the text was first written:

... I wondered what I could say to satisfy, at least in part, the expectations of an audience so well disposed towards me. I thought that a lecture of a purely theoretical nature, that failed to reference my direct experience as a militant architect, would be as inadequate as talking only about the work of my studio. So, I chose a subject that, while embracing the wider horizon of general problems, would be rooted in the generation to which I belong. I must confess my age straight away, so that the chronological definition of what I am going to say is at least clear. I am 46 years old, and I am going to talk about that class of architects who are a few years younger than me or a decade or so older. It goes without saying that allowing other people to know your age – when more than one wrinkle is beginning to appear, one's hair (the little that remains) is turning grey and one's belly is beginning to show in spite of repeated exercise on too many spring mornings – is in itself not a pleasant experience, and, believe me, men find this just as difficult as women; one's pride and vanity are hurt and the hopes for one's own physique are dashed, as well as those for one's spiritual being. No matter what age you are, there is always some consolation to be found in contemplating your life and all that has happened in it.

CASABELLA CONTINUITÀ NO. 211, JUNE–JULY 1956

Real culture lives by sympathies and admirations, not by dislikes and disdain.
— William James[I]

When the architects of my generation began to emerge in the artistic firmament, four primary stars dominated the heavens: Frank Lloyd Wright, Walter Gropius, Mies van der Rohe and Le Corbusier. Perhaps I should have said planets and not stars, as their light is to some extent a reflection of other stars which rose much earlier; to name only three of the most brilliant: Sullivan, Van de Velde and Perret.

I know, too, that other stars shone in the heavens besides this great foursome but allow me to dwell on these major figures for they represent a moment of synthesis in the architectonic consciences of those young men (of whom I was one) who were developing around 1930. This was – alas! a quarter of a century ago and, more importantly, history is not just made-up of a cold study of facts but comprises, and to a far greater extent, cherry-picking from among those facts, like bees hovering over fields and sucking more enthusiastically from some flowers than from others to make their honey.

I should say, by way of elucidation, that much of Frank Lloyd Wright's personality has been conveyed to us through the mediation of Mies van der Rohe, who, as he himself has written, was greatly influenced by Wright as early as 1910 when the American master gave an exhibition of his works in Berlin.

It can be said that for the most part it was Wright's principles of space which were introduced to European thought by Mies – like pollen borne on his wings.

I In a post scriptum at the end of his editorial (not reproduced here), Rogers clarifies that, after completing his tour in the USA, he was the guest of Frank Lloyd Wright at Taliesin in Wisconsin and then of Mies van der Rohe in Chicago. 'It was', he writes, 'the most remarkable experience that I could have had for checking on what I had just said [in my lectures]: a fresh and bracing experience resulting from the different temperatures to which my two generous hosts subjected me through the benign influence of their widely differing personalities ... The teachings of William James, the great American thinker, whose philosophy embraced the plurality of experience, were a useful guide in my attempts to gain as much as possible from my meetings with the two great masters.'

Since, at the time, the epicentre of the architectonic movement was in Europe – and I rather think its reverberations were felt throughout the whole world of culture – what I have to say about Europe also applies, I suppose, to the rest of the world.

These four giants – Wright, Gropius, Mies and Le Corbusier – are our immediate masters, but it is rather difficult to demonstrate this critically and to support it with precise reasons. At first sight, the differences between them seem to be much more in evidence than any identity which might emerge from a study of the totality of their works; but if we dig down to the very foundations of our modern artistic heritage we discover that they are solid and indispensable pillars of the structure of our culture – it is natural that the diverse elevations of this edifice reflect the differences between us.

The main contribution of these men – and this is why we came to love them when we were young – is that aesthetic and ethical problems were fused in their work; this is a matter of great historical importance and its originality should be underlined. For these men the problem of the *coerenza*, coherence, of thought and action was of such vital importance that the entirety of their artistic activity can be summed up by or identified with the stand they have taken: they live, fight, suffer and sacrifice themselves for architecture, deliberately never distinguishing between the problems of form and those of content, whether it be in their works (as is to be expected with any skilled artist) or in their lives.

Not that they consider life as a work of art, as did the hedonistic and sceptical, if not downright cynical, artists of the Renaissance; quite the contrary, they consider a work of art to be a vital part of existence and it becomes a vehicle for all their moral, social and sometimes even political aspirations. Van de Velde spoke of a '*morale de raison*' and trusted to reason to control every aspect of feeling, and certainly of artistic feeling, the latter validated only by being submitted to logical proof. From this logical proof he derived the moral justification for artistic feeling, which is, after all, its real and historical meaning.

I believe that this philosophical principle, while fully lived out by the Belgian master, is for Wright, Gropius, Mies and Le Corbusier a source of energy capable of still more dramatic and exciting results. These find their most completely unified form of expression in Gropius's concept of an architecture that serves life.

Admitting difficulties of character, human weaknesses, a certain vanity and even presumptuousness on the part of some of the four masters, we have nevertheless considered them as models of an artistic refusal to compromise. And that - in view of the difficult medium in which they have had to work - is to recognise them as courageous fighters who have never given way to pressure from either public or private clients.

The poetic feeling and the figurative language with which each of these great artists expresses his own particular style lie within the framework of a wider vision; this vision confers on their aesthetic statements the force of a manifesto which rises beyond that of art for art's sake to a veritable way of living, a way of living which, through the artist, strives to encompass the entire social structure. Even Gropius's realism cannot be separated from a strong vein of idealism deriving from his conviction that architecture - that is to say good architecture - contains in itself an intrinsic healing power capable of bettering the human lot. In Gropius this aspect of his work finds its expression in his pedagogical activity, which is informed by a method aimed at the scientific improvement of man. Whereas in Wright and Le Corbusier this idealism overflows into utopianism, and their words and projects are filled with messianic zeal for a perfect humanity.

Van der Rohe's architectural thinking reflects a fantastical world in which all human passions tend to be elevated to heights beyond the reach of the contradictory nature of life, pushed towards poetical summits.

The ways of living of these masters are to a large extent expressed in their architectural forms which are equally moral. If the stylistic character of this architecture can be summed up in a single phrase, I would say that it seeks to express in a more conscious manner than has ever been achieved before the functional relationship between utility and beauty inherent in architectonic phenomena of all ages.

Modern architecture expresses the reality of things, calling them by their names without resorting to literary embellishment, worldliness, analogy or allegory.

When designing a house or a city, Wright, Gropius, Mies and Le Corbusier do not borrow inspirations from other experiments. They do not try to deceive or adorn their work with superstructures. They do not draw on their memories or on those of others. Instead, they extract from the living reality around them a concrete response to the problems inherent in it. Their coherence and unity of style are guaranteed by *coerenza* and unity of method. That is why they defend their work so vigorously, for it is – they believe – something more than beautiful: it is just, honest, logical and true. The *coerenza*, though, is often only internal and one in which the dialectical terms of the problem, though resolved in artistic synthesis, do not always correspond to someone else's idea of reality. And this is their shortcoming: that they have championed an avant-garde architecture which is necessarily polemical.

Only a great man like Gropius would venture to be so modest as to underestimate the importance of his own works, and to think that they were at the same level as those of his contemporaries. But Wright and Le Corbusier want no association of any kind, and, against a background of calls for democracy and humanitarianism, they launch prophetic messages beyond the constraints of historical reality (Broadacre City, La Ville Radieuse). True, they do not attempt to build the City of God; but their plans and projects do shape human beings.

Frank Lloyd Wright has shown our age wonderful new spatial visions: he sings of individual liberty, and he interprets that liberty through the inexhaustible and truly original invention of form characteristic of his architecture: its organic development, even in geometric expression, follows a coherent interior process not unlike that of nature itself.

Gropius is the conscience of the modern movement: he is our conscience: he is the creator of a method which overrides the *a priori* principles of traditional styles and enables us to understand things, to grasp problems and to give logic and harmony to their form and spirit. Gropius is the Leon Battista Alberti of our age; Mies represents constructive purity and elegance – he is a Brunelleschi whom our age has wronged by failing to offer him the opportunity to build something of equal sublimity to the dome of Santa Maria del Fiore.

But our Michelangelo, the artist who loved to call himself '*pittor, scultor, architettor, poeta*' – painter, sculptor, architect and poet – is Le Corbusier. For it is Le Corbusier who has tried to achieve a synthesis of the plastic arts (*la synthèse des arts majeurs*), and to do this intrinsically rather than in the exercising of multiple separate activities.

In our culture, we have a clear understanding of what constitutes the Renaissance, even though many individuals contributed to it; the modern movement has emerged similarly as a unified activity in the history of artistic thought in spite of the diversity of its protagonists, the considerable differences between their temperaments and even between their starting points –where they come from, what their aims are.

When an artist looks into himself with sincerity and impartiality, he cannot fail to be aware of the contradictory forces that make up his life: he will discover the real energy of his personality as if he were an Adam without a sinful past and without conscious experience, and he will realise that the blood flowing to his heart and brain originates in a thousand rivulets which gradually unite to form great arteries; these arteries represent the influence of his masters, who have already taken on the historical process for him and given it character. We are all, ultimately, a combination of Adam and our antecedents: an individual and unmistakeable amalgam which we cannot ignore without renouncing the joys and sacrifices of taking responsibility for own destinies.

When we architects, now 40 to 50 years of age, first chose to follow a life of art, we felt the stimulus, the richness and the nurturing provided by these masters and we tried to define our task in terms of our having had such fathers and being obligated to build on their legacy.

CIAM 7 in Bergamo, Italy, 1949. From left Jacques Honneger, Sigfried Giedion, Josep Lluís Sert, Le Corbusier, Ernesto Rogers and Rudolf Steiger © GAMeC: Archivio Nino Zucchelli / Wells Foto

Once we have understood that these great artists have not handed down a practical manual, or a codebook or a dogma or anything else defined *a priori*, but rather the energy of a method which it is our duty to perpetuate amidst the continual vicissitudes of existence – those who have understood this realise that the true architect is not one who colludes in making a variety of elegant and tasteful forms, but rather a moralist whose task is to focus on the contents of life drawing from them the symbols needed to create the container. It follows that, if, instead of looking at the forms – the signature contributions of individuals – we had been able to draw directly from these widely differing masters, we could have taken whatever suited our personal preferences, and, from the group as a whole, the admirable character of their methodology and ethics.

Our artistic activity was not to be limited to making ideal clothes for an ideally conceived humanity, or to making beautiful clothes for the hunchbacked, distorted and dithering social body; it had to pursue the rehabilitation of that body and to foster its development.

Thus, while our masters had set us an example through their struggle, initiated in the name of a theoretical humanity, we had to get on with fighting in the ranks, shoulder to shoulder with other men; while our predecessors flew the flag of the *avant garde*, we fly the flag of *continuità*, continuity.

This is undoubtedly less striking, less piercing, much less brilliant; it could even be seen as rather dull, but I am convinced that, even within the limits of its deliberate modesty, it evidences a *continuità*, a historical awareness, from which we derive a sense of reality, a sense of the need to deepen our study of culture and to widen its effects. Some, it has to be admitted, used this to conceal the poverty of their imagination, labouring under the illusion that an architect requires only a passing acquaintance with politics and sociology or statistics or perhaps criticism and failing to realise that they need to draw out of these things, with the liveliest creative energy, expression, communication, in a word, art.

However it should also be said that many architects have completely understood the meaning of their mission and have sought to elaborate a style which, though becoming increasingly intelligible to the masses, has lost none of its vigour or immediacy, its objectivity or inventiveness; no language, in any age, is capable of satisfying the needs of the more sensitive members of society without these qualities. We have had to recuperate a sense of tradition which, although implicit in the works of modern architecture (if only because modernity is a profound cultural act), had been temporarily set aside in the polemics surrounding the revolutionary action [of the *avant garde*]. For those polemics were destined to pervade every contemporary activity so as to prevail over the resistance of academic, nostalgic and reactionary culturalism, perpetually ready to frustrate, with smoke bombs any advance of the *avant-garde*.

Once we were sure that modern ideas were no longer in danger of being corrupted or adulterated, at least by those who believed in them, we were able to extend our interests to embrace the most profound visions of history, and as we penetrated it more and more thoroughly, we became aware that we had acquired vital new energy from it.

The greatest danger in our age is not conformity to the academic styles against which the generation of masters had to struggle, at least this is now the case in the western world (and apparently even beyond), but the danger that lies in a new modernistic conformity; it is evident in the superficiality of those who believe they are of their time only because they ape the language of true artists or because they have confused the bizarre with the truly original, substituting the letter for the spirit of modern architecture. The real threat to modern architecture today is formalism, and it is therefore the task of the most enlightened spirits to prove their sincerity by basing their work on the experience of an assimilating culture and not by adopting mannerisms and mindlessly whistling someone else's tunes.

Against a cosmopolitanism that operates in the name of a superficial universal sentiment, and that erects the same architecture in New York, Rome, Tokyo or Rio, in the countryside as in the cities, we must try to harmonise our works with the *preesistenze ambientali*, the pre-existing conditions, – both those of nature and those created historically by human ingenuity.

We cannot overstate the importance of the task that has been entrusted to us. But the masters themselves continue to furnish richly creative examples. We need only consider Frank Lloyd Wright's sadly unrealised plans for a house in Venice, or Le Corbusier's work in the Punjab or at Ronchamp, or Mies's skyscrapers which build upon the lesson of the Chicago School, or Gropius's house in New England, to appreciate how attuned they were to the cultural specificity of their surroundings, in terms of both the natural and the artistic setting in which they worked, and how clear and honest their solutions are.

The difficulty, as we deepen our understanding of tradition, lies in harnessing the contribution of those in the avant-garde without betraying their intentions. This is because there are many who, in combatting modernistic formalism do not notice that they are falling foul of another type of formalism, that of folklorism and traditional styles, which are unable to respond to the multifarious needs of a healthy society.

It is true that the interconnectedness of ethics and aesthetics, which forms the bedrock of my understanding of modern architecture, does not allow for a separate consideration of these factors, but it has to be admitted that either one or the other has dominated the process from which modern architecture derives. The generation of masters certainly confronted the problem of aesthetics with great skill and forged a language capable of expressing new contents. It is for us to pick up on these new contents, to specify them, to characterise them, in order to create relevant forms, like an egg whose outer form expresses the life contained and protected within.

If, in spite of all the studies, projects and slogans lavished on urban planning in the last few years, we are still in a period of crisis and far from reaching our goals, we may attribute this to the lamentable lack of cohesion shown between theoretical and practical values in projects so far submitted.

It is far more difficult to define the city of today than the city of tomorrow for the very reason that it is extremely difficult to confront real problems. The Charte d'Athènes [Athens Charter] remains a symbol of the fundamental step that had to be taken if we were to break free from traditional schemes before advancing. It would be absurd to reject the brilliant notion which gave rise to that document, however, it is incumbent upon us to build real cities that work for all of us human beings, with all our joys and sorrows, and we have to forge the legal and political instruments needed to solve our pressing problems, for these can no longer be put off to some time in the future.

We have to dream, but let us dream with our eyes wide open. Architecture is the representation of time - that is the era - in space; but this definition is too abstract if it is not completed by a reciprocal action, that is to say if space is not concretely realised in time.

We are right to point to the lack of faith of the bureaucrat, to the faint of heart and the conservatives and the Pharisees; but we must, in our turn, take pains to build on solid ground.

The work of a greatly talented and prolific artist, who emerged between the generation of the masters and our own, has translated many of the achievements of the masters into a language that fits the problems we face. This is Alvar Aalto, as rich in experience as in a rare creative facility, who, with technical precision, was able to graft his own personality onto cultivated architecture (ancient, specifically Italian architecture), as well as onto the trunk of the vernacular architecture of his country. While Mies van der Rohe prepared the first synthesis, rationalising organic architecture, Aalto, more than 20 years later, has made rational architecture more organic: it is in this nimble dialectic between European and American culture - which shows even the most retrograde that the word is a fluid unit in space and time - that our generation's activities find their place.

It is worth noting that those masters who are still alive and working (may God preserve them for another 100 years!) are our older companions, accompanying us on the journey and sometimes going ahead of us on the path. As such, I am not so much making a comparison between generations as speaking of an epoch as a whole in which the accumulation of ideas has happened at a great rate, incorporating the thinking of our elders, our own thoughts and now those of the younger generation. The first half of the century has shown us that, although the elites have managed to achieve remarkable refinements to qualitative problems, these customs have not been disseminated more widely (the broadly recognised marks of a civilisation), accompanying the equally extraordinary development of solutions to quantitative problems. We must now quantify quality, which means - and this is no play on words - qualifying quantity.

I hope that no-one will think I am suggesting that we attempt to reach these goals by means of those convenient demagogical systems that entail the complete negation of civil progress. We must muster all our forces to enable architecture to become part of the language of everyone who aspires to free expression - not as a soliloquy, but as a friendly conversation with one's equals. Planning, although necessary for a rational vision, has too often put a straitjacket around the natural development of ideas, because the plans involve making extrapolations about things that do not actually come true for the simple reason that the future isn't a linear extension of the present, but rather another present for which do not yet possess the data and which we cannot tie down if it is to unfold freely from the dialectical succession of events.

We need to come up with urban planning which, while being developed along clear lines, does not attempt to determine the forms of future but will allow for changing relations between the multiple factors of existence.

The abstract problem of categories would now take on tangible energy if it were considered in the light of the empirical relationships between the categories themselves, because the different relationships between apparently similar elements substantially alter their substance: it is here that we find the practical limit of the Charte d'Athènes.

This is the most important consideration when thought is being translated into action.

These principles are beginning to come to the fore in our consciousness, now that utopian plans and technocratic plans, both illusory, have failed to come to fruition. In urban planning (as in industrial design, whose role is to regulate the relationship between quality and quantity for production in the building industry), we need to concentrate on the study of elements which are flexible and adaptable rather than attempting to crystallise a fixed typology unsuited to meeting the demands of potential and unforeseen destinies.

We will have acquitted ourselves well in administering the heritage of the masters and enriching the meaning of their message if we manage to adhere ever more closely to reality in our architectural culture, if we explore more thoroughly both a sense of tradition and a sense of the future, if we clarify, in particular, the sights of the present for the greater benefit of our contemporaries.

Some of this has already been achieved, but we have much more to do. I do not wish to provide a final analysis; life involves continual change and therefore does not allow this.

After the time he spent in Switzerland, London, Tucuman and the USA, Rogers began teaching at the Politecnico di Milano. This coincided with the years during which faculties of architecture were becoming centres of student revolt. He gathered together the most promising students, discussed and disagreed with them and even invited some to collaborate with him at *Casabella*. It wasn't until 1962, however, that he was finally made a full professor. Shortly after obtaining the chair in the faculty of Milan, Rogers suffered the first crisis of an illness that would seriously affect his voice and eventually lead to his death seven years later. Belgioioso recalls that 'he [Rogers] felt that he was suffering from a cruel fate that was depriving him of the means through which he was able to express the power of his thought and intellect, just when, after a long fight against the opposition of the academic authorities, he had finally been granted a full professorship.'

The excerpts below are from *Gli elementi del fenomeno architettonico* [The Elements of the Architectural Phenomenon], the only complete book written by Rogers (as the other two are collections of articles he wrote for other publications), which aimed to introduce architecture students to the problems of the profession. In an attempt to move away from the Beaux-Arts understanding of architectural composition, based on the theory of architectural orders, Rogers approaches the subject from a phenomenological rather than stylistic perspective. In this book, he illustrates the fundamental aspects – the elements – that make up the architectural phenomenon, as the modern movement has come to understand it, and the skills and qualities that need to be acquired during one's training in order to be able to analyse these aspects and bring them together into a coherent architectural whole.

The manuscript was originally published in 1961 by Laterza in the series 'Biblioteca di cultura moderna'. But Rogers's doubts, his rethinking of everything from first principles, induced him to withdraw the volume from the market immediately after publication, and it was pulped. Lodovico Belgioioso suggested that the reasons behind this drastic decision might have had to do with the fact that Rogers had been roundly rejected when he was examined for a full professorship at the Politecnico di Milano, something which he attributed to this little book, a draft of which he had sent to the examining commission. Thanks to the architectural historian Cesare de Seta, who rediscovered the manuscript over a decade after Rogers's death, the book was reissued by the Naples publisher Guida Editori in 1981 and subsequently in 2006 by Marinotti Edizioni in Milan. A collection of short essays, the book is organised into four sections:

THE ELEMENTS OF ARCHITECTURE

The Elements of the Architectural Phenomenon, Society as an Element of the Architectural Phenomenon, The Element of Tradition, and The New Meaning of Tradition, bookended by a short introduction and concluding remarks. The following selection, which is by no means exhaustive, is intended to give a flavour of the way in which Rogers approached his students and his task as an educator and a critic. As he writes in the introduction to this manuscript, for him this task was less about 'imparting rules and laying down tracks' than about 'opening up vast horizons' and allowing his students to advance towards them through their own efforts.

Bad Criticism

Criticism is essential to the architectural phenomenon, as are invention and figuration, and a school that teaches only according to figurative criteria, leaving aside critical criteria, is just as distorting as one that takes the opposite approach.

Frank Lloyd Wright's quip to Sigfried Giedion, 'we both work on history, but you write it and I make it', is debatable because it aims at *analysis* of an inseparable reality that presents itself as a synthesis, and can be examined from two distinct viewpoints, but only if we remember that they are inextricably linked.

Even worse than the schools described above, however, is one that is limited to practical instruction, and does not engage in serious thought or stimulate or refine sensibilities.

The elements of the architectural phenomenon that architecture schools are tasked with clarifying and passing on, have to contain – as an almost quintessential duty – the Vitruvian trilogy '*firmitas, utilitas, venustas*' [enduring strength, utility, beauty] and to continuously relate these values to one another, which must be understood, critically, in terms of their overarching function, leaving open all their quantitative and qualitative potential.

This kind of criticism really enhances this potential, because it stimulates continuing dialectical debate between reason and sensibility, reality and imagination, and inserts technique amongst these, with the deliberate intention of realising a tangible phenomenon.

Disegno and Design

In conclusion, the meaning of *disegno* (and therefore its resulting pedagogical and practical interpretation) should be understood as being more than the descriptive representation of an object by way of symbols, reflecting its ancient semantic value summed up by the English term 'design' (as opposed to 'drawing'), which contains the concepts of thought, concrete intention and projection of an object.

This term applies to the observation and representation of an existing architectural object, and to the specification of a work of architecture to be built, because in the first case one is retracing the trajectory followed by that object to become what it is, and in the second case one is embarking on the process involving the transmutation of the symbol into a real object.

To get back to my starting point, which was the ideal programme for an architectural school: in the first year of a course in Elements of Architecture the empirical observation of historical examples should prevail over theory, allowing students to draw general conclusions; in the second year. Theory can illuminate these experiences, and, without drawing any didactic conclusion, it should lead, in the experiencing of architecture (whether ancient or modern), to an awareness of the *coerenza* (coherence) of a method which has concentrated elements of the architectural phenomenon to produce a coherent style: something to aim at rather than a predetermined aim.

At the end of the second year, once the character and aptitude of the students are known, it becomes possible to encourage those who are sufficiently gifted to get to grips with the problems of composition, which, though they are more complex, will already have become evident through the observation of architectural elements.

Also, the heterogeneous classes of young people arriving from different types of high school will have become more homogeneous (without repressing individual qualities, but rather by drawing these out) thanks to the habitual practice of observing concrete humanism.

Invention and Memory

Let us now take a closer look at the connection that can always be found between the creation of new phenomena and the observation of existing ones (invention and drawing from reality): an artist's interpretation of history has an impact on his interpretation of the period in which he is living and, in turn, is manifested in art. Whether they are moving in time or in space, artists find themselves at the centre of a system of influences: the past is inflected with the whole range of the artist's spirit, and the present cannot help but be affected too. To a smaller and more directly observable extent, the influence of travel is always visible, both in those who make journeys and in those who are visited. We would not be able to understand Palladio without his studies on ancient Roman culture, or without appreciating the direct influences of the places (and people) he came across.

So the element of memory is intrinsic to artistic activity, both for the subject and for the object.

The master of the use of memory is Marcel Proust (*Le Temps retrouvé*): 'was not the re-creation by the memory of the impressions which had then to be deepened, illumined, transformed into equivalents of understanding, was not this process one of the conditions, almost the very essence of the work of art as I had just now ... conceived it?'

The creative act is influenced by two actions of memory, or more precisely by the dialectical relationship between two opposing forces. The first action is addressed to the past, drawing conscious or unconscious nourishment from experiences that have already happened to create new ones. It is the sense of ancestral memories (leaving aside psychoanalytic argument), of preserving, of rethinking; the reworking through which things that have already happened persist in us, lay down a *tradition*, that is, continue to move forward through our mediation, real in the present and granting the present stability on foundations broader than would have been created by us alone. Memory provides things in space with the dimension of time, of all the time that came before us. But it is the time of those who preceded us and to a large extent it is the time of the dead, uniting to urge us to be alive, just as they were in their own eras.

The Latin words *moneo* and *memini*, to admonish and to remind, have the same semantic root, traceable in the word *monument* and the symbolic idea it conveys. Monument, according to modern understanding (and already, to some extent for Palladio), is not just the house of God and the Prince, but above all the house of man and any other constructed organism that combines utility and beauty and satisfies the needs of a particular society.

Here is the other action of memory, not the one that moves from us towards things, but that which moves from things to us and beyond us.

An artist is not an artist if he does not have the memory of the experience of others and if he does not add to it the two meanings elaborated in contemplation and activity.

History as Utility

I hope I will not once again be accused of being paradoxical if I say that history is a succession of interpretations of an idea presumed to be true, which becomes true as the result of trust placed in it by men through the development of a system that is coherent in itself, which will be modified over time and will be negated by new systems that are, in their turn, coherently institutionalised.

The important thing is robust belief; so the '*credo quia absurdum*' [I believe because it is absurd] of St Paul takes on the quality of truth whether one reads it in the manner of the apostle who assigned the concept of the absurd a value that mystically negated itself in supernatural revelation, or one sees things as absurd because of a desire restrict oneself to logical verification.

What is important is that an idea has been useful for the evolution of humanity, and that people have remained faithful to certain existential principles until they no longer have any bearing.
It is up to us to establish the historical relevance of these principles, so that these inform our choices in a positive or negative relationship with historical reality, according to our ideological leanings.

It is also true for architecture that choice and taste become style only if they are able to establish themselves in a coherent system.
Today, to approach the problem of the elements of the architectural phenomenon, it is essential to believe that they are all available to us. But it is also necessary to harness their potential energy for an objective that can organically contain it.

It seems worth stating that the fundamental quality of a free style is its ability to stand out from arbitrary modes of expression, because they are inconsequential and superficial, while a free style is consequential, right down to the deepest roots that nourish its eventual form and provide its true justification.

The notion of history thus becomes a notion of continuously changing frameworks that are contradictory (that have, in other words, come about freely) but are nevertheless consistent with and organised within the phenomena.

This way of looking at human events implies that the study of a monument of any epoch (of which it is the physical representation), revealing it, penetrating it, makes us participate in its life to the point of identifying with it and making it part of our experience, thus altering it.

Far from our merely undertaking a passive academic observation of its outward appearance, it will help us to develop a new understanding of our responsibilities, as well as the stimulus to fulfil them.

Thus a cycle is established between knowing and creating, a process that characterises the life of the individual and is analogous to the process of history.

Above all, he who is setting forth, starting out on the *gradus ad Parnassum* [the steps to Parnassus], has to adopt a method that will allow him to find his own way so as to reach the destination as successfully as possible. He has to become aware of what is happening inside him, and if he is sure that his doubts are part of the psychological make-up of every man, and in particular of every artist, he will accept these doubts as an intrinsic condition of his own nature that allow him to create concrete forms. The young man will learn not to be frightened by his own doubts and not to assume moralistic positions as he stops struggling with them, and, as a result, he will recognise that his struggle - both with himself and with others - is characteristic of anyone who has affirmed himself and completed worthwhile works: the lives of his elders prove this, even the most outstanding of whom have gone through similar trials.

Drawing from Life

Drawing from life helps one to get to know objective reality. Naturally the aim of this operation - reaching an understanding of existing works of architecture - will not be evident to the student, but we cannot expect to teach this solely by means of more or less abstract explanations. Rather it is by coming to grips with the challenges of this operation that, little by little, its purpose becomes clear.

This act of taking ownership implies an attitude that is open to feelings and ideas, as well as a technical skill that can be learned more effectively through practical exercise. Those who are able to draw well can more accurately convey, to themselves and others, their own inner reality, expressed in the image.

Cennino Cennini (*Libro dell'Arte* in *Prosa dell'Arte del '400*, Florence) writes: 'and this is an occupation known as painting, which calls for imagination, and manual skill, so as to discover things unseen, hidden in the shadows of natural objects, and to give them form, presenting to plain sight what does not actually exist.'

Of course what applies to the other plastic arts also applies to architecture.

But due to the fact that the act of describing is a way of revealing something that comes from within, it is necessary for each of us to find the means most appropriate to our nature, or more particularly to our own personal development. When it comes to drawing, and the forms that one captures through drawing, one has to leave to one side the academic approach that promises to magically unravel any mystery.

And we can extend this to what Kandinsky writes, as well: 'For the creative artist who wishes to, and indeed should express his inner world, even successful imitation of natural phenomena cannot be an end in itself.'

The study of the monuments of any era, including those of our own, should not lead to their imitation; similarly the study of nature or of traditional systems serves not as a model, but as a stimulus: we have to find our own way.

Obviously the scientific discoveries of someone like Luca Pacioli and of humanistic perspectival drawing, or those of [Gaspard] Monge for descriptive geometry, represent indispensable knowledge for those who use drawing as a means of representation, but it will suffice to look back to the studies of Alois Riegl (*Late Roman Art Industry*), or, more particularly, those of Erwin Panofsky (*Perspective as Symbolic Form*), to be persuaded that the depiction of space and that of the objects arranged in it have been communicated in a variety of ways, invariably legitimately and with aesthetic validity. Today, many new and original avenues remain open for intelligent exploration allowing one to grasp and convey artistically the essence of reality.

Just consider the new meaning taken on by perspectival drawing in the sketches of [Erich] Mendelsohn or [Antonio] Sant'Elia, or the programmatic coherence with which, on the other hand, early rationalism excludes perspective and turns to isometric drawing as an 'objective' way of representing architecture, avoiding individual vantage points - useless in a composition that excluded the static axes of symmetry.

After all, there is a close kinship between the new modes of representation developed by modern architecture and those developed by contemporary figurative art: a kinship that becomes even more evident - extraordinarily close - in the purist drawings of Le Corbusier, those of [Amédée] Ozenfant and the architectural drawings of L'Esprit Nouveau; and in the drawings and paintings of De Stijl and the constructive graphics of [Theo] van Doesburg, [J.J.P.] Oud, [Gerrit] Rietveld and [Piet] Mondrian himself.

Just as in the modern movement there are new ways of representing space and the object, so there are new modes of communicating an architectural object to its builders both in its constituent parts, and as a whole, that harmonise with our cultural situation and with technical advances.

In the case of executive drawing, the idea is to offer a clear key for the interpretation of practical symbols, making it possible to access objectively the cultural world to which they aspire or from which they are derived.

I refute the idea that a modern individual, aware of the wider horizons opened up by art criticism in the evaluation of space, cannot freely interpret the relationship between architectural objects as well as their individual relationships with space.

The idea is to be as clear as those who rely on classical schemas, which are always valid, just as it is valid - within reasonable limits - to deploy Euclidean geometry, if we have no need to shift the representation into the ambit of the non-Euclidean geometries that were developed from the 1800s.

The Example of [Gropius and] Le Corbusier
Modern works, if they are treated as templates, contradict their reason for being, and this lies at the core of the architectural phenomenon, which is always open to a process of synthesising new forms, whether unforeseen or foreseeable. The critique suggested by Gropius is circumscribed by contemporary attitudes and this has an effect on the information we can draw from our experience of the whole history of western civilisation (as well as of those, more comprehensively, that are very different, such as oriental civilisations - though western culture is not always cognisant of these).

According to Gropius, if knowledge of history is left to one side at the beginning of an architect's training will afford a broader and more robust foundation.

In the theoretical-practical programme for architectural students, he states that: 'history studies should be started in the third year rather than in the first, to avoid *intimidation* and *imitation*'.

Here we can clearly see the sign of a complex with regard to history, which can also be linked back to the ancient myth of Oedipus who blinds himself after having killed his father in the wake of an impossible love for his own mother. The true irony of this approach is that it is advanced by people like Gropius (and other masters), who, despite knowing history very well, were not intimidated by it and did not feel compelled to imitate, but rather found that it contributed substantially to their progressive ideas.

So why deprive young people of an element necessary to their training?

I would like to quote from Gropius again, with a statement in which he contradicts himself, so as to be able to develop and to logically incorporate the dynamic principle of his methodology. The quote above is from 1939, while the one below, from 1934, seems to embrace much wider perspectives, though it does not explicitly talk about the study of history: he says he is convinced that 'our conception of a new architecture is not in any way at odds with traditional architecture since respect for tradition does not imply passive acceptance of obsolete aesthetic forms, but rather - and this has always been the case - involves an effort to capture their essential qualities, in other words, to grasp that which lies behind technique and finds expression through it.'

Here is the central question: studying history in order to identify what is essential. This is what should be taught from the outset, not least through the analysis and representation of monuments. The ability to engage with the elements of architecture will not be compromised, but will in fact be enriched by the inner dialogue that takes place in all of us between our inventions and what has already been invented.

No artist of our time, I believe, has made this exchange between himself and the experiences of history more vital than has Le Corbusier. Those who visit the priory of La Tourette immediately have a sense of this all-pervading vitality; it feels like entering an ancient monument because it gives the impression of somewhere that we have always known and that we have always belonged to - so profound is our relationship with the phenomenon that we are completely absorbed by it.

If we then examine the forms, we see that they are all new and invented: both those belonging to the typology of this organism so inflected by tradition, and those that could be compared to other forms in the works of Le Corbusier himself.

I have chosen this example because, given the typology of this organism, the *a priori* constraints might have seemed inescapable, and because, although he respects them, Le Corbusier has been able to create one of his most autonomous works: he has managed 'to capture their essential qualities'.

This editorial introduces an issue of *Casabella* featuring the work of several students from the Faculty of Architecture at the Politecnico di Milano. The title, an oxymoron often repeated by Rogers to his own students, and which echoes Edoardo Persico's reference to 'substance of things hoped for' in his book *Profezia dell'architettura* (*Prophecy of Architecture*), published in 1935, is an invitation to 'project the present into a possible future'. This, for Rogers, was the central civic responsibility of the architect and therefore fundamental to academic research. Luciano Patetta, a student of Rogers on his course 'Stylistic and constructive characteristics of monuments' at the Politecnico, recalls the conceptual difficulty presented by Rogers's lectures, which were 'more like those of a philosopher than of an architect or historian'. 'As a student', said Patetta in a speech in 2009, 'I was naturally in a hurry to learn how to be an architect, and I expected lessons that were immediately directly applicable. Rogers, on the other hand, involved us in a series of dialectical problems that, in his words, had to "evaluate the whole complexity of the phenomenological evolution of architecture ..." His definitions of "continuità" were new and difficult, and so were his reflections warning us against the dangers of modernist formalism and passive imitation. Even more difficult was his concept of a "utopia of reality", which was to be understood as the opposite of "abstract and extravagant utopianism".'

THE UTOPIA OF REALITY

PUBLISHED IN *EDITORIALI DELL'ARCHITETTURA* (TURIN: EINAUDI, 1968)

CASABELLA CONTINUITÀ NO. 259, JANUARY 1962

Utopia is not always a 'futile image without foundation', nor is it 'a chimera, a castle in the air, etc.' as indicated by the definitions found in dictionaries. It can be teleologically charged in its projection of the present into a possible future in spite of the fact that its forms are not yet achievable, and there being many obstacles to the expression of the ideas that underpin them as well as the actions needed to realise them.

The task at hand is to reframe the concept of utopia: to think concretely about a better society (certainly not just a world of the honest, the beautiful and the good, but a world constructed with real means for real ends). After all, progress has never happened without a drive to reach for higher goals, however distant they may be.

Nor is there a better place than school to approach such topics: here those who are not labouring under the weight of contingencies can more broadmindedly address those problems which, while they are neither abstract not extravagant, appear to have no immediate solution: it is enough to be able to penetrate reality, to extrapolate its meaning, to identify its immanent relationships so as to bring them alive and insert them into the evolutionary cycle in such a way that they can mature and engender further evolutionary change. The Academy, for example, which for Plato was the crucible of research whose validity increased in inverse relation to how far it concerned itself with immediate interests and the commonplace, narrowed its scope over time, coming to symbolise an attitude disconnected from life in the broadest sense of the word - characterised by passivity, rhetoric and the most pernicious form of alienation. Schools themselves, of art and architecture, have often become 'academic' in the negative sense of the term. The École des Beaux-Arts is responsible for forging the pre-eminent model of a static approach to learning and to existence that has pervaded practice leading to the adoption and reiteration of abstract schemas.

Van de Velde was one of the first to attempt to pre-empt these gathering threats; it was he who triggered the crisis that led to a complete rupture between Gropius's Bauhaus and the modern movement.

Undeniably the value of such revolutions, is that while being fuelled by reality, they are energised by a strong utopian impulse; we need only examine the Plan Voisin of Le Corbusier (and, of course, Frank Lloyd Wright's Broadacre City) to become aware of the profound discrepancy between the visions of artists and the *ambiente,* the built environment, shaped by the majority of their contemporaries, and to understand that those phenomena have emerged precisely as a reaction to the 'reality' of the conformists, the mediocre and the faint of heart.

We could also claim that some of the prophecies are merely hallucinations, but if we trace those phenomena back to the valid intentions from which they spring, we have to recognise that they correspond, at this point, to inalienable motives of architectural culture, although that culture - precisely because it is living - will need to reassess the solutions that are proposed and match them with new contents.

Some people, constrained, above all, by the exigencies of professional practice or unaware of current research, have imagined that the constructive and creative sense of culture could and should be replaced by practicalism (which is as limited a description of the entire architectural phenomenon, a muscles being taken as expressing someone's whole being).

Who would deny that techniques are required for the realisation of the phenomenon? On the other hand, who would claim - without implicitly revealing their own vapidity - that techniques are enough in themselves to allow the insertion of the phenomenon into the whole of history and to grant it vitality? There is no alternative to or contradiction between the technical and the theoretical activities of architecture as both must be present in the creation of the architectural phenomenon. Thoroughgoing research must be granted its rightful place, not least in order to rebalance the curriculum in schools of architecture, because in these eventful times, it is necessary to reconsider all human knowledge: to deepen our understanding of reality and to imagine the possibility of crossing its perceived boundaries. It is clear that while traditional academic schools erred on the side of abstraction, allowing only a partial formalistic understanding of the architectural phenomenon, schools dealing mainly with practice are equally lacking, because they are applying the template of a design office and fail to prepare students for other goals, or to make a proper contribution to current architectural training.

If we are not afraid of words and we want to get beyond mere nominalism, which is now somewhat discredited, we may nurse the hope that the school will become an academy, as it should be, rather than a place cut off from life where practices that are already sanctioned (and how miserable those sanctions can be!) are sanctified or at best simply perpetuated. Instead, it should offer a service to the whole of society, acting as a laboratory for creating culture.

There are some risks involved if one openly confronts the problems of life, in that evolution involves continuous struggle. Given how necessary it is to produce tools to respond to the challenges of the world rather than simply adapting to them, which might seem more certain, we will be obliged not just to accept but also to encourage criticism and imagination as the mainstays of architectural investigation.

The project by several students from the School of Architecture of Milan, is covered unusually comprehensively in this issue with fine drawings that clearly evidence courage in their preparation, development and execution.

It matters little if current legislation (the Aldisio Act, the Romita Act, the Fanfani Act, the Building Code, etc.) contains numerous impediments for the realisation of this project. It is still an intelligent and committed work (within its academic limits) and therein lies its value; it has to be assessed within those limits, and it is not hard to find flaws in it, the most obvious of which is immaturity, due to the fact - *felix culpa* - that it has been put together by young people. Having accepted that this is a brilliant academic exercise, we can of course delve into the thesis advanced by the students and make critical methodological observations (which is, of course, the job of pedagogy); we might observe, for example - though this is not the place for a full analysis - that the concentration of problems and structural proposals in a relatively small space partly invalidates the approach on a theoretical level, because full investigation of the principles that have been applied would require a much larger canvas.

What counts, instead, is that the writings and the drawings demonstrate enthusiasm, vitality and commitment; those who have collaborated on this work, both faculty and students, have been made stronger through their involvement; each of them will be able to translate this academic experience, to good advantage, in the challenges they encounter in professional practice.

Even existing regulations could be reframed, because we will find in the utopia expressed in these works new critical points of reference capable of broadening our understanding of reality.

In *Editoriali dell'architettura*, where this interview with artist and critic Gianemilio Simonetti is accompanied by two other texts dedicated to Le Corbusier, Rogers added the following note: 'the figure of Le Corbusier deserves much more space than the little afforded to him here. I will endeavour to repay him a little for the immense gift he gave to me of his work, his friendship and his presence with a publication titled *Le Corbusier Totale* (The Complete Le Corbusier), already committed to by the publisher Einaudi.' Rogers's ambition to write a book on Le Corbusier, previously announced in the series *Architetti del Movimento Moderno* (Architects of the Modern Movement) was, however, never to materialise.

LE CORBUSIER: ROGERS IN CONVERSATION WITH GIANEMILIO SIMONETTI

PUBLISHED IN *EDITORIALI DELL'ARCHITETTURA* (TURIN: EINAUDI, 1968)

MARCATRE NO. 16 18, 1965

What does the death of Le Corbusier represent?

The death of Le Corbusier undoubtedly represents a very great loss for culture. From another standpoint, as a friend, I feel his loss still more keenly, not least because I was planning an encounter with him for the book I have had in mind for some time. Who knows if I will still write it? A critical book that would capture the originality of the artist both in our culture and in terms of creativity. Much information is still lacking for this book, above all information about how Le Corbusier regarded himself. I have tried repeatedly to explore this very particular critical angle but have very seldom managed to stumble upon just the right perspective. Le Corbusier, in fact, is neither a critic nor a self-critic; he is a creator who transforms both life and himself.

What can be said about Le Corbusier and his presence in Italian architecture?

Le Corbusier has neither been abandoned, nor is he an acknowledged presence in architectural pedagogy. His is a vital presence for every student or teacher who thinks conscientiously about the moment in which we live. Neither in Italy nor elsewhere is there an artistic figure comparable to Le Corbusier, and yet everyone, from architects to activists, has absorbed his message, and the best have transformed it as well. As for a taking a position regarding his work in Italian architectural culture, we can respond with two negative reactions that are, at the same time, affirmative. There is no critical awareness of what Le Corbusier is as an architect or as regards the rest of his versatile activity, and yet here in Italy his influence is evident, not so much, fundamentally, in the works of the finest architects, where it is in any case easy to spot, as in the works of the worst ones, where it shows through in the imitative gestures of those who, consciously or not, have borrowed from his formal repertoire. On this subject, I remember a conversation I had with Le Corbusier on a train, when we were returning from Venice. He was praising the work of a young English architect who had a certain reputation at the time; I felt that this fame was undeserved, and I said to him, 'he is just an imitator, while your true disciples are not the ones in whose works your influence is immediately visible, but those who have absorbed it into their own world.' Le Corbusier closed his eyes for a while, and then told me I was right.

Personally, what do you owe the most to Le Corbusier?

What I owe, what all of us architects owe to Le Corbusier, is the ability and courage to approach freely the various themes that concretely present themselves to us.

Which work by Le Corbusier do you feel is of the greatest significance?

For me there is no single masterpiece in the work of this artist; instead there is the dialectical concatenation of works - sadly, at an end - which, now that it can be seen in its entirety, elicits that sense of perfection which makes us experience all his work as a masterpiece.

What do you think about the last work of the master: the hospital in Venice?

The hospital project in Venice offers tangible proof of Le Corbusier's impressive and enduring capacity for invention. It is in fact completely original. Once again his thematic has taken on a new guise, and this time its inherent characteristics have made it the object of intense criticism. For example, the patient cubicles, lit from above with no windows in their sides, have surprised and perplexed everyone. My personal opinion, not because I want to judge *in verba magistri* but because I believe in the cathartic power of genius, is that this world of the patient as envisioned by Le Corbusier has its own inner logic which is so powerful that it leads to a coherent result, whereby the patient himself takes on the role bestowed upon him by the work.

So, are you able to recommend a critical approach or system of interpretation that might be useful for developing an understanding of Le Corbusier's work?

I believe Le Corbusier cannot be understood critically unless we always take into consideration his particular world. He cannot be comprehended if you start with preconceptions, which many critics do, so that by the time they get to Ronchamp they have lost their bearings; in other words, they are unable to appreciate his profound intellectual and creative freedom.

What do you think people mean when they talk, as many do, about Le Corbusier's 'neo-Baroque detour', particularly in connection with Ronchamp?

For me, this is an error typical of nominalism. This story has deep roots in the book by Eugenio d'Ors where he refers to the Baroque as a category. Seen through this lens and by referencing certain characteristics of the historical Baroque (together with others from periods such as the 'Alexandrian'[1] with artistic moments moving in quite another direction), we could say that Ronchamp is Baroque. If, however, we want to understand the true essence of this work, that is, to approach it leaving aside formalistic analysis - which due to the presence of analogous stylistic elements, such as curves and counter-curves, for example, allows us to compare it to historical Baroque - we need to recognise what Le Corbusier himself made clear, namely that Ronchamp is an 'in itself' different from the other 'in themselves' in his artistic journey. In other words, Ronchamp is not Baroque at all, either by reference to the idea or in its documentation, which draw on the language of curves, but spring from a different source from that of the Baroque. Ronchamp is one of the many instances in which Le Corbusier reaffirms his own freedom: he gives it *coerenza* (coherence) and autonomy. It might seem like a paradox, but it is the very autonomy of each element that establishes a methodological continuity in his activity. Every one of his works frees itself phenomenologically from its predecessors to the extent that it presents itself as a completed experience. In other words, it is a total reinvention.

Modern architecture is usually distinguished from previous forms of architecture with reference to extrinsic characteristics, like those, for example deriving from socioeconomic changes in Western society. This leads, in architectural criticism, to particular emphasis being laid on

1 The Hellenistic-Alexandrian period is the one that started developing in Greece after the death of Alexander the Great (323 BC) and ended with the conquest of the Greek world by the Romans, a process well underway by 146 BC. Hellenistic Alexandria originated a distinctive architectural form language that is often referred to as baroque due to its liberal use of ornamentation and its repurposing of structural elements as ornamental elements.

Le Corbusier portrayed by Ernesto Rogers, 1952 © Fondation Le Corbusier

underlying socio-cultural elements. Were these elements central to the work of Le Corbusier?

I would say that Le Corbusier generally rejects that which is. He rejects it in the sense that he knows it is there, but he does not want it to be as it is; a kind of historical refusal: he does not close his eyes, but he does not accept. Neither acceptance nor compromise. This strength to resist acceptance of the status quo has allowed Le Corbusier to unfailingly preserve his inventive, elemental energy, which can be intuited in the drawings and is constructed in concrete visions. His has been a constant search for the strength to resist the commonplace.

Is Le Corbusier an ingenuous urbanist?

I would say that Le Corbusier is always ingenuous. In other words, he is a prodigy, an extroverted talent that gives of itself unstintingly in every direction – urban planning, architecture, painting. In urban planning, ingenuousness – which comes down to putting trust in people – is more evident as the planning reflects a vision of society corresponding to that of urban planning itself. A typical example is Le Corbusier's plan for Algiers. The entire city is imagined in a new way: it provides the opportunity to live in a world designed for that particular place. It could be said that Le Corbusier's ingenuousness is basically a true utopia, a sense of hope in a tomorrow aligned with his ideas, destined to be better. The actions of both Gropius and Le Corbusier have aimed at producing effective improvements to the way people live: for Gropius we refer to his '*Existenzminimum*', for Le Corbusier to his '*Ville Radieuse*'.

What are the differences between them from a political-social viewpoint?

We might say that sometimes Le Corbusier's ingenuousness leads to an incomprehensible absence of historical contact (he dreams while the world continues on its way). Gropius, on the other hand, arm-wrestles with society, deploying a logical, transmissible pedagogical method in order to change the world. Gropius wants to modify reality with his teaching, Le Corbusier according to his concrete actions: his is a conscious detachment from society as it is in order to attempt a step forward. In this sense, and paradoxically, Gropius is more inserted into the experience of life than is Le Corbusier.

In The Method of Le Corbusier and the Form of the Chapel of Ronchamp you refer to a quality in the poetics of Le Corbusier: humour. Tell us something about this.[2]

The attitude of Le Corbusier is one of absolute freedom, his own actions included. Unlike his slavish imitators, he never actually deployed his famous Five Points - or at least not all in the same work - because he understood, and this is worth emphasising, that it is 'things' that really dictate how to act rather than opinions: when he interrogates things, he discovers, on each occasion, a new way of proceeding, and this happens independently of his own principles.

The image of Le Corbusier, intolerant even of his own operative principles, inevitably evokes the figure of Joyce and the thematic structure of Ulysses, which is apparently based on a Homeric parallel, but is reduced, in the end, merely to sharing a name. Can a cultural hypothesis be identified in this?

There must be one: they breathed the same historical air. Le Corbusier accomplished in the figurative arts what Joyce achieved in literature. Certainly, they both freed themselves of the burden of existing notions; in fact, their true greatness lies precisely in getting beyond even the notions they had formulated themselves. Le Corbusier, in spite of this freedom and anti-conformism, is, in any case, the only architect of the twentieth century who attempted to create a framework similar to those of the Renaissance. Here, if we wish, we can identify a contradiction: but one that serves the artist's purpose.

There is an anecdote about Rossini that says much about the modernity of his way of 'doing music'. He was once late in delivering a score, so had to work for many hours each day, and he liked to do this in bed. The story goes that, in his haste he let one page of the score fall to the floor and, rather than getting out of bed and catching a chill, he decided to write

2 Published in *Casabella Continuità* nº 207 (October 1955); in this editorial Rogers recounts the experience of his first visit to Le Corbusier's Chapel of Ronchamp.

another from scratch. Can you tell us something equally revealing about Le Corbusier?

During a session of the 'committee of five' - Gropius, Le Corbusier, [Sven] Markelius, [Lúcio] Costa and the undersigned - in Paris, at the UNESCO headquarters, the position and size of one of the main doors was being discussed. Each of us made some suggestions in response to the drawings in front of them, and each idea was backed up with valid reasoning. Then Le Corbusier spoke up and completely changed the parameters of the discussion. Instead of talking about the position of the door, he said, 'let's change the mode of access by building a small wall in front of it [the doorway] so that the path of those entering has to change.' This apparently banal episode suddenly gave me the sense that while the others had been focusing on the drawing, Le Corbusier had already seen beyond it; and I shuddered, because I understood that this was the stuff of genius.

MAN IN THE MIDDLE
ERNESTO NATHAN ROGERS IN CONTEXT
JOAN OCKMAN

Previous page: Rogers (in the centre) with Alison and Peter Smithson (right) at CIAM 11 in Otterlo, Netherlands, 1949 © Bakema, J.B. Archief / Het Nieuwe Instituut

The destiny of an architect – we should say of an artist – is the destiny of his generation, just as the fate of a flower is that of the field to which the flower belongs.
– Ernesto Rogers, 'An Architect of Almost 30 Years Old', 1938[1]

Ernesto Nathan Rogers viewed his place in history in generational terms, arguably more than any other architect of the twentieth century. Born in 1909 and formed both intellectually and architecturally during the periods of fascism, antifascism, and wartime reconstruction in the 1930s and 1940s, Rogers's career was at its peak during the 'miracle' years of the 1950s. He died in 1969 at the age of 60. His life not only straddles the watershed of World War II but spans exactly two generations by the conventional measure of 30 years. Reading through his extensive body of essays, editorials, lectures and autobiographical reflections, one repeatedly encounters the trope of the generation, understood as a determinant of collective biography. The 'problem of the generations' was rarely absent from his thinking, from a reference in the epigraph above, which appeared in the Milanese newspaper *L'Ambrosiano* a year before the outbreak of war; to his letter to Giulio Einaudi proposing the publication of a collection of his writings that would appear in 1958 as *Esperienza dell'architettura*; to a lecture of six years later titled 'Modern Architecture after the Generation of the Masters'; to his return in the early 1960s to the never-resolved issue of his generation complicity with fascism. In his proposal to Einaudi, written in 1950, Rogers expressed the hope that his book might serve as a 'sincere biography, a confession of our generation of architects, born and raised under the political and cultural conditions of a particularly dramatic period.'[2] Several months later, not long after the suicide of the poet and antifascist Cesare Pavese, he recorded in an unpublished two-page note that in Pavese's death his generation had discovered a collective symbol: 'We are the generation between two wars, always between two wars...'[3]

What was it that so compelled Rogers to think of himself in generational terms, and what significance did this predisposition have for

1 Ernesto N. Rogers, 'Un architetto di quasi trent'anni', *L'Ambrosiano* nº 172 (22 July 1938); reprinted in Ernesto N. Rogers, *Esperienza dell'architettura* (Turin: Einaudi, 1958), 57. All subsequent citations are from this 1958 edition unless otherwise noted. All translations in this essay are my own unless otherwise noted.

2 Letter from Ernesto Rogers to Giulio Einaudi, 11 June 1950; published in Ernesto Nathan Rogers, *Esperienza dell'architettura*, ed. Luca Molinari (Milan: Skira, 1997): 305. This is a republication of the original edition with added critical material and a valuable afterword by Molinari, 'Alcune note sull'esperienza di Ernesto Nathan Rogers': 304–327.

3 Reproduced in *Molinari*, 'Alcune note': 307.

his life and work? The present essay begins by considering the meaning of *generation* in broad terms and then, more narrowly, in relation to the history of twentieth-century Italy. It then addresses the idea of a *middle generation*, an identity that Rogers himself embraced explicitly and that was applied to him by others. Finally, it explores the question of *experience*, reading Rogers's key concept of context (*preesistenze ambientali*) in both generational (temporal) and environmental (spatial) terms. Together these concepts – along with a handful of others, among them *continuity, evolution, coherence* – form an intellectual and moral constellation within which Rogers's thinking revolved and evolved over the course of his career, giving his activities as an architect, writer, editor, citizen and historical witness a rare level of, indeed, *coerenza*.

Generational history

Viewed as a linear flow of time, history is like a loaf of bread that can be cut at any point. Yet the location of the cut is not a neutral matter. The German language distinguishes between *Historie* and *Geschichte*, between history, in the former case, as a simple chronicle of facts and, in the latter, as a narration of those facts, thereby acknowledging, as English and the Latin languages do not, that history-writing involves the telling of a story, an act of construction. Precisely as such, it is always based on value judgments and subjective decisions, and the apparently innocent concepts we use to slice time into discrete chunks of temporality – centuries, decades, epochs, generations – beg critical examination.

How, then, does the generation differ from other temporal yardsticks? The century, in comparison, is not just a longer unit of time but ostensibly a more objective one: a hundred years. Ever since the Enlightenment, however, it has also been bound up with the telos of an advancing modernity – the 'long nineteenth century,' the 'American Century'. The epoch, era, or age, on the other hand, is nonspecific in length. It places the accent on unique and transformative events such as scientific breakthroughs and wars, or world-historical actors such as kings and inventors. It often harbours a certain grandeur – the 'Age of Napoleon'. In distinction to these temporal constructs, the generation is a biological metaphor. Although a calendrical fiction (inasmuch as individuals are born into time continuously), it personifies periods of history in terms of a life cycle of infancy, maturity and old age. Rather than placing an emphasis on civilisation's advance or on singular events, it privileges a pattern of repetition.[4]

Early twentieth-century Italy showed a particular affinity for thinking in terms of generations. The rhetoric of both Italian fascism and Italian futurism is suffused with generation-talk. Benito Mussolini's populist appeals were addressed directly to the nation's young people, while the firebrand poet and impresario Filippo Tommaso Marinetti enjoined his fellow avant-gardists to discard all those who were more than 40 years old 'like useless manuscripts'.[5] In the years leading up to World War I, fascism and futurism shared a militant sympathy not only with the rising generation but also with each other. Marinetti would remain committed to the *Duce* for most of his life. His early ally Giovanni Papini, an iconoclastic writer and right-wing thinker, likewise longed for broad-scale cultural and political renewal. Founder of the Florentine review *Lacerba* together with Ardengo Soffici in 1913, Papini welcomed the arrival of World War I as a catalyst for a national resurgence, declaring, 'We – young and free – have proclaimed the necessity of war.'[6] He also viewed his editorial activity as a generational project, writing in his autobiography:

Every time a generation presents itself on the terrace of life it seems that the world's symphony is going to have to strike up a new tempo. Dreams, hopes, plans of attack, the ecstasy of discoveries, the scaling of heights, challenges, fits of arrogance – and a journal.[7]

The opponents of fascism were also inclined to adopt a generational perspective. After the war, the historian Adolfo Omodeo was among those who saw themselves engaged in a dialectical and existential

4 On the relationship between modernity and historical periodisation, see Susan Sontag, *Tradities van het nieuwe, of: Moeten wij modern zijn?* (Amsterdam: Uitgeverij Bert Bakker, 1990), a Dutch translation of her 1989 Huizinga Lecture delivered in Leiden, 'Traditions of the New, or: Must We Be Modern?' Sontag summarises her definition of the generation as follows: 'The concept of the generation is used to describe a group of people who have an essential experience, orientation, world vision, and aspiration in common' (39; my translation). I am grateful to Max Risselada for drawing my attention to this lecture, unavailable in the original English.

5 F. T. Marinetti, 'The Founding and Manifesto of Futurism' (1909), trans. in Lawrence Rainey, Christine Poggi, and Laura Wittman, eds., *Futurism: An Anthology* (New Haven: Yale University Press, 2009): 53.

6 *Lacerba* (15 May 1915).

7 Giovanni Papini, *Un uomo finito* (Florence: Libreria della Voce, 1913): 85; cited in Robert Wohl, *The Generation of 1914* (Cambridge, Mass.: Harvard University Press, 1979): 161. Wohl's book focuses on French, German, English, Spanish and Italian society between the two world wars and provides a valuable intellectual history and cross-cultural account of the concept of the generation.

BBPR in the 1930s. From left Enrico Peressutti, Lodovico Belgiojoso, unknown, Gianluigi Banfi and Ernesto Rogers © Fondo Peressutti / IUAV Archivio Progetti

struggle with their bellicose countrymen. He intended his *Momenti della vita di guerra* (Moments in the Life of War), published in instalments between 1929 and 1933, to serve as a 'moral history', one that would absolve members of his generation from blanket associations with irredentism and irrationalism.[8] Antonio Gramsci too found the obsession with generations hard to avoid, although as a Marxist he viewed social conflict and historical change through the lens of class struggle, not biology; in his view, a generation was a superficial, or simply inevitable, temporal demarcation. Imprisoned by the regime in 1926, he spurned Mussolini's vitalist rhetoric; nor did he have much use for the moralism of academics like Omodeo. At the same time, he could not altogether deny the existence of generational dynamics: the older generation was always responsible for educating and passing power to the younger one, while the young, as he recognised, tended to be in a state of 'permanent rebellion' against their elders, all the more so in times of social and political tension.[9]

The generational habit of thought persisted in Italy through the 1930s and well beyond World War II, and it would become ingrained in subsequent interpretations of fascism. Yet by the 1960s, in an essay titled 'Il fascismo e il problema delle generazioni' (Fascism and the Problem of the Generations, 1964), the sociologist Renato Treves suggested that the concept had reached a point of exhaustion. Already in the late 1950s, he noted, commentators were complaining about its reflexive use and abuse.[10] In an overview of the 'problem', he identified three general positions. The first, harking back to nineteenth-century positivism and the ideas of Auguste Comte, treated the generation more or less like the century or decade, basically as a quantity of time, although instead of dividing history into multiples of one hundred or ten, it calibrated it in spans of fifteen or 30 years. A more modern approach was that of Karl Mannheim. In a classic essay originally published in 1927–28, 'The Problem of Generations', the German sociologist strove to give the generation an objective and non-ideological connotation, characterising it simply as a common location in society or a shared

8 Wohl, *Generation of 1914*: 181.

9 Antonio Gramsci, 'La questione dei giovani', *Quaderni del Carcere* I (1948): para 127; see also Wohl, *Generation of 1914*: 191–202.

10 See Renato Treves, 'Il Fascismo e il problema delle generazioni', *Quaderni di sociologia* (April–June 1964): 119–47. In 1959–60, over the course of seven issues, the review *Il Paradosso* had conducted an inquiry into the 'generazione degli anni difficili', and some of the older protagonists, including Norberto Bobbio and Ugo La Malfa, had expressed dissatisfaction with the term.

style of life.[11] The third position, however – and the one most typical of Italian usage – rested on a belief in the binding force of shared life experiences. Prominently expounded by Ortega y Gasset in a series of lectures presented in Madrid in 1933, the Spanish philosopher argued that 'the method of the generations' not only allowed the historian to see life 'from within itself, as it actually is', but also to see it as part of a genetically continuous present. 'Each human generation carries within itself all the previous generations', Ortega stated, continuing:

[O]ne must recognise that the past is here among us, that we are its summing up, that our present is made out of the material of that past, which past is therefore the moment at hand, the heart, the hidden core, of the present.[12]

This view of history was the one that infused and informed the thought of Ernesto Rogers.

Generation, continued

Ironically (or not), Treves's postmortem for the concept of generation in relation to the *anni difficili* – the years of fascism – coincided with a new moment of generational passage. Italians who were born after 1945 and came to maturity in the 1960s had not had the traumatic experience of their parents. Growing up in the heyday of the economic miracle, they had not suffered under Mussolini's persecutions or mourned over Gramsci's ashes. Yet the 'children of Marx and Coca-Cola' – as Jean-Luc Godard famously described the new generation in France, although he might just as well have been speaking of Italy – shared different bonds of solidarity. The young people who joined strikes in the factories of the north, shut down universities and fought on the barricades of 1968 forged another kind of collective identity.

We shall briefly return to the sixties generation, at the end of this essay. However, our subject here is Rogers, and let us now concern ourselves more directly with him. Not only was his consciousness fundamentally shaped by the experience of fascism in the 1930s and World War II, but his burning need to explain and expiate his guilt

11 Karl Mannheim, *Essays on the Sociology of Knowledge*, ed. and trans. Paul Kecskemeti (London: Routledge and Kegan Paul, 1952): 276–322.

12 José Ortega y Gasset, *Man and Crisis* (New York: w. w. Norton, 1958): 45–46, 53. The content of this book, including chapters titled 'The Idea of the Generation', 'The Method of the Generations in History', and 'Change and Crisis', was originally presented by the author in a series of lectures in Madrid in 1933–34. The book first appeared in Italian in 1946.

for participating in the events of those years led to a profound and protracted reflection on history and his generation's place in it. His essay 'Catharsis', published in *Costruzioni Casabella* in 1946, coincided with the completion of the Monument to the Dead in German Concentration Camps by his architecture firm, BBPR. Founded by Rogers and three of his fellow students upon their graduation from Milan's Politecnico in 1932, BBPR took its name from the initials of its four principals, Gianluigi Banfi, Lodovico Barbiano di Belgiojoso, Enrico Peressutti, and Rogers. One of the partners, Banfi, perished in a concentration camp at Mauthausen-Gusen in 1945. Another, Belgiojoso, was lucky to return from the same camp. Rogers himself, of Jewish descent on his mother's side, survived by taking refuge in Switzerland. The monument to the war dead, principally designed by Peressutti, was located on the primary axis of one of Milan's two main cemeteries. A diminutive steel cage elevated on a cruciform stone base, it was a statement of abstract, lyrical minimalism.

In 'Catharsis', Rogers painfully acknowledged that most Italian modern architects in the 1930s, even those who were not out-and-out adherents of the regime, had been collaborators by virtue of the role they had played in fascist culture – building, writing and contributing to its official exhibitions. Even if their intentions were idealistic, they had bought into a fatal syllogism: fascism was a revolution, modern art and architecture were revolutionary, therefore modern architecture might be folded into fascism's program.[13] Among the panels displayed on BBPR's wall-long installation at the VI Triennale in Milan in 1933 was one that read, *cittadini funzionali: architettura funzionale*, functional citizens: functional architecture.

In Rogers's view, the two most exemplary and most tragic architects of the period were Giuseppe Terragni (1904–43) and Giuseppe Pagano (1896–1945). In the early 1930s both had optimistically embraced the regime, hailing Mussolini's promise to renew Italian society and culture. Terragni, who went off to the Russian front in 1941 to serve as an artillery captain, had a nervous breakdown at Stalingrad and was institutionalised upon his return home. He would succumb in 1943 to the effects of his experience, dying, possibly by suicide, without undergoing any apparent change of heart. Pagano, for his part, would become increasingly disillusioned with the state's corrupt and reactionary politics. While staunchly defending modern architecture against the academic bombast of Mussolini's official architect Marcello Piacentini

13 'Catarsi', *Costruzioni Casabella* nos. 195–198 (December 1946); reprinted in *Esperienza dell'architettura*: 97.

'Sala della coerenza' (Room of Coherence), Studio BBPR, Gianluigi Banfi, Lodovico Belgiojoso, Enrico Peressutti, Ernesto Rogers, VI Triennale, Milan, 1936 © Triennale Milano – Archivi

– both in the pages of *Casabella*, which he co-directed with Edoardo Persico starting in 1933, and in his own architecture – he nonetheless remained a loyal party member through the 1930s. Yet after a stint in the army in Albania in 1941, he returned the following year as an outspoken adversary of the regime. His 'Presupposti per un programma di politica edilizia' (Presuppositions for a Program of Building Politics), published in *Casabella* in June 1943, was an impassioned statement defending democratic values and artistic integrity. Coming late to antifascism, his conversion was all the more decisive. After courageously throwing in his lot with the Resistance, he too ended up in prison, then paid the ultimate price at Mauthausen. Meanwhile, Rogers, five years younger than Terragni and a dozen years younger than Pagano, repudiated fascism in 1937, a year before Mussolini officially promulgated the Racial Laws.

Yet whatever the individual circumstances, the effects of living through modern Italy's most turbulent and violent period were defining for so many of the survivors. Over the years, and confirming the sense of destiny he had felt in 1938 at the age of 29, Rogers strove to come to terms with the events that had been thrust upon his generation and to translate this existential experience into a profound life-lesson, or *Bildung*. In 1962 he published yet another 'testimony' in *Casabella*. Reprinted under the title 'L'esperienza degli architetti' (The Experience of the Architects) in the collection *Fascismo e antifascismo: Lezioni e testimonianze* (Fascism and Anti-Fascism: Lessons and Testimonials),[14] it evinced his still unrequited need, seven years before his death, to speak out on behalf not just of himself but of 'my generation'. Reiterating the same arguments he had put forward sixteen years earlier in 'Catharsis', but now without any attempt to explain away the historical contradictions between fascist politics and rationalist architecture, he bluntly stated, 'There is a need to acknowledge, without reticence, that the majority of Italian architects contributed directly or indirectly, with distinction or without, to the works of the regime.'[15] Once again he singled out Terragni and Pagano, characterising them as not just the leading architects of his generation but also 'the most fascist among us'. Terragni's Casa del Fascio in Como was at once 'the most important public work of the regime' and 'the

14 Paolo Calzini, Bianca Ceva, Enzo Collotti, Mario Mauri, Rossana Rossanda Banfi and Brunello Vigezzi, eds., *Fascismo e antifascismo (1918–1936)* vol. 1 (Milan: Feltrinelli, 1962): 334–339.

15 Ernesto N. Rogers, 'Testimonianza sugli architetti del ventennio', *Casabella* no 268 (October 1962); reprinted in Ernesto N. Rogers, *Editoriali di architettura* (Turin: Einaudi, 1968): 82.

most beautiful building constructed during that epoch'.[16] Pagano, for his part, managed to outwit Piacentini at his own game in his collaboration on the Italian pavilion at the 1937 World's Fair in Paris, smuggling in modernism between the trabeated columns, as it were. Rogers also pointed to other admirable modernist projects realised under the regime, from Luigi Piccinato's new town of Sabaudia to Giovanni Michelucci's masterful train station in Florence. As ever, though, he underscored the theme of life experience, recalling his own decision to join the Partito d'Azione – the militant group founded in 1942 by Ferruccio Parri, which played a central role in the Resistance – as one of the most emotional days of his life. For him the enduring revelation of the 1930s would be the irreconcilability between fascism's 'superman', or 'dishuman man', and 'human measure' – a lesson both political and architectural.[17]

A young man of the modern movement

The experience of Italian fascism was not the only generational context in which Rogers located himself, however. Cosmopolitan both by family background and through his broad intellectual and cultural outlook, he saw himself as belonging to a cohort of international architects whose task it was to carry forward the achievements of the pioneering generation of modern architecture. In his lecture 'Modern Architecture after the Generation of the Masters', presented at the University of California at Berkeley in 1956 on one of his frequent trips abroad during that decade, he elaborated on the concept of modern architecture's succession. 'When the architects of my generation set out to insert themselves into the firmament of their art', he stated, 'four stars burned most brilliantly, illuminating our destinies.'[18] The four luminaries were Frank Lloyd Wright, Walter Gropius, Ludwig Mies van der Rohe and Le Corbusier. Planets as much as stars, with orbits of faithful followers, they also reflected the light of their own forebears – architects like Louis Sullivan, Henry van de Velde and Auguste Perret.

Another exceptional architect, of no less fertile talent in Rogers's view, was Alvar Aalto, who would emerge half a generation later. But it was the chain of relationships linking these protagonists not just to each other but to architecture's future that was now at stake. If the forefathers

16 Rogers, *Editoriali di architettura*: 85.

17 Ibid., 87. 'Measure' would be another central theme for Rogers in the postwar period. See note 49 below.

18 Ernesto N. Rogers, 'L'architettura moderna dopo la generazione dei Maestri' (1956), in *Esperienza dell'architettura*: 190.

Sven Markelius, Le Corbusier, Walter Gropius, Ernesto Rogers (left to right) discussing the competition entries for the UNESCO Headquarters, Paris, 1952 © Fondation Le Corbusier

had launched their architectural innovations under the banner of a radical modern movement, those 'formed in the years around 1930' – 40 to 50 years old at midcentury – had a less original, though no less important, role to play:

> Certainly a sign less glittering, less ringing, less brilliant, and maybe even a bit wan: but it is – I am convinced – within the limits of a deliberate modesty, the index of a historical knowledge from which will follow the sense of the real, the necessity to deepen the inroads of culture and enlarge their import.[19]

Rogers thus embraced his own historicity, rejecting avant-garde conceptions of his place in architecture's lineage. Like Walter Benjamin's angel blown backwards into the future, if more deliberately, he turned his back on the storm of perpetual newness. The midcentury, as he saw it, was destined to be a period of incremental rather than ground-breaking achievements. The project, once again, was one of *Bildung* – how, literally, to build on the lessons of the past, how to nurture both roots and ramifications. It was not a matter of passively receiving and repeating the breakthroughs of a quarter century earlier; to do so would be to turn the legacy of the masters into a style, into mere formalism. Rather it was a readiness to take one's place in 'the thousand rivulets flowing together to form the major arteries carrying the vital contribution of one's masters'[20] while at the same time responding to the dynamic forces of one's own time. For 'history is constituted not only of a cold study of the chronicle of events, but also – and often even more – of the choice we make of them'. Reaching once again into the natural world for a metaphor, he poeticised: 'like bees hovering over the meadows slipping their stingers into certain flowers and with their chosen juice making their own honey'.[21]

It was, in short, a different sort of agency that postwar architects had to embrace, reflecting their unique historical identity and experience. 'Our generation is the one that now is beginning, by historicising the works that were validated in the recent past, [to] achieve an active critical revision'.[22] *Active critical revision*: an evolutionary rather than

19 Ibid., 195.

20 Ibid., 194.

21 Ibid., 191.

22 Ibid., 190.

revolutionary task, dialectical rather than radical, underwrote Rogers's generational concept of history. It would find its summary expression in his signature concept of continuity, *continuità*. To accept the historicity of one's work was to chart a path forward while acknowledging one's indebtedness to the past.

Middle generation

I began by suggesting that no twentieth-century architect was more conscious of belonging to a particular generation than Ernesto Rogers. This claim now needs to be qualified slightly: a possible exception was Peter and Alison Smithson. Like Rogers, the Smithsons defined themselves in strongly generational terms. Of those who, as their colleague Reyner Banham nicely put it, 'interrupted their architectural training in order to fight a war to make the world safe for the modern movement',[23] they were younger than Rogers by more than a dozen years. Peter Smithson was born in 1923, Alison in 1928. But it was more than age difference that underlay the feud that erupted between the 'middle generation' of Rogers and the self-proclaimed 'youngers' who rallied around the Smithsons in the breakaway Team 10 group that emerged out of the International Congresses of Modern Architecture (CIAM). The respective protagonists of Italian and English architecture culture understood their historical roles differently, and this difference would surface at the postwar meetings of CIAM. It culminated in 1959 in a head-on clash at the organisation's final gathering in Otterlo, where Rogers presented the BBPR's recently completed skyscraper in Milan, the Torre Velasca.

It is hardly surprising that CIAM, the self-appointed standard-bearer and guardian of the legacy of modern architecture, was the arena in which the conflict between architectural generations played out most dramatically. The winds of succession could already be felt at CIAM's first postwar meeting, held in Bridgwater, England, in 1947. Even in the postwar atmosphere of urgent reconstruction and economic stringency, and likely in reaction to it, the 28-year-old Dutch architect Aldo van Eyck – soon to ally himself with the Smithsons in the group that called itself Team 10 – made a passionate plea for CIAM to move beyond its previous utilitarianism, and to inflect mechanistic functionalism with creative imagination. Several members of the old guard, notably Sigfried Giedion

23 Reyner Banham, 'Revenge of the Picturesque: English Architectural Polemics, 1945–1965', in John Summerson, ed., *Concerning Architecture: Essays on Architectural Writing Presented to Nikolaus Pevsner* (London: Penguin, 1968): 265.

Eduardo Paolozzi, Alison Smithson, Peter Smithson and Nigel Henderson, 1956 © Tate Archive

and Le Corbusier himself, fully concurred. During the war years, Giedion, one of van Eyck's mentors, had called for a 'new monumentality', urging his architectural colleagues to take people's spiritual and emotional needs into account and, with this aim in view, to focus attention on the previously neglected matter of civic representation. Moreover – and significantly apropos of Rogers – Giedion made his case precisely in terms of historical evolution. In the aftermath of World War I, architects had properly seen their immediate task as to provide functionally designed, affordable shelter. But now that modern architecture had reached a more mature phase of development, it could afford to look beyond bare minimum. In this sense, as he argued, his proposal for a new monumentality was not a break with previous developments but a logical outgrowth.[24]

A decade later, in the mid-1950s, Rogers made a similar case for neoliberty, a stylistic tendency that had recently emerged in Italy, and of which the BBPR's Torre Velasca would become an emblematic example. A recovery of craftsmanship, ornament, and history – turn-of-the-century values that the most militant wing of the modern movement had explicitly rejected – neoliberty was not so much a break with the ethos of the previous generation, in Rogers's view, as a sign of its maturation and growth, of 'revision and updating'. What appeared to orthodox modernists as heretical should instead be viewed as an enlargement of the modern tradition: of 'continuity' rather than 'crisis'.[25]

In fact, like Giedion, Rogers had begun calling for a richer remit for modern architecture a decade earlier. In 1946, in a programmatic statement that inaugurated his short-lived tenure immediately after the war as editor of the journal *Domus*, he outlined his vision of architecture's role in the formation of culture. Beginning by confessing some guilty pleasure in attending a concert at a moment when so many of his countrymen were still suffering, he concluded that beautiful music was no less essential to the construction of a humane society than practical activity. 'Why renounce beauty?' he asked. 'No problem is solved if [architecture] does not respond at once to utility, morals and aesthetics'.[26]

24 See Sigfried Giedion, 'The Need for a New Monumentality', in Paul Zucker, ed., *New Architecture and City Planning* (New York: Philosophical Library, 1944), 549–68; and J. L. Sert, F. Léger, S. Giedion, 'Nine Points on Monumentality', especially the fifth point, in Sigfried Giedion, *Architecture, You and Me* (Cambridge, Mass.: Harvard University Press, 1958): 49.

25 Ernesto N. Rogers, 'Continuità o crisi?', *Casabella Continuità* nº 215 (April–May 1957); reprinted in *Esperienza dell'architettura*: 203–210.

26 Ernesto N. Rogers, 'Programma: Domus, la casa dell'uomo', *Domus* nº 205 (January 1946); reprinted in *Esperienza dell'architettura*: 115–18; trans. in Joan Ockman, ed., *Architecture Culture 1943–1968: A Documentary Anthology* (New York: Rizzoli, 1993): 79.

At CIAM's second postwar meeting, held in Bergamo in 1949 and organised by the Italian members with Rogers taking a lead role, a direct confrontation occurred. Unlike at the meeting two years earlier in Bridgwater, the cause was more geopolitical than generational. In an early clash of Cold War ideologies, Helena Syrkus, a leading representative from Poland, now under Soviet domination, attacked the ideology of functionalism in the name of socialist realism. Although the architects from the West immediately closed ranks, it was clear that the postwar CIAM was fracturing along more than one axis. Two years later, at CIAM's eighth meeting, held in Hoddesdon, England, in 1951, the Smithsons were invited to attend their first congress as observers. Their entry on the scene proved decisive and divisive. By the next meeting, in Aix-en-Provence in 1953, generational conflict was again at the fore, with the Smithsons' 'Urban -Reidentification' grid serving as a rallying cry against the functionalist urbanism codified at CIAM's fourth congress in Athens exactly two decades earlier. Among the major agenda items at Aix was the drafting of a new Charter of Habitat, intended as a sequel to or revision of the Athens Charter. As little progress was made on it, the project was tabled for CIAM 10, and a committee of younger members, including Peter Smithson and van Eyck, was designated as Group 10 and tasked with doing the preparatory work. Out of this assignment, Team 10 was born and took its name.

All of those who would subsequently affiliate themselves with Team 10 – initially including (besides the Smithsons and van Eyck) Jacob Bakema, Georges Candilis, Shadrach Woods, John Voelker and, slightly later, Giancarlo de Carlo (introduced to the others by Rogers) – were no older than 45 in the 1950s. By the time CIAM 10 took place in Dubrovnik, Yugoslavia, in 1956, generational tensions were high. The meeting opened with the reading of a message from Le Corbusier by Josep Lluís Sert, who had succeeded to the presidency of CIAM at Bridgwater. (Rogers had been solicited for the position but declined.) Le Corbusier was not personally in attendance. Whether having astutely sized up the potential for a rancorous gathering and unwilling to engage in the Oedipal struggle playing out, or simply because his own work was more preoccupying at the moment, he elected to sit it out. In his message he explicitly posed 'the problem of the generations', calling it a question of 'crisis or evolution'.[27] The time had arrived, he declared, for the 'generation of 1928' – the founding fathers who had convened CIAM's first congress in

27 'Message de Le Corbusier adressé au X Congrès à Dubrovnik, Cap Martin, July 23, 1956', Fondation Le Corbusier, D3–7, 121–27.

La Sarraz, Switzerland, in 1928 and drafted the Athens Charter five years later – to pass the baton to the 'generation of 1956', those who were to become 'tomorrow's leaders', *réalisateurs pour demain*. They were the ones who must now assume responsibility, must translate theory into reality and pave the way for the implementation of CIAM's precepts on a worldwide basis. It was the generation 'born around 1916 during wars and revolutions, and those then unborn, now 25 years old, born around 1930 during the preparation of a new war and amidst a profound economic, social, and political crisis', who were, he averred,

... the only ones capable of feeling actual problems, personally, profoundly, the goals to follow, the means to reach them, the pathetic urgency of the present situation. They are in the know. Their predecessors no longer are, they are out, they are no longer subject to the direct impact of the situation.[28]

Born fifteen years apart 'in difficult times', these two generations were to constitute the 'SECOND-CIAM'. The second generation was to 'carry in its loins the fertile seed of the FIRST-CIAM'. Le Corbusier concluded his message: 'May CIAM continue in its creative passion, in disinterest, rejecting the opportunists and hotheads. Good luck. Long live the SECOND-CIAM! Your friend, Le Corbusier'.[29]

The Swiss-French architect did not spell out who the opportunists and hotheads were; there was no need. But if his message amounted to a voluntary surrender of power, it also presumed a natural and orderly succession. Seniority should pass from the founders – himself, Gropius, Giedion – to those next in line, the middle generation of Sert and Rogers. Yet the fledgling Team 10, restive proponents of new themes at Dubrovnik like 'the problem of Cluster', 'the problem of Mobility' and 'the problem of Growth and Change', had different ideas. More than three decades later, Alison Smithson would still be bitter over what she perceived to be the middle generation's 'bossiness' at Dubrovnik. She resented how they had bickered with her over the meaning of the word 'cluster' and had tried to shut out the English architects by insisting on French as the meeting's official language. Following the acrimony at Dubrovnik, efforts to reorganise CIAM along new lines sputtered along for another three years, even as personal

28 Ibid.; excerpt trans. in Oscar Newman, ed., *New Frontiers in Architecture: CIAM '59 in Otterlo* (New York: Universe Books, 1961), 16.

29 'Message de Le Corbusier adressé au x Congrès à Dubrovnik'.

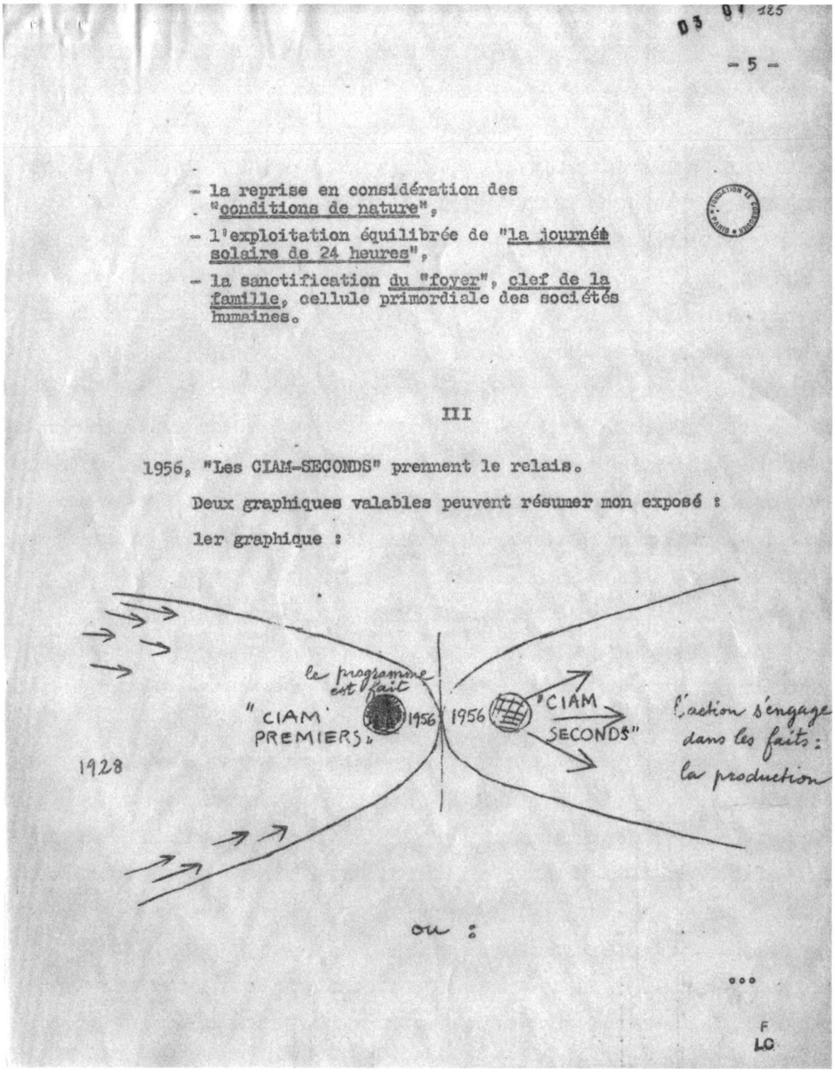

D3 01 125

- 5 -

- la reprise en considération des "conditions de nature",
- l'exploitation équilibrée de "la journée solaire de 24 heures",
- la sanctification du "foyer", clef de la famille, cellule primordiale des sociétés humaines.

III

1956, "Les CIAM-SECONDS" prennent le relais.

Deux graphiques valables peuvent résumer mon exposé :

1er graphique :

ou :

...

F
LC

From Le Corbusier's message in absentia to CIAM 10, Dubrovnik, 1956 © Fondation Le Corbusier

relations deteriorated to the point of open hostility. Rogers's editorial 'Continuità o crisi?' (Continuity or Crisis?) appeared in the April–May 1957 issue of *Casabella*.[30] But the tenth CIAM congress would be the organisation's last official meeting. In her retrospective account, published in 1991, Smithson noted that 'the behaviour of the middle generation at Dubrovnik – a very large Italian contingent – was basically the reason why the full force of my wrath descended upon them at Otterlo'. Nor could she resist a catty put-down: in between the sessions, 'the middle generation wives [went] shopping for "ethnic" embroidered sheepskin jackets'.[31]

The power shift that occurred at Dubrovnik came into full view in 1959, when what was billed as a 'working congress' and an 'outgrowth' of CIAM was staged at the Kröller-Müller Museum in Otterlo. The museum had been designed by the ageing Henry van de Velde just before the outbreak of World War II. Rogers's subsequent description of the Otterlo event as 'CIAM at the museum' in an editorial of that title in *Casabella* thus had more than one meaning.[32] Only 40 architects were invited to take part. Of those, as noted in the introduction to the official publication edited by Oscar Newman and published in German and English editions in 1961, the average age 'was about 40 – a generation of architects who had reached artistic maturity in the post-war period'.[33] In contrast to the group projects and grid layouts that had been mandated at earlier meetings, all the invitees were asked to present their own individual work, with the ultimate aim of determining 'if a true affinity of thought exists between participants not only in spoken and written words but, more profoundly, at the level of plastic invention'.[34]

The question on the table, in other words, was whether there was any basis for a reorganised CIAM-type institution to exist in the future, or whether modern architecture's latter-day representatives were already too factionalised and too much at odds in their vision of the way forward to justify the endeavour. The harsh exchange between Rogers and Peter Smithson over the Torre Velasca more or less sealed the issue. It is usually recalled that the initial volley was fired by Smithson against Rogers. In fact, Rogers spoke out first, criticising the Smithsons'

30 See note 26.

31 Alison Smithson, ed., *Team 10 Meetings* (New York: Rizzoli, 1991): 24–26.

32 'I CIAM al Museo', *Casabella Continuità* nº 232 (October 1959): 2.

33 *New Frontiers in Architecture*: 7.

34 Letter of invitation to Otterlo meeting, ibid.

London Roads Study. Calling into question the English couple's disregard for the pre-existing fabric of London's Soho district in their eagerness to accommodate new traffic patterns, he argued:

[T]he character of this kind of life - underground and immoral, as you would like to call it, but very pleasant - is what you are destroying. We cannot make rational a life which is typically irrational, a result of many, many years of evolution.... [Places like these] have acquired the irrational character they have through many years of evolving.

The Smithsons' claims notwithstanding, Rogers concluded by stating, 'what now exists will be drastically changed'.[35]

With the subjects of history and contextualism thus broached, discussion became much more contentious during Rogers's own presentation of the Torre Velasca. Just three months earlier, Reyner Banham had denounced neoliberty in the pages of *Architectural Review* as an 'infantile regression' and a 'retreat from modern architecture'.[36] Picking up where Banham left off, Peter Smithson now accused the BBPR's skyscraper of being not just irresponsible but 'dangerous'. The image it conjured up of a battlemented medieval Milan was that of a closed rather than open society, Smithson asserted, harking back (in an echo of Karl Popper's 1945 book *The Open Society and Its Enemies*) to a political system from which 'we are now in the most active evolution'.[37] In reply, Rogers insisted that it was not fidelity to particular forms that made a building of its time but rather – as Gropius had taught – its design methodology, its spatial conception, and its technology. Arguing that the Torre Velasca was not a thoughtless imitation of history but rather an embodiment of 'the essence of history', he vigorously defended it: 'we found it necessary that our building breathe the atmosphere of the place and even intensify it.' Once again, he reiterated his evolutionist argument concerning the course of modern architecture:

The attitude of the fathers of modern architecture was anti-historical. But this was an attitude born of a great revolution and it was necessary that the first premise of our culture be a new attitude to history. But this is now no longer necessary.[38]

35 Ibid., 78.

36 Reyner Banham, 'Neoliberty: The Italian Retreat from Modern Architecture', *Architectural Review* XXV 747 (April 1959): 235.

37 *New Frontiers in Architecture*: 94, 96.

38 Ibid., 93.

Members of Team 10 holding a mock funeral for CIAM, during the last CIAM meeting in Otterlo, Holland, 1959. From left Peter Smithson, Alison Smithson, John Voelcker, Jaap Bakema, Sandy van Ginkel, with Aldo van Eyck and Blanche Lemco below © John Voelcker Collection / AA Archives

Scornfully dismissing Smithson's claim that the Velasca tower was somehow immoral, Rogers declared, 'There is one difficulty that I see and that is that you think in English'.[39] This may sound like a throwaway line, but for Rogers it was more. His own Anglo-Italian background made him alert to cultural differences. In an essay that originally appeared in *Casabella* in February–March 1954 under the title 'Pretesti per una critica non-formalistica' (Pretexts for a Non-Formalistic Criticism), republished in *Esperienza dell'architettura* as 'Tradizione e talento individuale' (Tradition and Individual Talent), he used the reference to T. S. Eliot's eponymous essay to make the point that ingrained habits of mind tend to lead to blind spots and errors of judgement: 'Every nation has not only its own creative [capacities], but its own critical turn of mind; and is even more oblivious of the shortcomings and limitations of its critical habits than of those of its creative genius'.[40]

In the end, with each architect claiming the high ground, the controversy between Rogers and Smithson boiled down to their respective views on the meaning and value of historical experience. For Rogers, history entailed an authentic and irreducible connection between the past and present. For the Smithsons, history was more like a relay in which each generation took from its antecedents that which it deemed most usable. In an essay titled 'Three Generations' that would appear in 1981 in the publication of Giancarlo de Carlo's International Laboratory of Architecture and Urban Design (ILA&UD), Peter Smithson drew a parallel between three successive generations of Renaissance architects and three generations of modern architects. The transfer of architectural ideas from Filippo Brunelleschi in the 1420s to Leon Battista Alberti in the 1450s to Francesco di Giorgio in the 1470s and '80s was analogous, he suggested, to that from Walter Gropius, Mies van der Rohe and Le Corbusier in the 1920s to Jean Prouvé and Charles and Ray Eames in the 1940s to 'my own generation, the third generation' in the 1950s and 1960s. 'We feel we have a "natural right" ', he stated, using characteristic Smithson locution, 'both as apprentices-by-proxy, and as being members of the family who design-by-thinking-of-the-making, to inherit as a landscape of the mind, the thoughts and the ways of putting things together of Mies van der Rohe'.[41] It was the extended family – with its network of affective ties,

39 Ibid., 95.

40 Ernesto N. Rogers, 'Pretesi per una critica non formalistica', *Casabella Continuità* nº 200 (February–March 1954); reprinted as 'Tradizione e talento individuale', *Esperienza dell'architettura*: 289.

41 Peter Smithson, 'Three Generations', ILA&UD *Annual Report 1980* (Urbino, 1981): 88.

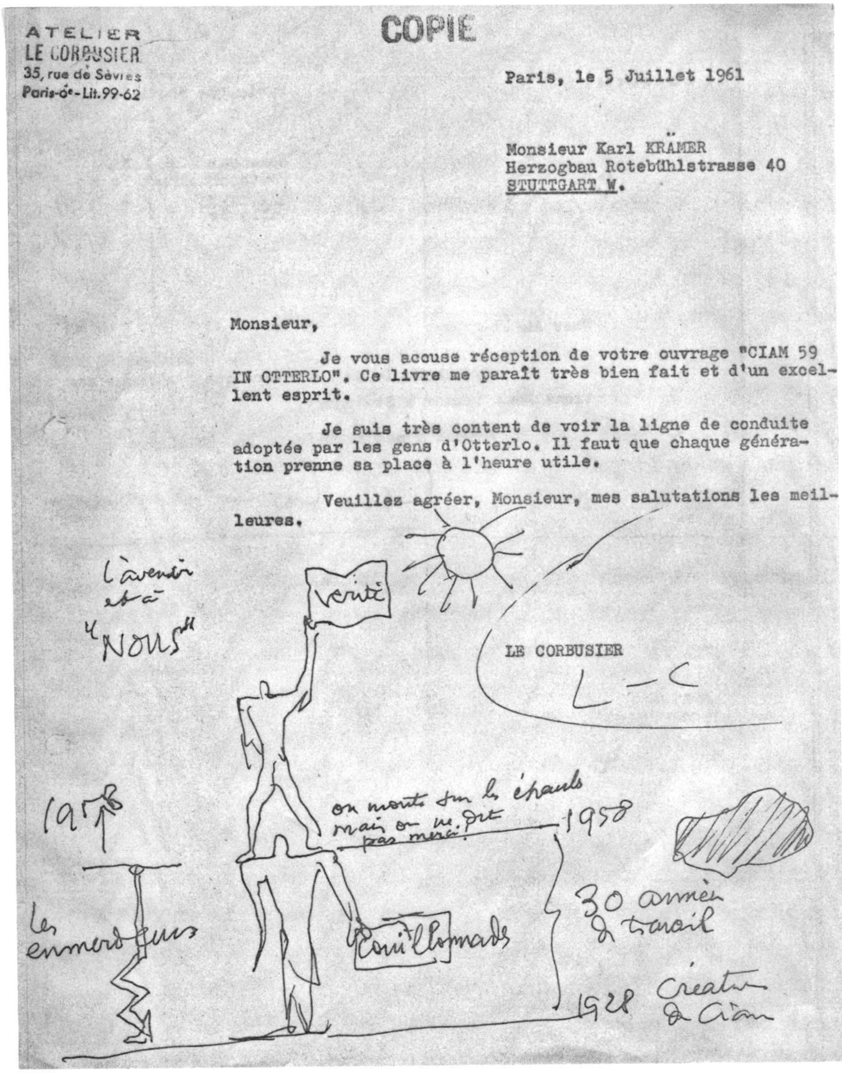

ATELIER
LE CORBUSIER
35, rue de Sèvres
Paris-6e - Lit.99-62

COPIE

Paris, le 5 Juillet 1961

Monsieur Karl KRÄMER
Herzogbau Rotebühlstrasse 40
STUTTGART W.

Monsieur,

Je vous accuse réception de votre ouvrage "CIAM 59 IN OTTERLO". Ce livre me paraît très bien fait et d'un excellent esprit.

Je suis très content de voir la ligne de conduite adoptée par les gens d'Otterlo. Il faut que chaque génération prenne sa place à l'heure utile.

Veuillez agréer, Monsieur, mes salutations les meilleures.

LE CORBUSIER
L-C

Le Corbusier, letter to publisher Karl Kramer, 1961, acknowledging receipt of the book *New Frontiers in Architecture: CIAM '59 in Otterlo* © Bakema, J.B. Archief / Het Nieuwe Instituut

internal loyalties, repressed Oedipal impulses and patrimonial rights of inheritance – that was the Smithsons' privileged metaphor for their understanding of generational relations. Along with 'team', it was also a countermodel to the postwar CIAM's unwieldy bureaucracy. Following CIAM's demise at Otterlo, the rebellious architects of Team 10 would go on to solidify their identity as an exclusive, close-knit and sometimes squabbling architectural family.

Rogers, on the other hand, deeply regretted the lack of comity that marked CIAM's demise. In a valedictory editorial in *Casabella* in October 1959, he paused to shed a tear for 'this glorious institution'.[42] From his standpoint, the ideal model for architecture's leading body of progressive representatives was neither the family nor the team but rather the dedicated cohort forged in shared historical experience. Such a model was epitomised by BBPR, who retained the extra 'B' in their acronym in permanent homage to their dead comrade Banfi. (It is worth noting parenthetically that Manfredo Tafuri's insistence in his writings on attributing the firm's postwar work to 'BPR' was, on this count, not a little insensitive).[43] It is also of note that in the final revised edition of *Space, Time and Architecture*, published in 1967, a year before Giedion's death, the Swiss architectural historian adopted the rubric of the 'third generation'. But rather than anointing the Smithsons and Team 10 as its representatives, he chose to pass the mantle to the Danish architect Jørn Utzon.[44] Le Corbusier himself, in a letter sent in 1961 to the publisher of the Otterlo proceedings acknowledging his receipt of the book, would redraw the generational diagram he had sent to CIAM in Dubrovnik, this time not without mixed feelings: 'On monte sur l'épaule mais on ne dit pas merci!' (They stand on one's shoulders but do not say thank you!).

Milieu

'Tradition is nothing but the continuous co-presence of experiences', wrote Rogers in his autobiographical preface to *Esperienza dell'architettura*, part of 'the active phenomenology of history'.[45] One of Rogers's close colleagues and philosophical mentors during the postwar period was Enzo Paci (1911–76). In moving 'from existentialism to

42 Ernesto N. Rogers, 'I CIAM al museo', *Casabella Continuità* nº 232 (October 1959); reprinted in Editoriali di architettura: 77.

43 See, among other books by Tafuri, *History of Italian Architecture*, 1944–1985, trans. Jessica Levine (Cambridge, Mass.: MIT Press, 1989), passim.

44 See S. Giedion, Space, *Time and Architecture: The Growth of a New Tradition*, 5th ed. rev. (Cambridge, Mass.: Harvard University Press, 1967): 672–695.

45 Ernesto N. Rogers, 'Prefazione. Il mestiere dell'architetto', *Esperienza dell'architettura*: 36.

relationism', as he elaborated in a book of that title published in 1957, Paci aimed to introduce a more dynamic sense of history and multiplicity into the Husserlian tradition of phenomenology.[46] Rejecting the sovereignty of 'the dogmatic and idealistic subject', he emphasised the continuously evolving nature of lived experience and of 'time's irreversible moments'. No longer was the human subject to be understood as a self-sufficient and circumscribed 'substance', as he put it, but rather as a living, environmental organism that 'always resolves itself into centers' of relationships'.[47]

Rogers absorbed Paci's relational philosophy and assimilated it into his architectural thinking. Like Paci, he took inspiration from the anti-essentialist thought of the American Pragmatist philosophers John Dewey and William James and drew on the insights of Gestalt psychology. Shortly after taking on the editorship of *Casabella* in 1953, he added the word *Continuità* to the journal's title. 'We believe', he stated in an editorial in the first issue bearing the new title, 'in the fertile cycle of *man–architecture–man* and want to represent its dramatic unfolding – its crises, its few but indispensable certainties and its many and even more necessary doubts'.[48] He had initially alluded to this 'cycle' at the Milan Triennale in 1951, in an installation titled 'Architettura, misura dell'uomo' (Architecture, Measure of Man). Man-architecture-man became another kind of continuity for Rogers, one that was not just temporal but also spatial: 'continuity in time, continuity in space', as he put it.[49] Within this humanist continuum, architecture was the midterm and mediator. Man-architecture-man was thus one more meaning of middleness for Rogers. For architecture to be in the middle ultimately meant for it to be *in relation to.*

For Rogers, as we have seen, to belong to a generation was to share in a collective experience, to be part of a moment in history, to enter into a community defined by its temporality. In Rogers's own biography, it was to straddle the eras of fascism and democracy and also to bridge early and late modern architecture. But, just as importantly,

46 See Rogers's note on Paci appended to 'Continuità o crisi?' in *Esperienza dell'architettura*: 210.

47 Enzo Paci, 'Introduzione', *Diario Fenomenologico* (Milan: Bompiani, 1973 [1961]); trans. Luigi Bianchi, https://www.yorku.ca/lbianchi/paci/diary_ver_02.html.

48 Ernesto N. Rogers, 'Continuità', *Casabella Continuità* nº 199 (January 1954); reprinted in *Esperienza dell'architettura*: 131. Rogers's italics.

49 Ibid., 132. For the text of Rogers's installation at the IX Triennale in Milan (co-curated with Vittorio Gregotti and Giotto Stoppino), see Ernesto N. Rogers, 'Architettura, misura dell'uomo', *Domus* nº 260 (July–August 1951): 1–5. The aim was to present architecture as a 'concrete expression of man, a synthesis of his physical and spiritual measure'.

'Architettura misura dell'uomo' (Architecture is the Measure of Man) exhibition, IX Triennale, Milan, 1951, by Ernesto Rogers, Vittorio Gregotti and Giotto Stoppino © Triennale Milano – Archivi

it was to be *in a context*, in the middle of a place, literally *mi-lieu* – like the Torre Velasca in its setting in Milan. This fundamental temporal-spatial homology underpins the entirety of Rogers's thinking. Another key concept that Rogers elaborated in the 1950s was that of *preesistenze ambientali*. Often translated into English – not without loss of meaning – as 'pre-existing conditions', or more literally as 'contextual preexistences', *preesistenze ambientali* were the spatial-environmental equivalents of the temporal-historical conditions that constituted *continuità*.[50]

As previously suggested, Rogers's thought reveals an extraordinary degree of coherence. Again, coherence, *coerenza*, is among the concepts repeatedly encountered in his writings, always with a positive or aspirational valence. At times the terms *coerenza* and *tendenza* seem dialectically related. Culture, Rogers writes in his preface to *Esperienza dell'architettura*, is 'choral'; it is composed of multiple voices and plural tendencies.[51] But when the disparate or dissonant tendencies are reflected upon consciously and historically, they acquire a degree of coherence. This, in Rogers's view, was the role of a journal of cultural tendency like *Casabella*: namely, to contribute to a continuous, and continuously revised, process of making coherent, of making sense of one's moment.

The pursuit of coherence was no less a task of the architectural project. In *Art as Experience*, John Dewey, a philosopher whom Rogers read and admired, described lived experience as unreflected and formless; his precise words are 'inchoate', 'slack and discursive', 'a mere succession of excitations'.[52] Only when lived experience is transformed into aesthetic experience, something that possesses pattern and structure, do meaningful relationships emerge. Until the end of his life Rogers strove to redeem and comprehend his generational experience of both fascism and modern architecture through intellectual and aesthetic reflection. By the time of his death, however, a new and different generation had come of age, one that grew up in very different circumstances from his own. For the generation of the 1960s – not just in Italy – youth would be a collective identity and would give rise to hopes, especially among those on the left, for social and political transformation. Yet by the end

50 On this important concept, see Ernesto N. Rogers, 'Le preesistenze ambientali e i temi pratici contemporanei', *Casabella Continuità* nº 204 (February–March 1955); reprinted in *Esperienza dell'architettura*: 304–10; trans. in Ockman, ed., *Architecture Culture 1943–1968*: 201–204.

51 Rogers, 'Prefazione. Il mestiere dell'architetto', *Esperienza dell'architettura*: 48.

52 See 'Having an Experience' in John Dewey, *Art as Experience* (New York: Minton, Balch & Company, 1934): 35, 40, 57.

Restoration and conversion into a museum of the Sforza Castle in Milan, carried out by BBPR between 1948 and 1956 © Luca Miserocchi

of that decade these hopes would to a large extent be dashed, and the counterculture's emancipatory aspirations would dissipate.[53] In hindsight, the 'sixties seem better described as a decade than as a generation, at least according to Ortega's definition. In her 1989 lecture 'Traditions of the New', cited at the beginning of this essay, Susan Sontag predicted that a preference for decade-speak – the 'seventies, the 'eighties, the 'nineties – would henceforth be in the ascendant.[54] Today we freely use terms like 'baby boomers', 'millennials', 'Gen X'. But these labels seem to be as much branding strategies as real historical distinctions.

53 On the narrative construction of generational identity, see an interesting book by John Downton Hazlett, although it is concerned with a different context, that of the USA in the 1960s: *My Generation: Collective Autobiography and Identity Politics* (Madison: University of Wisconsin Press, 1998).

54 Sontag, *Tradities van het nieuwe, of: Moeten wij modern zijn?* Sontag claims that the preference for the decade as a periodising device dates from the 1960s; thereafter, other decades were increasingly labelled as such. Characterising the decade as 'the smallest unit of time, least rich in meaning' (49), she associates its burgeoning usage at the end of the twentieth century with a late-modern consumer society in which popular trends in fashions and lifestyles have become the primary indices of historical change.

TIMELINE

1909
Born in Trieste to Ida Manni and Romeo Rogers.

1914
The Rogers family moves to Zurich, Switzerland.

1918
After a brief spell back in Trieste the family moves to Rome.

1921
Rogers moves to Milan and becomes a student at the Liceo Giuseppe Parini where he befriends Gianluigi Banfi and Lodovico Belgiojoso and attends lectures given by philosopher Antonio Banfi.

1927
Enrols in the Faculty of Architecture at the Politecnico di Milano where he meets Enrico Peressutti.

1932
Banfi, Belgiojoso, Peressutti and Rogers graduate and form BBPR. Rogers obtains Italian citizenship, renouncing British citizenship, and performs military service. Moves out of the family home and begins living in hotels and suffers economic hardship.

Makes occasional written contributions to *Casabella* from 1932 until 1940.

1933
With other BBPR associates, Rogers starts with contributing to *Quadrante* and does so until 1936.

1935
Becomes a member of CIAM and, together with Belgiojoso, is also active in the Sindacato Interprovinciale Fascista degli Architetti della Lombardia (SIFA), a fascist architects' union in Lombardy.

1937
On the occasion of the World Expo, Rogers lives in Paris for a month, following the construction of a pavilion designed by BBPR. During this time, he strengthens his ties with architects outside Italy, particularly with Le Corbusier.

1938
Following the promulgation of the Racial Laws in Italy, Rogers is forced into anonymity.

1939
Becomes a member of the Maison des Artistes at the Château de La Sarraz in Switzerland.

1941 to 1942
Writes the column 'Confessions of a Twentieth Century Anonymous Person' for Pagano's *Domus*.

1943
Rogers flees to Switzerland, where he is interned at the internment camp of Vevey and starts teaching urban and architectural theory at the Champ Universitaire Italien de Lausanne, alongside Giulio Einaudi, Amintore Fanfani and Adriano Olivetti.

1944
Becomes co-editor of the *Bulletin du centre d'études pour le bâtiment*, where he writes about reconstruction and education.

1945
Teaches at the Haute École d'Architecture in Geneva before moving back to Milan after Liberation and rejoining the other two surviving members of BBPR following Banfi's tragic death.

Joins the Consiglio Nazionale delle Ricerche (CNR) – the National Research Council of Italy – focusing on reconstruction as well as the Movimento di Studi per L'architettura (MSA) – the Movement for Architectural Studies. BBPR publishes the Piano AR for the reconstruction of Milan (*Costruzioni Casabella* nº 194)

1946
BBPR completes the memorial to those who died in the Nazi death camps at the Cimitero Monumentale in Milan. Becomes editor of *Domus* January 1946 to December 1947. With BBPR, edits the 'Architetti del movimento moderno' series (Milano: Il Balcone).

1947
Becomes a member of the CIAM Council and vice president of the CIAM Education Commission; Walter Gropius was president.

1948
Teaches at the Instituto de Arquitectura y Urbanismo de Tucuman in Argentina and gives lectures at the universities of Santiago de Chile, Lima in Peru and at the Institute of Design in Chicago.

1949
Rogers chairs the Educational Commission at CIAM VII in Bergamo and shortly afterwards teaches at the first CIAM Summer School which was held at the Architectural Association in London (between 8 August and 2 September). Also teaches two parallel courses on architecture at the Architectural Association.

1951
In collaboration with Vittorio Gregotti and Giotto Stoppino, Rogers designs the 'Architettura misura dell'uomo' exhibition at the IX Triennale in Milan.

1952
Serves on the advisory committee for the design of the new UNESCO Headquarters in Paris with Le Corbusier, Lucio Costa, Sven Markelius and Walter Gropius. Starts teaching at the Politecnico di Milano.

1953
Takes on the editorship of *Casabella*. Nominated as an expert in architecture and urbanism for the United Nations and acts as a consultant for the ECSC (European Coal and Steel Community).

BBPR completes the Olivetti showroom on Fifth Avenue in New York.

1955
Moves to an apartment in Via Bigli in Milan.

1956
BBPR completes the restoration of the museums at the Castello Sforzesco in Milan.

Rogers is made honorary member of the American Institute of Architects.

1958
BBPR completes the Torre Velasca in Milan which is presented at the final CIAM in Otterlo.

Rogers's *Esperienza dell'architettura* (Milan: Einaudi) is published.

1959
Teaches Italian culture at the University of California, Berkeley, and in the following years lectures widely around the world, including universities in Sweden, Norway, China, other universities in the USA and, of course, in Italy.

1962
Becomes a full professor of architecture at the Politecnico di Milano.

1963
Is made an Honorary Fellow of the Royal Institute of British Architects.

1968
Rogers's *Editoriali di architettura* (Milano: Einaudi) is published.

1969
After a long illness, Rogers dies at Gardone in the province of Brescia, Lombardy, on 7 November.

ACKNOWLEDGEMENTS

The ideas behind this book began to take shape while I was still a student, first at the Politecnico di Milano and then at the Architectural Association. They emerged from lectures and conversations with mentors and peers, and were first crystallised in an essay published in *AA Files* (n. 75, 2017), various papers presented at conferences in the UK and abroad, and then in a series of lectures at the Architectural Association.

Over the years, many people have taken the time to share their memories, insights and criticisms. These include the late Vittorio Gregotti and Mark Cousins, Pier Luigi Nicolin, Maria Vittoria Capitanucci, Peter Carl, Martino Stierli, Marina Lathouri, Maurizio Sabini, Pippo Ciorra, Manuel Orazi, Kurt Forster and, in particular, Joan Ockman, whose guidance has been invaluable and whose essay is an essential contribution to this volume and, more generally, to an understanding of the work and influence of Ernesto Nathan Rogers.

I would like to express my deepest gratitude to Pamela Johnston and especially to Jill Hollis, whose unparalleled patience, thoroughness and exceptional command of not only English and Italian, but also French and German, have been instrumental in making this book a reality, giving coherence to the text, eliminating all manner of errors, and truly helping to convey the meaning from one language to another, not only of Rogers's words, but especially of mine.

I am indebted to the Graham Foundation for Advanced Studies in the Fine Arts and the Architectural Association, School of Architecture for their support and generous funding of the book, and I think with gratitude and fondness of the tireless conversations with family, friends and colleagues who have contributed to this project. Most of all, I would like to thank my husband, Ivor Williams, who designed the book and supported me and this project in more ways than I can list, and my friends and colleagues, Shumi Bose and Aram Mooradian, who read and helped with parts of the manuscript, always inspiring imagination, confidence and fun.

Last but not least, I would like to thank Thomas Weaver, my editor, for his enthusiasm, persistence and belief in this project from beginning to end, despite the many hurdles and the years that have passed.

LIST OF SOURCES

Publications by Rogers
Auguste Perret (Milano: Il Balcone, 1955)

Esperienza dell'architettura, ed. Luca Molinari (Milan: Skira, 1997; original edition Turin: Einaudi, 1958)

Gli elementi del fenomeno architettonico, edited by Cesare De Seta (Rome-Bari: Laterza, 1961)

Editoriali di architettura, (Rovereto: Zandonai, 2009 [Torino: Einaudi, 1968])

Il senso della storia, continuità e discontinuità, including an English translation, *The Sense of History, Ex-cathedra* (Milano: Unicopli, 1999)

Lettere di Ernesto a Ernesto e viceversa, ed. Luca Molinari (Milano: Archinto, 2000)

Architettura, misura e grandezza dell'uomo. Scritti 1930–1969, anthology, ed. Serena Maffioletti (Padova: Il Poligrafo, 2010)

*Il pentagramma di Rogers. Lezioni universitarie di Ernesto N. Roger*s, collection of lectures by Rogers, ed. Serena Maffioletti (Padova: Il Poligrafo, 2009)

Articles by Rogers available in English
Many of Rogers's editorials for *Casabella* were translated into English (and French) and published in the form of blue inserts in the journal. However, these are often difficult to find and, even when available, the quality of the translations is frequently poor and they are often not complete but extracts from the original Italian texts.
Other English translations have appeared over the years, rendered by different translators at different times in a wide range of formats and amounting to an inconsistent and fragmentary representation of Rogers's writings.

'Towards a Unity of Plastic Arts', *The Architects' Journal* (London, September 1949)

'The Evolution of Present Day Italian Architecture', *Architects' Year Book* no. IV (London, 1950): 40

'The Heart: Human Problem of Cities', in Rogers, Sert & Tyrwhitt (eds), *The Heart of the City: Towards the Humanization of Urban Life* (New York: Pellegrini and Cudahy, 1952)

'Report on Brazil', *The Architectural Review* no. 694 (London, 1954)

'Architecture and Politics in the Soviet Union', *International Asbestos-Cement Review* no. 4 (October, 1956): 5

'Our Responsibilities Towards Tradition', *Italian Quarterly*, nos. 7-8 (1958–59): 73

Modern Architecture Since the Generation of the Masters (Milano: Editoriale Domus, 1956)

'Presentation of Torre Velasca at CIAM '59' and 'Response to Peter Smithson' in Jurgen Joedicke (ed.), *Documents of Modern Architecture* (London: Alec Tiranti, 1961); a much shorter version also appears in Mallgrave's anthology cited below.

'Continuity or Crisis?', *Italian Quarterly* vol. 2 (1959): 81–87

'The Problem of Building Within an Existing Environment', *Zodiac* no. 3 (1990)

'Tradition and Modern design' in the *Acts of the Seventh International Design Conference*, Aspen, Colorado, 1957; an extract was published in *Canadian Architect* vol. 3:2 (February 1958): 64–66

'City Planning a Cultural Assessment', *Zodiac* no. 3 (1990)

'The Future was not to be Seen at Brussels', *Architects' Year Book*, no. 9 (1960): 132–139

'Villa, Townhouse and Unite: The Utopian Spectrum' in *Four Great Masters of Modern Architecture: Gropius, Le Corbusier, Mies van der Rohe, Wright. The Verbatim Record of a Symposium Held at the School of Architecture, Columbia University*, New York: March–May 1961

'The Phenomenology of European Architecture', in *Daedalus* vol. 93, no. 1 (Winter 1964): 358–372

'The Image: The Architect's Inalienable Vision' in Gyorgy Kepes, ed., *Sign, Image and Symbol*, (London: Studio Vista, London, 1966)

'Pre-existing Conditions and Issues of Contemporary Building Practice', Program, Domus: The House of Man' and 'Continuity' in Joan Ockman, ed., *Architecture Culture 1948-1963* (New York: Rizzoli, 1993); an extract from 'Continuity' is also published in Harry Francis Mallgrave, ed., *Architectural Theory* vol. 2, 1871-2005 (Oxford: Blackwell, 2006)

Extended studies on the work and legacy of Rogers

In Italian

Chiara Baglione, *Ernesto Nathan Rogers 1909-1969* (Milan: Franco Angeli, 2012)

Ezio Bonfanti, Marco Porta, *Città, museo e architettura. Il gruppo Bbpr nella cultura architettonica italiana* (Florence: Vallecchi, 1973)

Aldo De Poli, Visentin Chiara, *Ernesto Nathan Rogers e la costruzione dell'architettura* (Parma: MUP, 2009)

Gabriella Errico, *Tra razionalismo e continuità. Ernesto Nathan Rogers e i Bbpr* (Naples: Massa, 2011)

Anna Giannetti, Luca Molinari, eds, *Continuità e crisi. Ernesto Nathan Rogers e la cultura architettonica italiana del secondo dopoguerra* (Florence: Alinea Editrice, 2009)

Serena Maffioletti, *BBPR* (Bologna: Zanichelli, 1994)

Antonio Monestiroli, *Ernesto Nathan Rogers. L'architettura come esperienza* (Bologna: Baiesi, 1999)

Eugenia López Reus, *Ernesto Nathan Rogers, Continuità e contemporaneità* (Milan: Martinotti, 2009)

Quaderni del Dipartimento di Progettazione dell'Architettura del Politecnico di Milano 15. Ernesto Nathan Rogers: testimonianze e studi (Milan: Città Studi, 1993)

In English

Luca Molinari, *Continuita: A Response to Identity Crises, Ernesto Nathan Rogers and Italian Architectural Culture After 1945* (Delft: TU, 2008)

Maurizio Sabini, *Ernesto Nathan Rogers. The Modern Architect as Public Intellectual* (London: Bloomsbury, June 2020)

The Hero of Doubt: Selected Writings by Ernesto Nathan Rogers

Edited with an introduction by Roberta Marcaccio
Translated by Steve Piccolo and afterword by Joan Ockman

Design
Ivor Williams

Editor for the MIT Press
Thomas Weaver

Copyeditor
Jill Hollis

Printer
Musumeci, Aosta, Italy

Typeset in Forma DJR by David Jonathan Ross; a revival of Aldo Novarese's late mid-century neo-grotesque for the Italian Nebiolo foundry, and Zenith by Matthieu Cortat; a contemporary interpretation of Zeno which was cut by Charles Manin in 1936 for the German-Italian publisher Giovanni Madersteig.

This book was supported by a generous grant from the Graham Foundation for Advanced Studies in the Fine Arts and by a Research Publication Fellowship awarded by the Architectural Association, School of Architecture.

Graham
Foundation

Library of Congress Cataloging-in-Publication Data

Names: Rogers, Ernesto N., author. | Marcaccio, Roberta, editor, writer of introduction. | Piccolo, Steve, translator. | Ockman, Joan, writer of afterword.
Title: The hero of doubt : selected writings by Ernesto Nathan Rogers / edited with an introduction by Roberta Marcaccio ; translated by Steve Piccolo ; and afterword by Joan Ockman.
Description: Cambridge, Massachussetts : The MIT Press, [2024] | Includes bibliographical references. |
Identifiers: LCCN 2023052518 | ISBN 9780262049047 (hardcover)
Subjects: LCSH: Architecture, Modern--20th century. | Architecture and society--History--20th century.
Classification: LCC NA680 .R575 2024 | DDC 724/.6--dc23/eng/20240301
LC record available at https://lccn.loc.gov/2023052518

Overleaf: Alexander Calder's portrait of Ernesto Rogers, 1952